THE SCIENCE FICTION and HEROIC FANTASY AUTHOR INDEX

Compiled by
Stuart W. Wells III

Purple Unicorn Books
Duluth, Minnesota

ISBN 0-931998-00-X (Cloth)
ISBN 0-931998-01-8 (Sftbd)

First Edition June, 1978

For further information, please address Purple Unicorn Books, 4532 London Road, Duluth, Mn. 55804. Printed in U.S.A. by Mason Publishing Co., St. Paul, Minnesota and bound at Midwest Editions, Minneapolis, Mn. Phototypesetting done at Paul Bunyan Press, Duluth, Mn.

For additional copies of this book see your local bookseller or write Purple Unicorn Books, 4532 London Road, Duluth, Mn. 55804. For a price catalog of the in-print titles in this book and/or catalogs of second hand out of print titles listed in this book send $1.00 to Purple Unicorn Books at the above address.

This book is printed in a limited 1,000 copy clothbound edition of which 300 copies are numbered and signed by the compiler, and designer. A softbound edition is also available.

Stuart W. Wells III

Keith T Henricksen, designer

TABLE OF CONTENTS

I. INTRODUCTION

The AUTHOR-TITLE section of this Index is intended to be a compilation of every SCIENCE FICTION and HEROIC FANTASY title published in America since 1945. It covers every novel and collection initially published or reprinted during this period in hardcover or paperback. Many earlier titles are included so that complete information is given for most authors. Anthologies are beyond the scope of this work as are pulp or magazine appearances of the various titles. Weird and Horror stories are also omitted.

This Index covers the type of books that you read and collect. It contains the information that you want to know about a book for reading or collecting: Is it a novel or a collection?; is it part of a series?; is it the first publication? This Index covers the works of over 1000 authors and includes over 5000 separate titles. It is complete through the middle of 1978 and has been updated with all information available at the actual date of typesetting. Certain forthcoming titles are also included.

Most of the information in the AUTHOR-TITLE section is from original sources--the books themselves. I have 1300 hardcover and 3000 paperbacks in my own collection and have seen countless others on dealers' shelves. . I gathered other information from everywhere I could find it including various reference works in my collection, dealers' catalogs, magazines and fanzines. These sources are not always in agreement on all points. I have resolved these problems as best I could.

It is common in works of this type to formulate a definition of the subject matter: SCIENCE FICTION & HEROIC FANTASY. I leave this task to others except only to say that by Heroic Fantasy I mean fantasy of the R. E. Howard and J. R. R. Tolkien variety. I have included all titles marketed as Science Fiction or Heroic Fantasy or published by publishers who specialize in this material (such as Fantasy Press, Gnome Press, DAW Books, etc.) even if the title is marginal. I have included all other titles I could locate that are clearly within these fields even though not marketed as such. I have included the marginal works of all authors who have attained any fame in these fields as well as their Juvenile titles and older works for completeness. I have omitted other juvenile and childrens works and marginal titles by other authors. I do not believe that every title with a small amount of fantastic content is secretly Science Fiction or Heroic Fantasy. I admit that the above method of selection means that a marginal title, such as a near-future adventure novel, has been included if it is by Isaac Asimov while the same novel by Ian Fleming would not be included. This method is therefore troublesome in theory. I find it works rather well in practice, at least for me. You are free to disagree, of course.

Stuart W. Wells III

II. QUICK REFERENCE TABLE OF TYPES OF WORKS INCLUDED AND EXCLUDED

	INCLUDED	EXCLUDED
Genre	Science Fiction Fantasy Sword and Sorcery Prehistorical Adventure	Weird Horror Ghosts - Demons Black Magic - Occult Near Future Fiction
Date	Published or reprinted 1945 to present (1977)	
Country	American	British - Canadian Foreign Language
Age Range	Adult Young Adult	Juvenile Childrens
Type	Novels Collections - Single Author	Anthologies Non-Fiction Poetry Plays Comic - Cartoon
Cover	Hardcover Bookclub Paperback Pamphlet	Pulps Magazines
Subject	Serious (more or less)	Humor Sex oriented Religious propaganda
Publishers Specially Covered	Fantasy Press Gnome Press SHASTA GRANT FPCI Ballantine Adult Fantasy Winston Adv. in S.F. Daw Books	Arkham House Vanity Publishers: Vantage & Exposition Garland, Gregg & Hyperion titles not otherwise reprinted since 1945

III. EXPLANATION OF SYMBOLS AND EDITION ENTRIES

This is an index or checklist of separately published editions of each title published by an author. Each title is on a separate line and is followed by the symbol for the type of work. Symbols are listed in subsection A. For example:

THE RINGS OF URANUS (C9)

Each edition of this title is given in order of appearance, separated by a semicolon. Each entry for a hardcover edition consists of the name of the publisher (often abbreviated-see subsections B & C) followed by the year of appearance. Each entry for a paperback edition consists of the name of the publisher followed by the publisher's code number for that edition. Bookclub and paperback editions do not include the year of appearance unless they are the first edition. Bookclub editions have no code numbers. For example:

THE RINGS OF URANUS (C9) Dday 1955; SFBC; Sig Y2345; Walker 1966

Reprints by the original hardcover publisher and paperback reprints without change in code number are not listed.

If a work appeared under more than one title, the title changes are noted immediately below the original title entry. Where the work is subsequently published under its original title the publication sequence is shown by insertion of the symbol "(=)" in the proper place. For example:

CENTIPEDE EFFECT (N) S & S 1960; (=); DAW 1975
=CENTIPEDE POWER (N) Major 5432, 1966

Other changes in subsequent editions of a title such as a change in the number of stories in a collection or the revision of a novel are noted by a symbol in parenthesis immediately preceding the entry for the changed edition.

All authors are listed alphabetically under their most commonly used name. Thus Will Jenkins books are listed under "Murray Leinster" even though he has published a few titles under his own name. The authors true name (if known) is given together with any other known pseudonyms used on titles appearing in this work. Pseudonyms used only in magazines, etc. are not listed.

Works that form a series of two or more titles are listed first in the order of their internal chronology (reading order). Series names are the popular name most commonly used for the series or the name of the main character. Not all series are named. Other titles not part of any series follow in alphabetical order. Example of Author Entry:

SMITH, JOHN[1] = John Smith Jones[2]
also Rock Hardnose

MARS SERIES
MARS (N) Dday 1966; Ace F[3]+233; 11566;
SONS OF MARS (S5) Dday 1967; SFBC; (S4)[4] BB U2111; DAW 111
IDIOTS OF MARS (N) Daw 112, 1974; UY 1231;

ANDY AND HIS STAR TURNIP (JN) Atheneum 1957;
KERK ON VENUS (N) Fantasy 1959; SFBC; (=); Dell 5432;
=BARBARIAN OF VENUS (N) (as Hardnose)[5] Major 6969, 1966;
NIGHTS OF THE JEDI (S) CRAWFORD pb 1945;

Explanation:
1. Authors most commonly used name.
2. Authors true name.
3. This is part of an Ace double.
4. Paperback editions have only four of the original stories but same title was used.
5. This book was published under the pseudonym "Rock Hardnose".

A. SYMBOLS

(N)	NOVEL (and certain unitary works of fiction even though not novels in the true sense of having a plot)
(C6)	COLLECTION - of six stories by the same author (s)
(S)	STORY - separate title not long enough to be a novel.
(S7)	SERIES - a collection of seven stories in a series using the same main character or setting, etc.
(B)	BIOGRAPHY
(P21)	POETRY - a collection of 21 poems. Such collections are generally not covered in this work.
(A5)	ANTHOLOGY - of five stories by different authors - few anthologies appear in this work. See the introduction.

These symbols are mixed when necessary to describe a work. Thus:

(N+2)	Novel plus two short stories
(2N)	Two novels

(S3+S2) Three stories in one series and two in another

(C9+P2) Collection of nine stories plus two poems.

= This title is the same work as the title above.

=& These two titles together equal the title above. For instance a hardcover that has been split into two paperbacks. If used alone the title given is one of novels included in the work above.

=+ A later or expanded version of the title above.

*= An earlier or condensed version of the title above.

**= The title above is a entirely rewritten and expanded version on the title given. See J. Brunner in particular.

rev. A revised version. Used where no title change has been made.

pb Paperback - used where there is no publisher number or none is known. Publisher s numbers are given for paperbacks but not for hardcovers.

+ When used as part of the publisher index number of a paperback book this means that the edition is a double novel consisting of the listed title and another title. This includes Ace doubles which were printed back to back and a few other double novels by other publishers with both titles on the front cover.

+ When used as the last item at the end of a list of editions this means that subsequent reprints are not listed. Certain famous titles by Asimov, Heinlein and others have been reprinted so many times that I gave up keeping track.

(FC1978) Forthcoming Title. Complete information on the title may not be available and so it may be part of a series even though not so listed. I have only included titles by publishers who usually produce what they advertise but there is no guarantee that the title will be published.

B. ABBREVIATIONS OF HARDCOVER PUBLISHERS

BBHC	BALLANTINE HARD COVER
BC	BOOK CLUB - NOT SFBC
Berk/Put	BERKLEY-PUTNAM
Bobbs-M	BOBBS MERRILL
Coward M	COWARD McCANN
Dday	DOUBLEDAY
DMG	DONALD M. GRANT
Dodd-M	DODD MEAD
ERB	EDGAR RICE BURROUGHS
FPCI	FANTASY PUBLISHING CO., INC.
F-S&C	FARRAR STRAUS & CUDAHY
F-S&G	FARRAR STRAUSS & GIROUIX
F-S&Y	FARRAR STRAUS & YOUNG
G&D	GROSSET & DUNLAP
H-B-J	HARCOURT BRACE & JOVANOVICH
H-B-W	HARCOURT BRACE & WORLD
H&R	HARPER AND ROW
H-R-W	HOLT RINEHART & WINSTON
Houghton -M	HOUGHTON MIFFLIN
Lipp	J.B. LIPPINCOTT
Little-B	LITTLE BROWN
McGraw -H	McGRAW HILL
Macmil	MACMILLAN
Metro	METROPOLITAN
NAL	NEW AMERICAN LIBRARY
NESFA	NEW ENGLAND S.F. ASSOCIATION
P&C	PELLEGRINI & CUDAHY
Scrib	CHARLES SCRIBNER'S & SONS
SFBC	SCIENCE FICTION BOOK CLUB
S&S	SIMON & SCHUSTER
W&T	WEYBRIGHT & TALLEY

C. ABBREVIATIONS OF PAPERBACK PUBLISHERS

Avon E	AVON EQUINOX REDISCOVERY
Avon MMM	AVON MURDER MYSTERY MONTHLY
Bant	BANTAM BOOKS
BB	BALLANTINE BOOKS
BBAF	BALLANTINE BOOKS ADULT FANTASY
BBDR	DEL REY BOOKS - BALLANTINE
Bart	BARTHOLEMEW HOUSE
Begl	BEAGLE
Belm	BELMONT
B-T	BELMONT TOWER
Berk	BERKLEY
Coll	COLLIER
Crest	FAWCETT CREST
Curt	CURTIS
Galx	GALAXY
G-M	FAWCETT GOLD MEDAL
GSFL	GOLDEN SCIENCE FICTION LIBRARY
Lanc	LANCER
Leis	LEISURE
M-B	MacFADDEN BARTELL
PBL	PAPERBACK LIBRARY
Perm	PERMABOOKS
Pinn	PINNACLE
Play	PLAYBOY
Poc	POCKET
Pop	POPULAR
Prmd	PYRAMID
SBS	SCHOLASTIC BOOK SERVICE
Sig	SIGNET (NEW AMERICAN LIBRARY)
Warn	WARNER
WPBL	WARNER PAPEBACK LIBRARY

IV AUTHOR CROSS INDEX AND CO-AUTHOR INDEX

CROSBY, Harry C. Jr.	ANVIL, Christopher
CRUMLEY, Thomas W.	FANTHORPE, R. L.
CULBREATH, Myrna	Star Trek Series
DAVIS, Gerry	PEDLER, Kit co-author
DEL MARTIA, Astron	FEARN, John Russell
DE REYNA, Jorge	DETZER, Diane
DICKSON, Carter	CARR, John Dickson
EDMONDS, Helen Woods	KAVAN, Anna
EDWARDS, Norman	CARR, Terry & WHITE, Ted
ELLIOT, John	HOYLE, Fred co-author
FANE, Bron	FANTHORPE, R. L.
FINNEY, Walter B.	FINNEY, Jack
FISHER, Gene	LANCOUR, Gene
FLETCHER, George U.	PRATT, Fletcher
FOLEY, Dave	HATCH, Gerald
FOSTER, Richard	CROSSEN, Kendell Foster
FRENCH, Paul	ASIMOV, Isaac
GILLMAN, Robert Cham	COPPEL, Alfred
GLEMSER, Bernard	CRANE, Robert
GRAHAM, Robert	HALDEMAN, Joe and Attar the Merman Series
GRAHAM, Roger Phillips	PHILLIPS, Rog
GRIDBAN, Volstad	FEARN, John Russell
GRINNELL, David	WOLLHEIM, Donald
HADLEY, Franklin	WINTERBOTHAM, Russ
HALL, D. W.	GILMORE, Anthony
HALL, John Ryder	ROSTLER, William
HANNES, Alfven	JOHANNESSON, Olof
HARRIS, John Beynon	WYNDHAM, John
HARRIS, Larry Mark	JANIFER, Lawrence
HART, Harry	FRANK, Pat
HARTMAN, Darlene	LANG, Simon
HOAR, Roger Sherman	FARLEY, Ralph Milne
HOLLY, Joan C.	HOLLY, J. Hunter
HOLMES, H. H.	BOUCHER, Anthony
HOUGH, S. B.	GORDON, Rex
HOYLE, Geoffrey	HOYLE, Fred co-author
HUNGER, Anna	MILLER, R. Dewitt co-author
HUNTINGTON, Charles	Space Probe 6 Series
HYNAM, John	MORGAN, Dan co-author
JACKSON, John	SILENT, William T.
JACOB, Piers A. D.	ANTHONY, Piers
JAHN, Michael	Six Million Dollar Man Series
JAMES, Lawrence	Rack Series
JARDINE, Jack O.	MADDOCK, Larry
JAY, Mel	FANTHORPE, R. L.
JENKINS, Will F.	LEINSTER, Murray
JOHNS, Marston	FANTHORPE, R. L.
JONES, Robert Page	PAGE, Thomas

JORGENSEN, Ivar	FAIRMAN, Paul W.
JORGENSON, Ivar	SILVERGERG, Robert
JUDD, Cyril	MERRIL, Judith & KORNBLUTH, Cyril
KERN, Gregory	TUBB, E. C. and Cap Kennedy Series
KIPPAX, John	MORGAN, Dan co-author
KLASS, Phillip	TENN, William
KNOX, Calvin	SILVERBERG, Robert
LANGART, Darrell T.	GARRETT, Randall
LANGE, John F. Jr.	NORMAN, John
LEE, Wayne C.	SHELDON, Lee
LEY, Robert Arthur	SELLINGS, Arthur
LINEBARGER, Paul	SMITH, Cordwainer
LIONEL, Robert	FANTHORPE, R. L.
LOMBINO, S. A.	HUNTER, Evan
LORD, Jeffrey	Richard Blade Series
LORRAH, Jean	Star Trek Series
LOTTMAN, Eileen	Bionic Woman Series
LUKENS, Adam	DETZER, Diane
LUTHER, Ray	SELLINGS, Arthur
LYNCH, Jane D.	GASKELL, Jane
MCCANN, Edson	DEL REY, Lester & POHL, Fred
MACGREGOR, James Murdoch	MCINTOSH, J. T.
MCGAUGHY, Dudley Dean	OWEN, Dean
MCILWAIN, David	MAINE, Charles Eric
MCNEILLIE, John	NIALL, Ian
MAJORS, Simon	FOX, Gardner
MARSTEN, Richard	HUNTER, Evan
MARTIN, Thomas A.	THOMAS, Martin
MATHESON, JOan	TRANSUE, Jacob
MARSHAK, Sondra	Star Trek Series
MOORE, Walker	Balzon Series
MULLER, John E.	FANTHORPE, R. L.
NORTH, Andrew	NORTON, Andre
NORWAY, Nevil Shute	SHUTE, Nevil
NUTT, Charles	BEAUMONT, Charles
O'DONNELL, K. M.	MALZBERG, Barry
OSBORNE, David	SILVERBERG, Robert
PADGETT, Lewis	KUTTNER, Henry
PARKES, Lucas	WYNDHAM, John
PAYES, Rachel Cosgrove	ARCH, E. L.
PAYNE, Donald Gordon	CAMERON, Ian
PEEBLES, J. E.	KENNAWAY, James
PHILLIPS, Mark	GARRETT, Randall & JANIFER, Lawrence
PRITCHARD, John	WALLACE, Ian
PAYNE, Robert	LEONARDO DA VINCI Co-author
RACKHAM, John	PHILLIFENT, John
RANDALL, Robert	GARRETT, Randall & SILVERBERG, Robert

RANKINE, John	MASON, Douglas R.
RAYMOND, Alex	Flash Gordon Series
REYNOLDS, Dallas McCord	REYNOLDS, Mack
RICHARDS, Evan	Six Million Dollar Man Series
RICHARDS, Henry	SAXON, Richard
RICHARDSON, R. S.	LATHAM, Phillip
RILEY, Frank	CLIFTON, Mark co-author
ROCKLIN, R. L.	ROCKLYNNE, Ross
ROBERTS, Lionel	FANTHORPE, R. L.
ST. JOHN, Phillip	DEL REY, Lester
SANDERS, Leonard M.	THOMAS, Dan
SAXON, Peter	THOMAS, Martin
SCHOEPFLIN, Harl Vincent	VINCENT Harl
SCOTT, J. M.	THEOBOLD, Robert co-author
SCOTT, Peter T.	WERPER, Barton
SHANNON, Fred	RUBEN, Williams
SILVERBERT, Mrs. William	STONE, Leslie F.
SKEELS, Vernon	ROSSITER, Oscar
SLAVITT, David R.	SUTTON, Henry
SHELDON, Alice	TIPTREE, James Jr.
SMITH, Ernest Bramah	BRAMAH, Ernest
SNYDER, Gene	WATKINS, William Jon co-author
SOLER, Antonio Robles	ANTONIORROBLES
SOMERS, Bart	FOX, Gardner
SPANO, Charles A. Jr.	Star Trek Series
STATTEN, Vargo	FEARN, John Russell
STEFFANSON, Con	Flash Gordon Series
STEINER, D. T.	Star Trek Series
STERLING, Brett	HAMILTON, Edmund
STEWART, Will	WILLIAMSON, Jack
STINE, G. Harry	CORREY, Lee
STREIB, Daniel Thomas	PAGE, Thomas
STUBBS, Harry C.	CLEMENT, Hal
THOMPSON, Anthony A.	ALBAN, Anthony
THORPE, Trevor	FANTHORPE, R. L.
TORRO, Pel	FANTHORPE, R. L.
TROUT, Kilgore	FARMER, Philip Jose'
TUCKER, Arthur Wilson	TUCKER, Wilson
TUCKER, Bob	TUCKER, Wilson
UPCHURCH, Boyd	BOYD, John
VAN LHIN, Erik	DEL REY, Lester
VERN, David	REED, David V.
WALDROP. H.	SAUNDERS, Jake co-author
WALL, John W.	SARBAN
WARD, Arthur S.	ROHMER, Sax
WEISS, Henry George	FLAGG, Francis
WHITE, William A. P.	BOUCHER, Anthony
WILSON, John Anthony Burgess	BURGESS, Anthony
WILSON, Robert Anton	SHEA, Robert co-author
WOOD, Robert W.	TRAIN, Arthur co-author
WOODCOTT, Keith	BRUNNER, John
WOODWARD, Wayne	BOK, HANNES

YOUD, Christopher Sam	CHRISTOPHER, John
ZACHARY, Hugh	HUGHES, Zach
SEIGRFEID, Karl	FANTHORPE, R. L.
ZETFORD, Tully	Ryder Hook Series, Ken Bulmer
ZIEGLER, Edward William	TYLER, Theodore

V. NOTES

A. PARTIAL LISTINGS:

Partial listings are given on many authors whose works appeared prior to 1947 and have not been substantially reprinted since then. In these cases only the titles which have appeared in paperback since 1947 have been listed. The reader is referred to the bibliography section for works listing these titles.

Notes on other partial listings:

1. ROBERT BLOCH - only the Science Fiction and Fantasy titles are included. Bloch's many titles in the weird and horror gendre are excluded as well as his famous novel 'Psycho'.

2. EDGAR RICE BURROUGHS - Burroughs wrote some other novels which are largely mainstream. All Science Fiction and Fantasy titles are included (although only the first hard cover printing is given). A few titles are included which are not strictly fantasy, in order to give a complete listing of the early Ace and Ballantine titles.

3. JAMES BRANCH CABELL - Only the titles reprinted in the Ballantine Adult Fantasy Series are listed together with his famous novel 'Jurgen' which has appeared several times in paperback.

4. JOHN CREASEY - Creasey wrote over 500 books under many names. Almost all are mysteries. The Dr. Palfrey series contains many titles which are Science Fiction as well as mysteries. I was unable to locate more precise information.

5. LORD DUNSANY - Ballantine Adult Fantasy reprints and a few other recent editions only.

6. H. RIDER HAGGARD - Only titles reprinted in paperback are shown.

7. ROBERT E. HOWARD - I have included selected non-fantasy titles by Howard in a separate category. This information is included because of the extraordinary popularity of Howard's works and the large number of recently published titles. I have omited certain pamphlets published by small specialty publishers

due to incomplelte information. Several biographies and bibliographies of Howard have been published recently and the reader is referred to these for more complete information.

8. DAVID H. KELLER - Other titles are weird and horror fiction. I have included the few titles that seemed to be Science Fiction or Fantasy (at least in part) and some titles published by specialty publishing companies for completeness purposes.

9. TALBOT MUNDY - Only a few of Mundy's many novels of adventure fiction are also fantasy. I don't really think the Tros series should be included but I liked it too much to leave it out and it appeared in part in Gnome Press Editions.

10. SAX ROHMER - I included the Fu Manchu series largely because I enjoy the movie 'The Mask of Fu Manchu' staring Boris Karloff. The insidious Doctor does use a few weird inventions and so I believe I can defend the series as at least marginally Science Fiction.

11. JULES VERNE & H. G. WELLS - The main difficulty with these authors is that their titles are almost all in the public domain and therefore can be reprinted by anyone without indication of the original publications. The more famous works by both authors have been printed so many times that it is probably impossible to compile a complete list. In any event I did not try to do so. The more obscure works are difficult to locate and more difficult to separate Science Fiction and Fantasy from other works. I have done the best I could with my resources.

B. A NOTE ON SERIES NOT INCLUDED:

Doc Savage - Omitted because it is to long a series and I am not a collector of it. Also it is as much mainstream adventure as Science Fiction.

Perry Rhodan - Omitted because it is really an anthology and because it is too long a series. Two excellent indexes of Perry Rhodan 1-25 and 26-50 are available at $1.00 each for Rhodan fans who are interested.

C. A NOTE ON AUTHORS NOT INCLUDED:

AUGUST DERLETH
H. P. LOVECRAFT
Other Arkham House Authors
Other authors good and bad of Weird and Horror Fiction.

Weird and Horror fiction is not my bag. I don't read it or collect it. I am not competent to prepare a bibliography of it and have therefore excluded it. I do not apologize for this, however. I do apologize for any unintended exclusion of any titles by these authors that are Science Fiction or Fantasy and also for including some Weird and Horror titles by possibly lesser authors thru ignorance. I will gladly correct any such sins brought to my attention if I ever am foolish enough to prepare a second edition. Some Weird & Horror Fiction is intentionally included for the purpose of completeness of certain authors or publishers.

KENNETH ROBESON DOC SAVAGE (1) (9) (72) (75)

A

ABE', KOBO

THE BOX MAN (N) Knopf 1974;
INTER ICE AGE 4 (N) Knopf 1970; SFBC; Berk N2118;
THE WOMAN IN THE DUNES (N) Knopf 1964; Berk S1104;

ADAMS, JOHN

WHEN THE GODS CAME (N) Arcadia 1967;

ADAMS, RICHARD

THE PLAGUE DOGS (N) Knopf 1978; (Marginal)
SHARDIK (N) Macmil 1975; BC; Avon 27359
WATERSHIP DOWN (N) Macmil 1974; Avon 19810; E25759;

ADAMS, ROBERT

HORSECLANS SERIES
THE COMING OF THE HORSECLANS (N) Pinn 662, 1975; 25759;
SWORDS OF THE HORSECLANS (N) Pinn 991, 1977;
REVENGE OF THE HORSECLANS (N) Pinn 40-132, 1977;

ADLARD, MARK

T-CITY TRILOGY
INTERFACE (N) Ace 37090, 1978;
VOLTEFACE (N) Ace 86607, 1978;
MULTIFACE (N) Ace 54500, (fc 4/78)

ADLER, ALLEN

MACH 1: A STORY OF THE PLANET IONUS (N) F-S&C 1957;
=TERROR ON PLANET IONUS (N) PBL 52-941, 1966; 63-048;

AIKEN, JOHN

WORLD WELL LOST (N) Dday 1971;

AKERS, ALAN BURT =

DRAY PRESCOT OF ANTARES
DELIAN CYCLE
TRANSIT TO SCORPIO (N) DAW 33, 1972; UY 1169
THE SUNS OF SCORPIO (N) DAW 49, 1973; UY 1191
WARRIOR OF SCORPIO (N) DAW 65, 1973; UY1212;
SWORDSHIPS OF SCORPIO (N) DAW 81, 1973; UY 1231;
PRINCE OF SCORPIO (N) DAW 97, 1974; UY 1251

HAVILFAR CYCLE
MANHOUNDS OF ANTARES (N) DAW 113, 1974;
ARENA OF ANTARES(N) DAW 129, 1974

FLIERS OF ANTARES (N) DAW 145, 1975;
BLADESMAN OF ANTARES (N) DAW 159, 1975;
AVENGER OF ANTARES (N) DAW 173, 1975;
ARMANDA OF ANTARES (N) DAW 189, 1976;

KROZIAN CYCLE

THE TIDES OF KREGEN (N) DAW 204, 1976;
RENEGADE OF KREGEN (N) DAW 221, 1976;
KROZIAR OF KREGEN (N) DAW 237, 1977;

VALLIAN CYCLE

SECRET SCORPIO (N) DAW 269, 1977;
SAVAGE SCORPIO (N) DAW 285, 1978;

ALBAN, ANTHONY = ANTHONY A. THOMPSON

CATHARSIS CENTRAL (N) Berk X1687, 1969;
THE DAY OF THE SHIELD (N) Berk N2275, 1973;

ALDISS, BRIAN W.

BAREFOOT IN THE HEAD (N) Dday 1970; Ace 04758;
THE BOOK OF BRIAN ALDISS (C9) DAW 29, 1972;
BOW DOWN TO NUL (N) Ace D+443, 1960; F-382;
BROTHERS OF THE HEAD (N) Two Continents 1978;
CRYPTOZOIC (N) Dday 1968; SFBC; Avon V2295: 33415;
THE DARK LIGHT YEARS (N) Sig D2497, 1964; T4586;
EARTHWORKS (N) Dday 1966; SFBC; Sig P3116;
THE EIGHTY MINUTE HOUR (N) Dday 1974; Leis 237ZK;
ENEMIES OF THE SYSTEM (N) Harper (fc 7/78)
FRANKENSTEIN UNBOUND (N) Random 1974; Crst Q2473;
GALAXIES LIKE GRAINS OF SAND (S8) Sig S1815, 1960; T4781; Y7044; Gregg 1977;
GREYBEARD (N) Harcourt 1964; Sig P2689; Q5141; Y6929;
THE LONG AFTERNOON OF EARTH (N) Sig D2018, 1962; T4577;
=HOTHOUSE (N) Gregg 1976;
THE MALACIA TAPESTRY (N) H&R 1977; Ace 51647;
THE MALE RESPONSE (N) Galx 305, 1961;
MOMENT OF ECLIPSE (C14) Dday 1972;
NEANDERTHALL PLANET (C4) Avon V2322, 1970; SFBC;
NO TIME LIKE TOMORROW (C12) Sig S1683, 1959; T4605; Y6969;
THE PRIMAL URGE (N) BB F555, 1961;
REPORT ON PROBABILITY A (N) Dday 1969; Lanc 74-677;
STARSHIP (N) Criterion 1959; Sig S1779; D2271; Avon V2321; 22558;
STARSWARM (S8) Sig D2411, 1964; T4558; Y6883; Gregg 1978;
VANGUARD FROM ALPHA (N) Ace D+369, 1959;
WHO CAN REPLACE A MAN (C14) Harcourt 1966; Sig P3311, T5055; Y7083;

ALEXANDER, THEA

2150 A.D. (N) Warn 89-124, 1976;

ALLEN, HENRY WILSON

GENESIS FIVE (N) Morrow 1968; Prmd T2162;

ALPER, GERALD A.
MY NAME IS VLADIMIR SLOIFOISKI (N) Curt 7088, 1970;

ALTER, ROBERT EDMOND
PATH TO SAVAGERY (N) Avon S380 1969;

AMIS, KINGLSEY
THE ALTERATION (N) Viking 1977;
THE ANTI-DEATH LEAGUE (N) H-B-W 1966; BB U6114;

AMOSOFF, N
NOTES FROM THE FUTURE (N) S&S 1970;

ANDERSON, CHESTER
THE BUTTERFLY KID (N) Prmd X1730, 1967; Gregg 1977;
TEN YEARS TO DOOMSDAY (N) (with M. Kurland) Prmd R1015, 1964; Jove 04458;

ANDERSON, COLIN
MAGELLAN (N) Walker 1970; Berk S2262;

ANDERSON, POUL
TRADER VAN RIJN & POLESOTECHNIC LEAGUE
WAR OF THE WINGMEN (N) Ace D+303, 1958; G-634; 87201; Gregg 1976;
= THE MAN WHO COUNTS (N) Ace 51902, 1978;
TRADER TO THE STARS (S3) Dday 1964; SFBC; Berk F1284; Z3199;
THE TROUBLE TWISTERS (S3) Dday 1966; Berk X1417; Z3245;
SATAN'S WORLD (N) Dday 1969; SFBC; Lanc 74-698; 75-388; Berk 3361;
MIRKHEIM (N) Berk/Put 1977; SFBC; Berk 03596;
THE EARTH BOOK OF STORMGATE (C12) Berk/Put 1978;

PSYCHOTECNIC HISTORY
UN-MAN AND OTHER NOVELLAS (C3) Ace F+139, 1962;
THE SNOWS OF GANYMEDE (N) Ace D+303, 1958;
VIRGIN PLANET (N) Avalon 1959; Galaxy 270; PBL 63-333; Warn 75-462; 88-334;
STAR WAYS (N) Avalon 1956; Ace D+255; D-568; 78410;
= THE PEREGRINE (N) Ace 65949, 1978;

DOMINIC FLANDRY
ENSIGN FLANDRY (N) Chilton 1966; Lanc 73-677; 75-374;
A CIRCUS OF HELLS (N) Sig T4250, 1970;
THE REBEL WORLDS (N) Sig T4041, 1969; Q5714;
AGENT OF THE TERRAN EMPIRE (S4) Chilton 1965; — #III
=& WE CLAIM THESE STARS (N) Ace D+407, 1959; G-697;
FLANDRY OF TERRA (S3) Chilton 1965;
=& EARTHMAN, GO HOME (N) Ace D+479, 1960;
=& MAYDAY ORBIT (N) Ace F+104, 1961;
A KNIGHT OF GHOSTS AND SHADOWS (N) SFBC 1975; Sig Y6725;

HOLGER DANSKE
THREE HEARTS AND THREE LIONS (N) Dday 1961; SFBC; Avon G1127; S412; Berk 03680;
A MIDSUMMER TEMPEST (N) Dday 1974; BB 24404;

AFTER DOOMSDAY (N) BB 579, 1962; 1888;
THE BEST OF POUL ANDERSON (C9) Poc 80671, 1976;
BEYOND THE BEYOND (C6) Sig T3947, 1969; SFBC; Y6084; W7760;
BRAIN WAVE (N) BB 80, 1954; 393K; U2342; 1889; Walker 1969; 23668; 24685;
THE BROKEN SWORD (N) Abelard 1954; (rev)BB2107; 23526; BBDA 25512;
THE BYWORLDER (N) Sig T4780, 1971; Gregg 1978;
THE CORRIDORS OF TIME (N) Dday 1965; SFBC; Lanc 73-505; 74-536; 74-742; Berk 03659;
THE DANCER FROM ATLANTIS (N) SFBC 1971; Sig Q4894; Y6166; 7806;
THE DAY OF THEIR RETURN (N) SFBC 1973; Sig Y6371; W7941;
EARTHMAN'S BURDEN (S6) (with G. Dickson) Gnome 1957; Avon ZS166;
THE ENEMY STARS (N) Lipp 1959; SFBC; Berk G289; F1112;
FIRE TIME (N) Dday 1974; SFBC; BB 24628;
GUARDIANS OF TIME (S4) BB 422K, 1960; 1890;
THE HIGH CRUSADE (N) Dday 1960; Dolphin C351; M-B 50-211; 60-349; 95-374;
HOMEBREW (C14) NESFA 1976;
HOMEWARD AND BEYOND (C9) Dday 1975; Berk D3162;
THE HORN OF TIME (C6) Sig P3349; 1968; Q5480; Gregg 1978;
HROLF KRAKI'S SAGA (N) BBAF 23562, 1973; BBDR 25846;
INHERITORS OF EARTH (N) (see G. Eklund-author)
LET THE SPACEMEN BEWARE (N) Ace F+209, 1963;
=THE NIGHT FACE (N) Ace 57450, 1978;
THE NIGHT FACE AND OTHER STORIES (S4) Gregg 1978;
THE MAKESHIFT ROCKET (N) Ace F+139, 1962;
THE MANY WORLDS OF POUL ANDERSON (C10) Chilton 1974;
=THE BOOK OF POUL ANDERSON (C10) DAW 153, 1975; UJ1347;
NO WORLD OF THEIR OWN (N) Ace D+110, 1955; D-550;
= THE LONG WAY HOME (N) Ace 48922, 1978; Gregg 1978;
OPERATION CHAOS (N) Dday 1971; Lanc 75-319; Berk 03750;
ORBIT UNLIMITED (N) Prmd G615, 1961; F818; T2870; N3274; Gregg 1978;
THE PEOPLE OF THE WIND (N) Sig Q5479, 1973; Gregg 1977;
PLANET OF NO RETURN (N) Ace D+199, 1956;
= QUESTION AND ANSWER (N) Ace 69770, 1978;
TWO WORLDS (2N) Gregg 1978; (= Question and Answer & World Without Stars)
THE QUEEN OF AIR AND DARKNESS (C6) Sig Q5713, 1973; Gregg 1978;
SEVEN CONQUESTS (C7) Macmil 1969; SFBC; Coll 907;
SHIELD (N) Berk F743, 1963; X1862; N2673;
THE STAR FOX (S3) Dday 1965; SFBC; Sig P2920; T4763; Berk 03772;
STAR PRINCE CHARLIE (JN) (with G. Dickson) Putnam 1975; Berk Z3078;
STRANGERS FROM EARTH (C8) BB 483K, 1961;
TALES OF THE FLYING MOUNTAINS (S7) Macmil 1970; Coll 1626;
TAU ZERO (N) Dday 1970; Lanc 75-185; Berk D3210;
THERE WILL BE TIME (N) SFBC 1972; Sig Q5401; Y6925;
THREE WORLDS TO CONQUER (N) Prmd F994, 1964; X1875; N3541;
TIME AND STARS (C6) Dday 1964; SFBC; M-B 60-206; 75-330; 95-391; Berk 03621;
TWILIGHT WORLD (N) Torquil 1961; SFBC;
VAULT OF THE AGES (JN) Winston 1952; Avon ZS161;
THE WAR OF TWO WORLDS (N) Ace D+335, 1959; 87201;
THE WINTER OF THE WORLD (N) SFBC 1975; Sig W7003;

THE WORLDS OF POUL ANDERSON (3N) Ace 91055. 1974; (Planet of No Return + War of Two Worlds + World Without Stars)
WORLD WITHOUT STARS (N) Ace F-425, 1966; 91706;

HISTORICAL NOVELS
THE GOLDEN SLAVE (N) Avon T388, 1959;
ROGUE SWORD (N) Avon T472, 1960

ANDERSON, WILLIAM C.

PENELOPE SERIES
PENELOPE (N) Crown 1963; Poc 50126;
PENELOPE, THE DAMP DETECTIVE (N) Crown 1974;

ADAM M-1 (N) Crown 1964;
PANDEMONIUM ON THE POTOMAC (N) Crown 1966

ANTHONY, PIERS =PIERS ANTHONY DILLINGHAM JACOB

SOS SERIES
SOS THE ROPE (N) Pyramid X1890, 1968;
VAR THE STICK (N) Bantam N6948, 1973;
NEQ THE SWORD (N) British
ALL = BATTLE CIRCLE (3N) Avon 35469, 1978;

ATON SERIES
CHTHON (N) BB U6107, 1967; Berk Z2984;
PHTHOR (N) Berk Z3011, 1975;

CAL, VEG & AQUILON SERIES
OMNIVORE (N) BB 72014, 1968; SFBC; Avon E23026;
ORN (N) SFBC 1971; Avon V2405; 22699; 29892;
OX (N) SFBC 1976; Avon 29702;

GALAXY WAR SERIES
CLUSTER (N) Avon 34686, 1977;
CHAINING THE LADY (N) Avon 35121, 1978;
KIRLIAN QUEST (N) Avon 35113, 1978; (fc 7/78)

BUT WHAT OF EARTH (N) (with R. Coulson) Laser 44, 1976;
THE E.S.P. WORM (N) (see R. Margroff-coauthor)
HASAN (N) Newcastle B215, 1977;
MACROSCOPE (N) Avon W166, 1969; 22145; 36798;
PROSTHO PLUS (N) Berk S2137, 1973;
THE RING (N) (with R. Margroff) Ace A-19, 1968;
RINGS OF ICE (N) Avon 19448, 1974;
A SPELL FOR CHAMELEON (N) BBDR 25855, 1977;
TRIPLE DETENTE (N) DAW 118, 1974;

ANTONIORROBLES = ANTONIO ROBLES SOLER

THE REFUGEE CENTAUR (N) Twayne 1952;

ANVIL, CHRISTOPHER = HARRY C. CROSBY JR.

THE DAY THE MACHINES STOPPED (N) Monarch 478, 1964;

PANDORA'S PLANET (N) Dday 1972; DAW 66; UY1178;
STRANGERS IN PARADISE (N) Tower T-075-4, 1969; BT 40136;
WARLORD'S WORLD (N) DAW 168, 1975;

APPEL, BENJAMIN

THE FUNHOUSE (N) BB 345K, 1959;
=DEATH MASTER (N) Pop 220, 1974;
THE DEVIL AND W. KASPAR (N) Pop 3190, 1977;

ARISS, BRUCE WALLACE JR.

FULL CIRCLE (N) Avalon 1963;

ARIOSTA, LUDOVICO

ORLANDO FURIOSO (N) (1503-trans R. Hodgens) *= BBAF 3057, 1973; Penguin L311

ARNOLD, EDWIN LESTER - (Partial Listing)

LIEUT, GULLIVAR JONES: HIS VOCATION (Brit 1905) Arno 1975;
=GULLIVER OF MARS (N) Ace F-296, 1964; 30600;
PHRA THE PHOENICIAN (N) Harper 1890; Newcastle F110, 1977;

ARCH E. L. =RACHEL COSGROVE PAYES

BRIDGE TO YESTERDAY (N) Avalon 1963;
THE DEATHSTONES (N) Avalon 1964;
THE DOUBLE MINDED MAN (N) Avalon 1966;
THE FIRST IMMORTALS (N) Avalon 1965;
THE MAN WITH THREE EYES (N) Avalon 1967;
PLANET OF DEATH (N) Avalon 1964;
FORBIDDEN ISLAND (N) (As Payes) Berk 2396, 1973;

ARCHER, RON = TED WHITE & DAVE VAN ARNAM

ASHBY, RICHARD

ACT OF GOD (N) Leis LB8, 1971;

ASIMOV, ISAAC ALSO PAUL FRENCH

FOUNDATION SERIES
FOUNDATION (N) Gnome 1951; (=); Avon S224; V2248; N304; 23168; 29-579;
*=THE 1,000 YEAR PLAN (N) Ace D+110, 1955; D-110; D-538;
FOUNDATION AND EMPIRE (N) Gnome 1952; (=); Avon S234; V2236; N305; 23176; 30627;
=THE MAN WHO UPSET THE UNIVERSE (N) Ace D-125, 1955; F-216;
SECOND FOUNDATION (N) Gnome 1953; SFBC; Avon T232; G1248; S237; N306; 23814; 29280
ALL = FOUNDATION TRILOGY (3N) SFBC 1964; Avon E20933; 26930;

ROBOT STORIES
I ROBOT (S9) Gnome 1950; Gnome pb; G&D 1952; Sig S1282; S1885; Dday 1963; SFBC; Sig D2458; P3540; Crst T1453; +
EIGHT STORIES FROM THE REST OF THE ROBOTS (S8) Prmd R1283, 1966; R1783; T2085; +
THE CAVES OF STEEL (N) Dday 1954; SFBC; Sig S1240; Prmd F784; X1824; T1659+
THE NAKED SUN (N) Dday 1957; SFBC; Bant A1731; Lanc 72-753; 72-108; 73-702+

LAST 2 = THE ROBOT NOVELS (2N) SFBC 1969;
LAST 3 = THE REST OF THE ROBOTS (S8+2N) Dday 1964; SFBC;

TRANTORIAN EMPIRE
PEBBLE IN THE SKY (N) Dday 1950; Galx 14; Bant A1646; FP 47; Crst T1567; +
THE STARS LIKE DUST (N) Dday 1951; SFBC; (=): Lanc 74-815; 72-103; 73-704; +
=THE REBELLIOUS STARS (N) Ace D+84, 1954
THE CURRENTS OF SPACE (N) Dday 1952; SFBC; Sig 1082; Lanc 74-816; 72-104+
ALL 3 = TRIANGLE (3N) SFBC 1961; (Dday 1961)

ASIMOV'S MYSTERIES (C14) Dday 1968; SFBC; Dell 0307; Crest 23223;
THE BEST OF ISAAC ASIMOV (C12) Dday 1974; Crst Q2694
THE BICENTENNIAL MAN (C12) Dday 1976; SFBC Crest 23573;(fc 6/78)
HAVE YOU SEEN THESE (C8) NESFA 1974;
=+BUY JUPITER AND OTHER STORIES (C24) Dday 1975; SFBC; Crst Q3062;
THE EARLY ASIMOV (C27) Dday 1972; SFBC
=& THE EARLY ASIMOV BOOK ONE (C13) Crst P2087, 1974;
=& THE EARLY ASIMOV BOOK TWO (C14) Crst P2323, 1974;
EARTH IS ROOM ENOUGH (C15) Dday 1957; SFBC; Bant A1978; Crst T1401; T1718; +
THE END OF ETERNITY (N) Dday 1955; SFBC; Sig S1493; Lanc 74-818; 72-107; +
FANTASTIC VOYAGE (N) Houghton-M 1966; SFBC; Bant H3177; S5257; N7137;
THE GODS THEMSELVES (N) Dday 1972; SFBC; GM P1829; Q2460;
GOOD TASTE (s) Apocalypse 2, 1976;
THE HEAVENLY HOST (JN) Walker 1976;
THE MARTIAN WAY (C4) Dday 1955; SFBC; Sig S1433; Crst R1289; T1606; P2555; +
NINE TOMORROWS (C9) Dday 1959; SFBC. Bant A2121; Crst 1344; M1642; +
NIGHTFALL AND OTHER STORIES (C20) Dday 1969; SFBC; Crst M1486; 23118

DAVID STARR JUVENILE NOVELS (AS PAUL FRENCH)
DAVID STARR, SPACE RANGER (JN) Dday 1952; Sig T4849; Cres 23493;
LUCKY STARR & THE PIRATES OF THE ASTEROIDS (JN) Dday 1953; Sig T4850; Cres 23421;
LUCKY STARR AND THE OCEANS OF VENUS (JN) Dday 1954; Sig T4926 Crest 23461;
LUCKY STARR AND THE BIG SUN OF MERCURY (JN) Dday 1956; Sig T4925; Cres 23492;
LUCKY STARR AND THE MOONS OF JUPITER (JN) Dday 1957; Sig T4975; Cres 23422;
LUCKY STARR AND THE RINGS OF SATURN (JN) Dday 1958; Sig T4976; Q7669;

ASPRIN, ROBERT

THE COLD CASH WAR (N) St Martins 1977; Dell 11364;(fc 8/78)

AUGUST, LEE

SUPERDOLL (N) Award A427, 1969;

AUGUSTUS, ALBERT JR. = CHARLES NEUTZEL

AYLESWORTH, JOHN B.

FEE FEI FO FUM (N) Avon G1199, 1963;

AYME, MARCEL

THE WALKER THROUGH WALLS (C12) Berk F634, 1962;

B

BAHNSON, AGNEW H. JR.

THE STARS ARE TOO HIGH (N) Random 1959; Bantam A2048;

BALCHIN, NIGEL

KINGS OF INFINITE SPACE (N) Dday 1968; Curtis 7019;

BALL, BRIAN N.

TIME SERIES

TIMEPIECE (N) BB 1903, 1970;
TIMEPIVOT (N) BB 2095, 1970;

PROBABILITY SERIES

THE PROBABILITY MAN (N) DAW 3, 1972;
PLANET PROBABILITY (N) DAW 40, 1973;

THE REGIMENTS OF NIGHT (N) DAW 19, 1972;
SINGULARITY STATION (N) DAW 84, 1973;
SUNDOG (N) Avon V2193, 1969;
See Space 1999 series

BALLARD, J.G.

BILLENIUM (C10) Berk F667, 1962;
THE BURNING WORLD (N) Berk F961, 1964;
=THE DROUGHT (N) Gregg 1976; Penguin 2753;
CRASH (N) FS&G 1973; Pinn 423 (Marginal)
CHRONOPOLIS (C16) Putnam 1971; SFBC; Berk Z2212 (from prior collections)
CONCRETE ISLAND (N) FS&G 1974;
THE CRYSTAL WORLD (N) F-S-G 1966; SFBC; Berk X1380; Avon E30429;
THE DROWNED WORLD (N) Berk F655, 1962; F1266 Penguin 2229;
THE DROWNED WORLD & THE WIND FROM NOWHERE (2N) Dday 1965; SFBC;
HIGH RISE (N) H.R.W 1977; Pop 04181; (Borderline)
THE IMPOSSIBLE MAN (C9) Berk F1204, 1966;
LOVE & NAPALM, EXPORT USA (C15) Grove 1972;
PASSPORT TO ETERNITY (C9) Berk F823, 1963;
TERMINAL BEACH (C9) Berk F928, 1964; Penguin 2499;
VERMILLION SANDS (S8) Berk S1980, 1971;
THE VOICES OF TIME (C7) Berk F607, 1962; F1243;
THE WIND FROM NOWHERE (N) Berk F600, 1962; F1198; Penguin 2591;

BAMBER, GEORGE

THE SEA IS BOILING HOT (N) Ace 75690, 1971;

BANISTER, MANLEY

CONQUEST OF EARTH (N) Avalon 1957; Airmont SF 7;

BARBET, PIERRE

BAPHOMET'S METEOR (N) DAW 35, 1972;
THE ENCHANTED PLANET (N) DAW 156, 1975;
GAMES PSYBORGS PLAY (N) DAW 83, 1973;
THE JOAN-OF-ARC REPLAY (N) Daw 287, 1978;
THE NAPOLEONS OF ERIDANUS (N) DAW 199, 1976;

BARJAVEL, RENE'

ASHES, ASHES (N) Dday 1967; Curt 7015;
FUTURE TIMES THREE (C3) Award AS743, 1970;
THE ICE PEOPLE (N) Morrow 1970; SFBC; Prmd V2913; A4048;
THE IMMORTALS (N) Morrow 1974; BB 24626

BARKER, THOMAS W.

FIVE FOR INFINITY (N) Major 3050, 1976;

BARNES, ARTHUR K.

INTERPLANETARY HUNTER (S5) Gnome 1956; Ace 37100

BARR, DONALD

SPACE RELATIONS (N) Charterhouse 1973; Crest P2370;

BARR, TYRONE C.

THE LAST 14 (N) Chariot CB 150, 1960;

BARRETT, NEAL JR.

ALDAIR SERIES
ALDAIR IN ALBION (N) DAW 195, 1976;
ALDAIR, MASTER OF SHIPS (N) Daw 259, 1977;

HIGHWOOD (N) ACE + 33710, 1972;
THE GATES OF TIME (N) Ace +27400, 1970;
THE LEAVES OF TIME (N) Lanc 74-721, 1971;
KELWIN (N) Lanc 75113, 1970;
STRESS PATTERN (N) DAW 128, 1974;

BARRETT, WILLIAM E

THE EDGE OF THINGS (C3) Dday 1959;
FLIGHT FROM YOUTH (N) Lipp 1939;
THE FOOLS OF TIME (N) Dday 1963; Cardinal 50003; Avon W243;

BARRINGER, LESLIE

NEUSTRIAN
GERFALCON (N) Newcastle F106, 1976;
JORIS OF THE ROCK (N) Newcastle F108, 1976;
SHY LEOPARDESS (N) Newcastle F-112, 1977;

BARTH, JOHN

CHIMERA (N) RANDOM 1972; Crest Q1984,
GILES, GOAT BOY (N) Dday 1966; Crest P1052; 23524;

BARTON, WILLIAM

HUNTING ON KUNDERER (N) Ace +48245, 1973;
A PLAGUE OF ALL COWARDS (N) Ace 66780, 1976;

BARZMAN, BEN

TWINKLE, TWINKLE, LITTLE STAR (N) Putnam 1960; SFBC;
= ECHO X (N) PBL 52-130, 1962; 52-329; 54-684;

BASS, T. J. =THOMAS J. BASSLER

HALF PAST HUMAN (N) BB 2306, 1971; 24635;
THE GODWHALE (N) BB 23712, 1974; 24647;

BATEMAN, ROBERT

WHEN THE WHITES WENT (N) Walker 1964;

BAUM, TOM

COUNTERPARTS (N) Dial 1970;

BAXTER, JOHN

THE OFF-WORLDERS (N) Ace G+588, 1966;

BAYLEY, BARRINGTON J.

ANNIHILATION FACTOR (N) Ace +33710, 1972;
COLLISION COURSE (N) DAW 43, 1973;
EMPIRE OF TWO WORLDS (N) Ace 20565, 1972;
THE FALL OF CHRONOPOLIS (N) DAW 105, 1974;
THE GARMENTS OF CAEN (N) Dday 1976;
THE GRAND WHEEL (N) Daw 255, 1977;
SOUL OF THE ROBOT (N) Dday 1974;
THE STAR VIRUS (N) Ace +78400, 1970;
STAR WINDS (N) Daw 294, 1978;

BEAGLE, PETER S.

A FINE AND PRIVATE PLACE (N) Viking 1960; Dell 2530; BB 1502; 3206; 23206; 24754;
THE LAST UNICORN (N) Viking 1968; BB1503; 2892; 22892; 24345; 25484;
LILA THE WEREWOLF (N) Capra 1974

BEAUMONT, CHARLES = CHARLES NUTT

THE HUNGER AND OTHER STORIES (C17) Putnam 1958; Bant A1917;
THE MAGIC MAN AND OTHER S.F. STORIES (C18) GM DI586, 1965;
NIGHTRIDE AND OTHER JOURNEYS (C15) Bant A2087, 1960
YONDER (C16) Bant A1759, 1958;

BECHDOLT, JOHN ERNEST "JACK"

THE TORCH (N) Prime 1948

BECKFORD, WILLIAM

VATHEK (N) (Brit 1834) BBAF 2279, 1971;

BEECHING, JACK

THE DAKOTA PROJECT (N) Delacorte 1969; Dell 1711;

BELL, NEAL

GONE TO BE SNAKES NOW (N) Pop 582, 1974;

BELL, THORNTON

SPACE TRAP (N) Arcadia 1966;

BELLAMY, EDWARD (partial listing)

LOOKING BACKWARD 2000-1887 (N) Ticknor 1888; Sig CD26, 1960; Lanc 73-440;

BELLAMY, FRANCIS RUFUS

ATTA (N) Wyn 1953; Ace D+79; Poc 77692;

BENFORD, GREG

DEEPER THAN THE DARKNESS (N) Ace 14215, 1970;
THE JUPITER PROJECT (N) Nelson 1975
IF THE STARS ARE GODS (N) (With G. Eklund) Berk/Put 1977; Berk 03761;
IN THE OCEAN OF NIGHT (N) Dial 1977; SFBC;Dell 13999;(fc 8/78)

BENNETT, MARGOT

THE LONG WAY BACK (N) Coward McCann 1955;

BENNETT, ROBERT

THE BOWL OF BAAL (N) Centaur pb 1972; DMG 1975;

BENOIT, PIERRE

ATLANTIDA (N) Duffield 1920; Ace F-281, 1964;

BENTLEY, JOHN

WHERE ARE THE RUSSIANS? (N) Dday 1967; Curtis 7023;

BERESFORD, JOHN DAVYS

THE HAMPDENSHIRE WONDER (N) (Brit 1911) Garland 1975;

BERGAMINI, DAVID

VENUS DEVELOPMENT (N) Pop 380, 1976;

BERGER, THOMAS

REGIMENT OF WOMEN (N) S&S 1973; Pop 8330;

BERK, HOWARD

THE SUN GROWS COLD (N) Delacorte 1971; Dell 8433;

BERNANOS, MICHEL

THE OTHER SIDE OF THE MOUNTAIN (N) Houghton-M 1968; Dell 6741;

BERRY, JAMES R.

THE GALACTIC INVADERS (N) Laser 31, 1976;

BERTIN, JOHN

BROOD OF HELIOS (N) Arcadia 1966;
THE INTERPLANETARY ADVENTURERS (N) Lennox Hill 1970;
THE PYRAMIDS FROM SPACE (N) Lennox Hill 1970; M-B 75-440; 12-502;

BESTER, ALFRED

THE COMPUTER CONNECTION (N) Berk/Put 1975; SFBC; Berk D3039;
THE DARK SIDE OF THE EARTH (C7) Sig D2474, 1964; T4402;
THE DEMOLISHED MAN (N) Shasta 1953; SFBC; Sig 1150; S1593; D2679; T4461; Q6625; Y7585; Garland 1976
STARBURST (C11) Sig S1524, 1958; D2672; T4460;
STARLIGHT (C16) SFBC 1976 (followed hard cover collections); Berk 3451;
=& STAR LIGHT, STAR BRIGHT (C10) Berk/Put 1976
=&THE LIGHT FANTASTIC (C7) Berk/Put 1976;
THE STARS MY DESTINATION (N) Sig S1389, 1956; S1931; Berk Z2780; Bant H4875; Berk 3376; Gregg 1976;

BETHANCOURT, T. E.

THE MORTAL INSTRUMENTS (N) Holliday 1977; (S.F. ?)

BEVIS, H. U. =HERBERT URLIN BEVIS

THE STAR ROVERS (N) Lennox Hill 1970
SPACE STADIUM (N) Lennox Hill 1970
THE TIME WINDER (N) Lennox Hill 1970;
TO LUNA WITH LOVE (N) Lennox Hill 1971;
THE ALIEN ABDUCTORS (N) Lennox Hill 1971;

BEYER, WILLIAM GRAY

MINIONS OF THE MOON (N) Gnome 1950;

BIERCE, AMBROSE (Partial Listing)

IN THE MIDST OF LIFE (C19) Putnam 1898; (C26) Signet CP60, 1961;
THE COMPLETE SHORT STORIES OF AMBROSE BIERCE (C) DDay 1971;

BIGGLE, LLOYD JR.

CULTURAL SURVEY SERIES

THE STILL, SMALL VOICE OF TRUMPETS (N) Dday 1968; Curt 7036; LB 310ZK;
THE WORLD MENDERS (N) Dday 1971; DAW 15;

JAN DARZEK SERIES

ALL THE COLORS OF DARKNESS (N) Dday 1963; SFBC; PBL 52-514; 53-746; LB295ZK;
THIS DARKENING UNIVERSE (N) Dday 1975;
WATCHERS OF THE DARK (N) Dday 1966; SFBC; Curt 7033; LB 275NK;
SILENCE IS DEADLY (N) Dday 1977; SFBC;

THE ANGRY ESPERS (N) Ace D485, 1961;
THE FURY OUT OF TIME (N) Dday 1965; Berk X1393; LB318ZK;
A GALAXY OF STRANGERS (C8) Dday 1976;
THE LIGHT THAT NEVER WAS (N) Dday 1972; DAW 52;

THE METALIC MUSE (C7) Dday 1972; SFBC; DAW 106;
MONUMENT (N) Dday 1974; SFBC; Bant 02877;
THE RULE OF THE DOOR (C9) Dday 1967; Curt 7024
=THE SILENT SKY (C9) BT 51122;

BINDER, EANDO =EARL AND OTTO BINDER

LATER TITLES =OTTO BINDER, ALSO JOHN COLERIDGE

ADAM LINK - ROBOT (S7) PBL 52-847, 1965; 53-763; Warn 75-460;
ANTON YORK - IMMORTAL (S4) Belm B50-627, 1965; B60-1033;
THE AVENGERS BATTLE THE EARTH-WRECKER (N) Bant F3569, 1967;
THE DOUBLE MAN (N) Curt 7167, 1971;
ENSLAVED BRAINS (N) Avalon 1965;
FIVE STEPS TO TOMORROW (N) Curt 7106, 1971;
GET OFF MY WORLD (N) Curt 7121, 1971;
THE IMPOSSIBLE WORLD (N) Curt 7113, 1971;
LORDS OF CREATION (N) Prime 1949; Belm B50-852;
MARTIAN MARTYRS (S)(as John Coleridge) Columbia 1; about 1940;
THE NEW LIFE (S) (as John Coleridge) Columbia 4; About 1940;
MENACE OF THE SAUCERS (N) Belm B60-1050, 1969;
NIGHT OF THE SAUCERS (N) Belm B75-2116, 1971; B-T 50808;
THE MIND FROM OUTER SPACE (N) Curt 7188, 1972;
PUZZLE OF THE SPACE PYRAMIDS (N) Curt 7134, 1971;
SECRET OF THE RED SPOT (N) Curt 7163, 1971;

BISCHOFF, DAVID

THE SEEKER (N) (with C. Lampton) Laser 30, 1976;

BISHOP, MICHAEL

A FUNERAL FOR THE EYES OF FIRE (N) BB 24350, 1975;
AND STRANGE AT ECBATAN THE TREES (N) H&R 1976;
=BENEATH THE SHATTERED MOONS (N) DAW 246, 1977;
STOLEN FACES (N) H&R 1977; Dell 18328; (fc 7/78)
A LITTLE KNOWLEDGE (N) Berk/Put 1977; Berk 03671;

BISHOP GEORGE
THE SHUTTLE PEOPLE
B-1983

BIXBY, JEROME =DREXEL J. BIXBY

DEVIL'S SCRAPBOOK (C19) Brandon 625, 1964;
= CALL FOR AN EXORCIST (C19) Brandon 6374, 1974;
SPACE BY THE TALE (C11) BB U2203, 1964;

BLANKENSHIP, WILLIAM D.

THE HELIX FILE (N) Walker 1972;

BLISH, JAMES

CITIES IN FLIGHT

THEY SHALL HAVE STARS (N) Avon S210, 1966; V2216;
=YEAR 2018 (N) Avon T193, 1957;

A LIFE FOR THE STARS (N) Putnam 1962; Avon H107; G1280;
EARTHMAN, COME HOME (N) Putnam 1955; SFBC; Avon T225; S218;
THE TRIUMPH OF TIME (N) Avon T279, 1958; S221;
ALL = CITIES IN FLIGHT (4N) Avon W187, 1969; Avon 09258; SFBC; (Dday 1973) Avon 27987;

AFTER SUCH KNOWLEDGE
DOCTOR MIRABILIS (N) Dodd Mead 1971; (Not S. F.)
BLACK EASTER (N) Dday 1968; Dell 0653; Avon E31724;
THE DAY AFTER JUDGEMENT (N) Dday 1971
A CASE OF CONSCIENCE (N) BB 256, 1958; U2251; Walker 1969; BB2755 24480;

AND ALL THE STARS A STAGE (N) Dday 1971; Avon 19216; 27177;
ANYWHEN (C7) Dday 1970; SFBC;
THE DUPLICATED MAN (N) (with Lowndes) Avalon 1959; Air SF8;
THE FROZEN YEAR (N) BBHC 1957; BB197;
GALACTIC CLUSTER (C8) Sig S1719, 1959; D2790; T4965; Q5441;
JACK OF EAGLES (N) Greenberg 1952; Galx 19; (=); Avon S337;
=ESP-ER (N) Avon T-268, 1958
MIDSUMMER CENTURY (N) Dday 1972; SFBC; (N+2) DAW 89;
MISSION TO THE HEART STARS (JN) Putnam 1965;
THE NIGHT SHAPES (N) BB F647, 1962;
THE QUINCUNX OF TIME (N) Dell 7244, 1973;
THE SEEDLING STARS (N) Gnome 1957; Sig S1622; D2549; Q4964; Q5440; Y6977;
SO CLOSE TO HOME (C10) BB465K, 1961; F632;
THE STAR DWELLERS (N) Putnam 1961; Avon F122; G1268; Berk S1922;
TITAN'S DAUGHTER (N) Berk G507, 1961; F1163;
*= GIANTS IN THE EARTH (N) in A Pair From Space; Belm 92+612, 1965; 50+813;
A TORRENT OF FACES (N) (with N. Knight) Dday 1967; SFBC; Ace A-29; 81781;
THE VANISHED JET (JN) W&T 1968;
VOR (N) Avon T238, 1958; S313; S415;
THE WARRIORS OF DAY (N) Galx 16, 1953; Lanc 73-580
WELCOME TO MARS (JN) Putnam 1967;
See Star Trek Series

BLOCH, ROBERT (Partial Listing)

ATOMS AND EVIL (C13) GM s1231, 1962;
THE BEST OF ROBERT BLOCH (C22) BBDR 25757, 1977;
DRAGONS AND NIGHTMARES (C4) Mirage 1968; (C3) Belm B75-1060; B-T 40119;
FEAR TODAY, GONE TOMORROW (C12) Award AS 811, 1971; AQ 1469;
REUNION WITH TOMORROW (N) Pinn (fc 1978)
SNEAK PREVIEW (N) PBL 64-660-, 1971;
THIS CROWDED EARTH & LADIES DAY (2N) Belmont B60-080, 1968; BT 50759;
See also Bloch & Bradbury (C6+C4) Tower 43-246, 1969;

BLOODSTONE, JOHN See STUART J. BYRNE

BLUM, RALPH

THE SIMULTANEOUS MAN (N) Little-B 1970; Bantam N5878;

BLUMGARTEN, JAMES

THE ASTRONAUT (N) Warn 76-521, 1974;

BODELSEN, ANDERS

FREEZING DOWN (N) H&R 1971; SFBC; Berk S2186;

BOGGON, MARTYN

THE INEVITABLE HOUR (N) Award A398, 1969;

BOK, HANNES = WAYNE WOODWARD

BEYOND THE GOLDEN STAIR (N) BBAF 2093, 1970;
THE SORCERER'S SHIP (N) BBAF 1795, 1969;
(See also A. Merrit co-author)

BOLAND, JOHN

WHITE AUGUST (N) Arcadia 1966;

BOND, J. HARVEY See RUSS WINTERBOTHAM

BOND, NELSON S.

EXILES OF TIME (N) Prime 1949; PBL 52-804
LANCELOT BIGGS: SPACEMAN (S13) Dday 1950; SFBC;
MR. MERGENTHWIRKER'S LOBBLIES (C13) Coward-McCann 1946;
NIGHTMARES AND DAYDREAMS (C15) Arkham 1968;
NO TIME LIKE THE FUTURE (C12) Avon T80, 1954;
THE 31ST OF FEBRUARY (C13) Gnome 1949; Gnome pb;

BONE, JESSE FRANKLIN

GIFT OF THE MANTI (N) (with R. Myers) Laser 56, 1977;
THE LANI PEOPLE (N) Bant J2363, 1962;
LEGACY (N) Laser 18, 1976;
THE MEDLERS (N) Laser 37, 1976;

BOORMAN, JOHN

ZARDOZ (N) (with Bill Stair) Sig Q5830; 1974;

BOUCHER, ANTHONY =WILLIAM ANTHONY PARKER WHITE

also H. H. Holmes

THE COMPLETE WEREWOLF (C10) S&S 1969; Ace 11622;
FAR AND AWAY (C11) BBHC 1955; BB 109;
ROCKET TO THE MORGUE (N) Duell-Sloan 1942 (as Holmes) Dell 591; Sig X1681; Prmd X1681; N3567; (Marginal)

BOULLE, PIERRE

THE GARDEN ON THE MOON (N) Vanguard 1965; Sig P3031; Q5806;
PLANET OF THE APES (N) Vanguard 1963; SFBC; Sig D2547; P3399; Q5646; N8033
TIME OUT OF MIND AND OTHER STORIES (C12) Vanguard 1966; Sig T3812; Y5871;

BOULT, S. KYE = WILLIAM E COCHRAN

SOLO KILL (N) Berk 3560, 1977

BOUNDS, SYDNEY J.

THE ROBOT BRAINS (N) Arcadia 1967; M-B 60-410;

BOVA, BEN

EXILES

EXILED FROM EARTH (JN) Dutton 1971; Dutton pb;
FLIGHT OF EXILES (JN) Dutton 1972;
END OF EXILE (JN) Dutton 1975

AS ON A DARKLING PLAIN (N) Walker 1972; Dell 3211; 13211;(fc 8/78)
CITY OF DARKNESS (N) Scribners 1976;
THE DUELING MACHINE (JN) H-R-W 1969; Sig Q 5328;
ESCAPE (JN) H-R-W 1970;
FORWARD IN TIME (C10) Walker 1973; SFBC; Pop 8310;
MILLENNIUM (N) Random 1976; SFBC; BBDR 25556;
THE MULTIPLE MAN (N) Bobbs-M 1976; BBDR 25656
OUT OF THE SUN (JN) Holt 1968;
THE SHINING STRANGERS (JN) Walker 1973;
STAR CONQUERORS (JN) Winston 1959;
THE STARCROSSED (N) Chilton 1975; Prmd A4105;
STAR WATCHMAN (JN) H-R-W 1964;
THX 1138 (N) (with G. Lucas) PBL 64-624, 1971; Warn 89-711;
THE WEATHERMAKERS (JN) H-R-W 1967; Sig Q5329
WHEN THE SKY BURNED (N) Walker 1973; Pop 207
THE WINDS OF ALTAIR (JN) Dutton 1973;

BOWEN, JOHN

AFTER THE RAIN (N) BB 248K 1959; Random 1968; BB U2248;

BOYCE, CHRIS

CATCHWORLD (N) Dday 1977;

BOYD, JOHN =BOYD UPCHURCH

ANDROMEDA GUN (N) Berk/Put 1974; Berk N2878;
BARNARD'S PLANET (N) Berk/Put 1975; Berk Z3239;
THE DOOMSDAY GENE (N) W-T 1973;
THE GIRL WITH THE JADE GREEN EYES (N) Viking 1978;
THE GORGON FESTIVAL (N) W-T 1972; Bant N8018;
THE I.Q. MERCHANT (N) W-T 1972;
THE LAST STARSHIP FROM EARTH (N) W-T 1968; SFBC; Berk S1675; S2214; Penq 004875;
THE ORGAN BANK FARM (N) W-T 1970; Bant S7049;
THE POLLINATORS OF EDEN (N) W-T 1969; SFBC; Dell 6996; Penq 004876;
THE RAKEHELLS OF HEAVEN (N) W-T 1969; Bant S5479; Penq 004877;
SEX AND THE HIGH COMMAND (N) W-T 1970; Bant N6551;

BRACKETT, LEIGH MARRIED TO EDMOND HAMILTON)

ERIC JOHN STARK
SECRET OF SINHARAT (N) Ace M+101, 1964; +75781;
PEOPLE OF THE TALISMAN (N) Ace M+101, 1964; +75781;
THE GINGER STAR (N) BB 23963, 1974; 24932;
THE HOUNDS OF SKAITH (N) BB 24230, 1974; 25586;
THE REAVERS OF SKAITH (N) BB 24438, 1976;
LAST 3 = THE BOOK OF SKAITH (3N) SFBC 1976;

ALPHA CENTAURI OR DIE (N) Ace F+187, 1963; 01770;
THE BEST OF LEIGH BRACKETT (C10) SFBC 1977; BBDR 25954;
THE BIG JUMP (N) Ace D+103, 1955; G-683; 06060;
THE COMING OF THE TERRANS (S5) Ace G-669, 1967; 11546;
THE HALFLING AND OTHER STORIES (C7) Ace 31590, 1973;
THE LONG TOMORROW (N) Dday 1955; SFBC; Ace F-135; BB 24289;
THE NEMESIS FROM TERRA (N) Ace F+123, 1961; 56940;
THE STARMEN (N) Gnome 1952;
=THE GALACTIC BREED (N) Ace D+99, 1955;
=THE STARMEN OF LLYRDIS (N) BB 24668, 1976;
THE SWORD OF RHIANNON (N) Ace D+36, 1953; F-422; 79141;

BRADBURY, EDWARD P. See MICHAEL MOORCOCK

BRADBURY, RAY

THE AUTUMN PEOPLE (C8) BB U2141, 1965; (stories in cartoon form)
DARK CARNIVAL (C27) Arkham 1947;
FAHRENHEIT 451 (N+2) BBHC 1953; BB 41; (N) BB 382K; F676; S&S 1967; BB U2138; U2843; SFBC; U5060; +
GOLDEN APPLES OF THE SUN (C22) Dday 1953; Bant A1241; J2306; S4867;+
THE HALLOWEEN TREE (JN) Knopf 1972; Bant QP8470;
I SING THE BODY ELECTRIC (C18) Knopf 1969; SFBC; Bant N5752; Q6652; X2882;
THE ILLUSTRATED MAN (C18) Dday 1951; Bant 991; 1282; F2588; H3484; S4482;+
LONG AFTER MIDNIGHT (C22) Random 1976; Bant 10882,
THE MACHINERIES OF JOY (C20) S&S 1964; Bant H2988; S5258; N8304; 02834;
THE MARTIAN CHRONICLES (SN) Dday 1950; SFBC; Bant 886; 1261; A1885; F2438;+
A MEDICINE FOR MELANCHOLY (C22) Dday 1958; Bant A2069; F2637; H3398; S5268;+
THE OCTOBER COUNTRY (C19) BBHC 1955; BB F139; F580; U2139; 72138; 1637; 2301;+
R IS FOR ROCKET (C17) Dday 1962; Bant F2915; FP164; FP4078; HP4398; SP5748;
S IS FOR SPACE (C16) Dday 1966; Sig S5621; N7961;
SOMETHING WICKED THIS WAY COMES (N) S&S 1962; Bant H2630; S3408; Q6438; N7202;
TOMORROW MIDNIGHT (C8) BB U2142, 1966; (stories in cartoon form);
TWICE 22 (C44) Dday 1966; SFBC; =Golden Apples Of The Sun + Medicine for Melancholy
THE VINTAGE BRADBURY (C26) Vintage 1965 V294;
THE WONDERFUL ICE CREAM SUIT (3 Plays) Bant SP7297, 1972; N8297;
SEE ALSO BLOCH AND BRADBURY (C6+C4) Tower 43-246, 1969;
DANDELION WINE (Not S. F.)
Recent collections contain only a few stories not from previous collections

BRADBURY, WILL

THE GOD CELL (N) Berk/Put 1976;

BRADLEY, MARION ZIMMER

The Ruins of ISIS 79 TMS

DARKOVER

STAR OF DANGER (N) Ace F-350, 1965; 77945;
THE BLOODY SUN (N) Ace F-303, 1964; 06851;
THE SWORD OF ALDONES (N) Ace F+153, 1962; 79200; Gregg 1977;
THE PLANET SAVERS (N) Ace F+153, 1962; (n+1) 67020;
THE WINDS OF DARKOVER (N) Ace +89250, 1970; 89251;
THE WORLD WRECKERS (N) Ace 91170, 1971;
DARKOVER LANDFALL (N) DAW 36, 1972; UY1256; Gregg 1978;
THE SPELL SWORD (N) DAW 119, 1974; UY1284;
THE HERITAGE OF HASTUR (N) DAW 160, 1975; Gregg 1977; Daw 1307;
THE SHATTERED CHAIN (N) DAW 191, 1976; UJ1327;
THE FORBIDDEN TOWER (N) DAW 256, 1977;
STORM QUEEN (N) Daw 292, 1978;

THE BRASS DRAGON (N) Ace +37250, 1969;
THE COLORS OF SPACE (N) Mon 368, 1963;
THE DARK INTRUDER AND OTHER STORIES (C7) Ace F+273, 1964; +22576;
THE DOOR THROUGH SPACE (N) Ace F+117, 1961;+ 15890;
ENDLESS VOYAGE (N) Ace 20660, 1975;
FALCONS OF NARABEDLA (N) Ace F+273, 1964; +22576;
HUNTERS OF THE RED MOON (N) Daw 71, 1973; UY1230; UW1407;(fc 7/78)
IN THE STEPS OF THE MASTER (N) Temp 5595, 1973;
THE JEWEL OF ARWEN (S) T-K Graphics pb 1974;
THE PARTING OF ARWEN (S) T-K Graphics pb 1974;
SEVEN FROM THE STARS (N) Ace F+127, 1961;

BRAMAH, ERNEST =ERNEST BRAMAH SMITH

KAI LLUNG'S GOLDEN HOURS (C11) Dday 1928; XANADU X-2, 1962; BBAF 2574;
KAI LUNG UNROLLS HIS MAT (C12) Dday 1923; TACOMA 1974; BBAF 23787;

BREGGIN, PETER

AFTER THE GOOD WAR (N) Stein-Day 1972; Pop 192

BRETNOR, REGINALD

A KILLING IN SWORDS (N) Pocket 81313; 1978;

BRETT, LEO See R. L. FANTHROPE

BRINTON, HENRY

PURPLE - 6 (N) Walker 1962; Avon S135;

BRISCO, PAT

THE OTHER PEOPLE (N) Powell PP24, 1970;

BRITAIN, DAN See DON PENDLETON

BROOKS, TERRY

THE SWORD OF SHANNARA (N) Random 1977; DR 24804; BBDR 27444;

BRODERICK, DAMIEN

SORCERER'S WORLD (N) Sig P4401, 1970;

BROWN, CARTER

GIRL FROM OUTER SPACE (N) Sig T5321, 1972; (Marginal)

BROWN, FREDRIC

ANGELS AND SPACESHIPS (C17) Dutton 1954; SFBC;
=STAR SHINE (C17) Bant 1423; 1956;
THE BEST OF FREDRIC BROWN (C29) SFBC; 1977; BBDR25700;
DAYMARES (C7) Lanc 73-727, 1968
HONEYMOON IN HELL (C21) Bant A1812, 1958; J2650;
THE LIGHTS IN THE SKY ARE STARS (N) Dutton 1953; SFBC; Bant 1285; J2578; S6917;
MARTIANS, GO HOME (N) Dutton 1955; SFBC; Bant A1546; BB 25314;
THE MIND THING (N) Bant A2187, 1961;
NIGHTMARES AND GEEZENSTACKS (C47) Bant J2296, 1961;
PARADOX LOST (C13) Random 1973; Berk N2656;
ROGUE IN SPACE (N) Dutton 1957; Bant A1701; S6763;
SPACE ON MY HANDS (C9) Shasta 1951; Bant 1077;
WHAT MAD UNIVERSE (N) Dutton 1949; Bant 835; 1253; Bant 10336; (fc 6/78)

BROWN, JAMES COOKE

THE TROIKA INCIDENT (N) Dday 1970;

BROWN, ROSEL GEORGE

SYBIL SUE BLUE SERIES
SYBIL SUE BLUE (N) Dday 1966;
=GALACTIC SYBIL SUE BLUE (N) Berkley X1503, 1968;
THE WATERS OF CENTAURUS (N) Dday 1970; Lancer 75-278;

A HANDFUL OF TIME (C12) BB F703, 1963;
EARTHBLOOD (N) (see K. Laumer-coauthor);

BROWN, WENZELL

POSSESS AND CONQUER (N) Warn 76-935, 1975;

BROWNE HOWARD

SERIES
WARRIOR OF THE DAWN (N) Reilly & Lee 1943;
RETURN OF THARN (N) Grandon 1956;

BRUNNER, JOHN ALSO KEITH WOODCOTT

AS KEITH WOODCOTT
I SPEAK FOR EARTH (N) Ace D+497, 1961;
LADDER IN THE SKY (N) Ace F+141, 1962;

THE MARTIAN SPHINX (N) Ace F-320, 1965;
PSIONIC MENACE (N) Ace F+199, 1963;

AGE OF MIRACLES (N) Ace 01000, 1973;
**=THE DAY OF THE STAR CITIES (N) Ace F-361; 1965;
THE ALTAR ON ASCONEL (N) Ace M+123, 1965;
THE ATLANTIC ABOMINATION (N) Ace D+465, 1960; 03300;
THE AVENGERS OF CARRIG (N) Dell 0356, 1969;
**=SECRET AGENT OF TERRA (N) Ace F+133, 1962;
BEDLAM PLANET (N) Ace G-709, 1968; 05301;
THE BOOK OF JOHN BRUNNER (C35) DAW 177, 1976;
BORN UNDER MARS (N) Ace G-664, 1967; 07160;
CATCH A FALLING STAR (N) Ace G-761, 1968; 09250;
**=THE 100TH MILLENNIUM (N) Ace D+362, 1959;
DOUBLE, DOUBLE (N) BB 72019, 1969;
THE DRAMATURGES OF YAN (N) Ace 16668, 1972;
THE DREAMING EARTH (N) Prmd F829, 1963; T2325; N3457;
ENDLESS SHADOW (N) Ace F+299, 1964;
ENIGMA FROM TANTALUS (N) Ace M+115, 1965;
ENTRY TO ELSEWHEN (C3) DAW 26, 1972; UY1154;
THE EVIL THAT MEN DO (N) Belm B60+1010, 1969; BT+50787;
FATHER OF LIES (N) Belm B60+081, 1968;
FROM THIS DAY FOREWARD (C13) Dday 1972; SFBC; DAW 72;
GIVE WARNING TO THE WORLD (N) DAW 112, 1974;
**=ECHO IN THE SKULL (N) Ace D+385, 1959;
INTO THE SLAVE NEBULA (N) Lanc 73-797, 1968; 75-346;
**=SLAVERS OF SPACE (N) Ace D+421, 1960;
INTERSTELLAR EMPIRE (C4) Daw 208, 1976; UE1362;
(=Altar on Asconel + Space Time Juggler +)
THE JAGGED ORBIT (N) Ace 38120, 1969; SFBC; 38121;
THE LONG RESULT (N) BB U2329, 1966; 1887;
MEETING AT INFINITY (N) Ace D+507, 1961; 52400;
MORE THINGS IN HEAVEN (N) Dell 5824, 1973;
**=THE ASTRONAUTS MUST NOT LAND (N) Ace F+227, 1963;
NO FUTURE IN IT (C11) Dday 1964; Curt 7008;
NOW, THEN (C3) Avon S323, 1968;
OUT OF MY MIND (C13) BB U5064, 1967;
A PLANET OF YOUR OWN (N) Ace G-592, 1966;
POLYMATH (N) DAW 85, 1974; UY1217;
**=CASTAWAYS WORLD (N) Ace F+242, 1963;
THE PRODUCTIONS OF TIME (N) Sig P3113, 1967; DAW 261
QUICKSAND (N) Dday 1967; SFBC; Bant H4212; DAW 203,
THE REPAIRMEN OF CYCLOPS (N) Ace M+115, 1965;
THE RITES OF OHE (N) Ace F+242, 1963;
SANCTUARY IN THE SKY (N) Ace D+471, 1960;
THE SHEEP LOOK UP (N) H&R 1972; SFBC; BB23612; 23926; 24948;
THE SHOCKWAVE RIDER (N) H&R 1975; SFBC; BB 24853; BBDR 27472;
THE SKYNAPPERS (N) Ace D+457, 1960:
TOMORROW MAY BE EVEN WORSE (P) Nesfa, 1978;

THE SPACE-TIME JUGGLER (N) ACE F+227, 1963;
THE SQUARES OF THE CITY (N) BB U6035, 1965; 1886; 23436;
STAND ON ZANZIBAR (N) Dday 1968; SFBC; BB 1713; 2758; 22758; 24082; 25486;
THE STONE THAT NEVER CAME DOWN (N) Dday 1973; SFBC; DAW 133;
THE SUPER BARBARIANS (N) Ace D+547, 1962;
THE STARDROPPERS (N) DAW 23, 1972; UY1197;
**=LISTEN THE STARS (N) Ace F+215, 1963;
THRESHOLD OF ETERNITY (N) Ace D+335, 1959;
TIMES WITHOUT NUMBER (N) Ace 81270, 1969;
**=TIMES WITHOUT NUMBER (N) Ace F+161, 1962; 81270;
TIME JUMP (C10) Dell 8917, 1973;
TO CONQUER CHAOS (N) Ace F-277, 1964;
TOTAL ECLIPSE (N) Dday 1974; SFBC; DAW 162
TIMESCOOP (N) Dell 8916, 1969;
THE TRAVELER IN BLACK (C4) Ace 82210, 1971
WEB OF EVERYWHERE (N) Bant Q8398, 1974
THE WHOLE MAN (N) BB U2219, 1964; 1885; 23437; Walker 1969; BBDR 27088
THE WORLD SWAPPERS (N) Ace D+391, 1959; 91051;
THE WRONG END OF TIME (N) Dday 1971; SFBC; DAW 61, UY1246;

BRYANT, EDWARD

AMONG THE DEAD (C17) Macmil 1973; Coll 1780;
CINNABAR (C8) Macmil 1976; Bant 10599;
PHOENIX WITHOUT ASHES (N) (With H. Ellison) G-M M3188, 1975;
from screenplay for the Starlost

BRYANT, PETER See PETER GEORGE

BUCKNER, ROBERT

STARFIRE (N) Perm M4185, 1960;
MOON PILOT (N) Perm M4241, 1962;

BUDRYS, ALGIS

THE AMSIRS AND THE IRON THORN (N) GMD1852, 1967;
BUDRYS INFERNO (C9) Berk F799, 1963;
THE FALLING TORCH (N) Prmd G-416, 1959; F693; F1028; X1837; N2776; N3430;
FALSE NIGHT (N) Lion 230, 1954;
=+SOME WILL NOT DIE (N) Regency RB110, 1961;
MAN OF EARTH (N) BB243, 1958;
MICHAELMAS (N) Berk/Put 1977; SFBC;
ROGUE MOON (N) G M s1057, 1960; L1474; Avon E 20925; Gregg 1977; Avon 38950;
THE UNEXPECTED DIMENSION (C7) BB 388K, 1960;
WHO? (N) Prmd G-339, 1958; Lanc 73-810, BB 24569;

BULMER, KENNETH

THE KEYS OF THE DIMENSIONS SERIES
THE KEY TO IRUNIUM (N) Ace H+20, 1967;
THE KEY TO VENUDINE (N) Ace H+65, 1968; +52500;

THE WIZARDS OF SENCHURIA (N) Ace +12140, 1969;
THE SHIPS OF DUROSTORUM (N) Ace +76096, 1970;
THE HUNTERS OF JUNDAGAI (N) Ace +68310, 1971;

BEHOLD THE STARS (N) Ace M+131, 1965;
BEYOND THE SILVER SKY (N) Ace D+507, 1961;
BLAZON (N) Curt 7099, 1970;
THE CHANGELING WORLDS (N) Ace D+369, 1959;
THE CHARIOTS OF RA (N) Ace +10293, 1972;
CITY UNDER THE SEA (N) Ace D+255, 1957; Avon E 26187;
CYCLE OF NEMESIS (N) Ace G-680, 1967;
DEMONS' WORLD (N) Ace F+289, 1964;
THE DOOMSDAY MEN (N) Dday 1968; Curt 7002;
THE EARTH GODS ARE COMING (N) Ace D+453, 1960;
THE ELECTRIC SWORD-SWALLOWERS (N) Ace +05595, 1971;
THE INSANE CITY (N) Curt 7122, 1971;
KANDAR (N) PBL 62-120, 1969;
LAND BEYOND THE MAP (N) Ace M+111, 1965;
THE MILLION YEAR HUNT (N) Ace F+285, 1964;
NO MAN'S WORLD (N) Ace F+104, 1961;
ON THE SYMB—SOCKET CIRCUIT (N) Ace 63165, 1972;
ROLLER COASTER WORLD (N) Ace 73438, 1972;
THE SECRET OF ZI (N) Ace D+331, 1958;
THE STAR VENTURER (N) Ace +22600, 1969;
SWORDS OF THE BARBARIANS (N) BT 50983, 1976;
TO OUTRUN DOOMSDAY (N) Ace G-625, 1967
THE WIZARD OF STARSHIP POSEIDON (N) Ace F+209, 1963
WORLDS FOR THE TAKING (N) Ace F-396, 1966;
See Ryder Hook Series

BULYCHEV, KIRILL

HALF A LIFE AND OTHER STORIES (C-) Macmil 1977;

BUNCH, DAVID R.

MODERAN (S46) Avon V2403, 1971;

BURGESS, ANTHONY =JOHN ANTHONY BURGESS WILSON

A CLOCKWORK ORANGE (N) Norton 1962; BB U5032; 1708; 02624; 22624; 24696;
THE WANTING SEED (N), Norton 1963; BBU 5030; 2011; 2654;

BURKE, JOHN

MOON ZERO TWO (N) Sig P4165, 1970;

BURKETT, WILLIAM R. JR.

SLEEPING PLANET (N) Dday 1965, PBL 54-445; 64-337;

BURROUGHS, EDGAR RICE (Partial Listing)

JOHN CARTER
A PRINCESS OF MARS (N) McClurg 1917; BB 701; BBU2031; 1521; 23578; SFBC;

THE GODS OF MARS (N) McClurg 1918; BB 702; BB U2032; 1522; 23579; SFBC
WARLORD OF MARS (N) McClurg 1919; BB 711; BB U2033; 1523; 23580;
THUVIA, MAID OF MARS (N) McClurg 1920; Ace F-168; BB770; U2034; 1524; 23581; SFBC
CHESSMEN OF MARS (N) McClurg 1922; Ace F-170; BB776; U2035; 1525; 23582;
MASTERMIND OF MARS (N) McClurg 1928; Ace F-181; BB U2036; 1526; 23583; SFBC
A FIGHTING MAN OF MARS (N) Metro 1931; Ace F-190; BB U2037; 1527; 23584;
SWORDS OF MARS (N) ERB 1936; BB 728; BB U2038; 1528; 23585; SFBC
SYNTHETIC MEN OF MARS (N) ERB 1940; BB 739; BB U2039; 1529; 23586;
LLANA OF GATHOL (N) ERB 1948; BB 762; BB U2040; 1530; 23587; SFBC
JOHN CARTER OF MARS (N) Canaveral 1964; BB U2041; 1531; 23588;

CARSON NAPIER

PIRATES OF VENUS (N) ERB 1934; Ace F-179; 66500;
LOST ON VENUS (N) ERB 1935; Ace F221; 49501;
CARSON OF VENUS (N) ERB 1939; Ace F-247; 09200;
ESCAPE ON VENUS (N) ERB 1946; Ace F-268; 21561;
THE WIZARD OF VENUS (N+1)Ace 90190, 1970;

PELLUCIDAR

AT THE EARTHS CORE (N) McClurg 1922; Ace F-156; G733, 03321; SFBC;
PELLUCIDAR (N) McClurg 1923; Ace F-158; G-734; 65851;
TANAR OF PELLUCIDAR (N) Metro 1930; Ace F-171; G-735; 79791;
TARZAN AT THE EARTH'S CORE (N) Metro 1930; Ace F-180; G-736; 79851; BB U2013;
BACK TO THE STONE AGE (N) ERB 1937; Ace F-245; G-737; 04631;
LAND OF TERROR (N) ERB 1944; Ace F;-256; G-738; 46996;
SAVAGE PELLUCIDAR (N) Canaveral 1963; Ace F-280; G-739; 75131;

THE MOON MAID (N) McClurg 1926;
=& THE MOON MAID (N) Ace F-157, 1963; G-745; 53700;
=& THE MOON MEN (N) Ace F-159, 1963; G-748; 53750;

THE LAND THAT TIME FORGOT (N) McClurg 1924; SFBC;
=& THE LAND THAT TIME FORGOT (N) Ace F-213, 1963; 47020;
=& THE PEOPLE THAT TIME FORGOT (N) Ace F-220, 1963; 65941;
=& OUT OF TIME'S ABYSS (N) Ace F-233, 1963 64481;

THE WAR CHIEF (N) McClurg 1927; BB U2045; 3082; 24634; (Western)
APACHE DEVIL (N) ERB 1933; BB U2046; 24605; (Western)

THE MUCKER (N) McClurg 1921; BB U6039; (Not SF)
THE RETURN OF THE MUCKER (N) Ace 71815, 1974; (Not SF)

THE OAKDALE AFFAIR & THE RIDER (2N) ERB 1937; (Not SF)
=& THE OAKDALE AFFAIR (N) Ace 60563, 1974; (Not SF)
=& THE RIDER (N) Ace 72280, 1974; (Not SF)

BEYOND THE FARTHEST STAR (N) Ace F-282, 1964; 05651;
BEYOND THIRTY (N) Eshbach pb 1955; SFFP; 1957 (With Man Eater - not SF)
=THE LOST CONTINENT (N) Ace F235, 1963; 49291;
THE CAVE GIRL (N) McClurg 1925; Dell 320, 1949; Ace F-258; 09280;
THE ETERNAL LOVER (N) McClurg 1925;
=THE ETERNAL SAVAGE (N) Ace F-234, 1963; 21801;
JUNGLE GIRL (N) ERB 1932;
=THE LAND OF HIDDEN MEN (N) Ace F-232, 1963; 47015;

THE LAD AND THE LION (N) ERB 1938; BB U2048; Ace 46870;
THE MAD KING (N) McClurg 1926; Ace F-270; 51401; (Not SF)
THE MONSTER MEN (N) McClurg 1929; Ace F-182; 53587;
THE OUTLAW OF TORN (N) McClurg 1927; Ace A-25; (Not S.F.)
TALES OF THREE PLANETS (3N) Canaveral 1964;

TARZAN

TARZAN OF THE APES (N) McClurg 1914; BB 745; U2001;+
THE RETURN OF TARZAN (N) McClurg 1915; BB746; U2002;+
THE BEASTS OF TARZAN (N) McClurg 1916; Ace F-203; BB747; U2003;+
THE SON OF TARZAN (N) McClurg 1917; Ace F-193; BB748; U2004;+
TARZAN AND THE JEWELS OF OPAR (N) McClurg 1918; Ace F-204; BB749; U2005;++
JUNGLE TALES OF TARZAN (N) McClurg 1919; Ace F-206; BB750; U2006;+
TARZAN THE UNTAMED (N) McClurg 1920; BB751; U2007;+
TARZAN THE TERRIBLE (N) McClurg 1921; BB752; U2008;+
TARZAN AND THE GOLDEN LION (N) McClurg 1923; BB753; U2009;+
TARZAN AND THE ANT MEN (N) McClurg 1929; BB754; U2010;+
TARZAN, LORD OF THE JUNGLE (N) McClurg1928; BB772; U2011;+
TARZAN AND THE LOST EMPIRE (N) Metro 1929; Dell 536; Ace F-169; BB OF777;+
TARZAN AT THE EARTH'S CORE (N) Metro 1930; Ace F-180; G736; BB U2013; Ace 79851 ;
TARZAN THE INVINCIBLE (N) ERB 1931; Ace F-189; BB U2014; +
TARZAN TRIUMPHANT (N) ERB 1932; Ace F-194; BB U2015;;+
TARZAN AND THE CITY OF GOLD (N) ERB 1933; Ace F-205; BB U2016;+
TARZAN AND THE LION MAN (N) ERB 1934; Ace F-212; BB U2017;+
TARZAN AND THE LEOPARD MEN (N) ERB 1935; BB U2018;+
TARZAN'S QUEST (N) ERB 1936; BB; U2019;+
TARZAN AND THE FORBIDDEN CITY (N) ERB 1938: BB; U2020;
TARZAN THE MAGNIFICANT (N) ERB 1939; BB; U2021;+
TARZAN AND THE FOREIGN LEGION (N) ERB 1947; U2022;+
TARZAN AND THE MADMAN (N) Canaveral 1964; BBu2023;
TARZAN AND THE CASTAWAYS (S3) Canaveral 1965; BB U2024;
TARZAN AND THE VALLEY OF GOLD (N) (See Fritz Leiber)

BURROUGHS, JOHN COLEMAN son of E R Burroughs

TREASURE OF THE BLACK FALCON (N) BB U6085, 1967;

BURROUGHS, WILLIAM S.

EXTERMINATOR (N) Viking 1973;
NOVA EXPRESS (N) Grove 1964; Evergreen BC 102
THE SOFT MACHINE (N) Grove 1966; BB 23604;
THE TICKET THAT EXPLODED (N) Grove 1967; Evergreen B164;
THE WILD BOYS: A BOOK OF THE DEAD (N) Grove 1971

BUSBY, F. M.

THE SAGA OF RISSA

RISSA KERGUELEN (N) Berk/Put 1976;
THE LONG VIEW (N) Berk/Put 1976;
BOTH=RISSA KERGUELEN (2N) Berk 3411, 1977;

BARTON SERIES

CAGE A MAN (N) SFBC 1973; Sig Q5918;
THE PROUD ENEMY (N) Berk N2846, 1975;

BUTLER, OCTAVIA

PATTERNMASTER (N) Dday 1976
MIND OF MY MIND (N) Dday 1977;
SURVIVOR (N) Dday 1978;

BUTLER, SAMUEL

EREWHON (N) (Brit 1880) Sig CD41, 1961; Coll HS 16; Air CL30;

BUTLER, WILLIAM

THE BUTTERFLY REVOLUTION (N) Putnam 1967; BB U6099; 24045 (Marginal)

BYRNE, STUART J. ALSO JOHN BLOODSTONE

THE ALPHA TRAP (N) Major 3059, 1976; 194;
GODMAN (N) (as Bloodstone) Pow PP 205, 1970;
STARMAN (N) Pow PP 165, 1969;
THUNDAR, MAN OF TWO WORLDS (N) (as Bloodstone) Leis LB 25S, 1971;

C

CABELL, JAMES BRANCH (partial listing)

THE CREAM OF THE JEST (N) McBride 1922; BBAF 2364, 1971
DOMNEI (2N) McBride 1920; BBAF 2345, 1972
FIGURES OF EARTH (N) McBride 1921; BBAF 1763, 1969;
THE HIGH PLACE (N) McBride 1923; BBAF 1855, 1970
JURGEN (N) McBride 1919; Penguin 601; Xanadu pb; Avon VS 7;
THE SILVER STALLION (N) McBride 1926; BBAF 1678, 1969;
SOMETHING ABOUT EVE (N) McBride 1927; BBAF 2067, 1971;

CAIDIN, MARTIN

STEVE AUSTIN

CYBORG (N) Arbor 1972; WPBL; 66986; 76-643
OPERATION NUKE (N) Arbor 1973; Warn 76-061;
HIGH CRYSTAL (N) Arbor 1974; Warn 76408;
CYBORG IV (N) Arbor 1975; Warn 78-655;

AQUARIUS MISSION (N) Bant 11267, 1978;
FOUR CAME BACK (N) Mckay 1968; Bant N4870
THE GOD MACHINE (N) Dutton 1968; Bant S3959;
THE LAST FATHOM (N) Meredith 1967; Pinn 483;
THE LONG NIGHT (N) Dodd-Mead 1956
MAROONED (N) Dutton 1964; Bant S2965; N5206;
THE MENDELOV CONSPIRACY (N) Meredith 1969; Pinn 458
NO MAN'S WORLD (N) Dutton 1967;

CALISHER, HORTENSE

JOURNAL FROM ELLIPSIA (N) Little-B 1965;

CALLENBACH, ERNEST

ECOTOPIA (N) Banyan Tree 1975; Bant 10489, 1977;

CALVINO, ITALO

THE BARON IN THE TREES (N) Harbrace HPL 72, 1977;
THE CASTLE OF CROSSED DESTINIES (C16) H-B-J 1977;
COSMICOMICS (C12) H-B-W 1968; HPL 69; Coll 1820; Harbrace 6226;
INVISIBLE CITIES (N) H-B-J 1975; HBJ 645380;
THE NON-EXISTENT KNIGHT & THE CLOVEN VISCOUNT (2N) Harbrace HPL 73, 1977;
T ZERO (N) H-B-W 1969; HPL 70; Coll 1821; Harbrace 6924;
THE WATCHER (C3) H-B-J 1971;

CAMERON, IAN = DONALD GORDON PAYNE

THE LOST ONES (N) Morrow 1968 Avon V2327,
=ISLAND AT THE TOP OF THE WORLD (N) Avon 20966, 1974; BC;
THE MOUNTAINS AT THE BOTTOM OF THE WORLD (N) Morrow 1974; Avon 21402;

CAMERON, LOU

CYBERNIA (N) G-M T2593, 1972

CAMPBELL, JOHN W. JR.

ARCOT, MOREY AND WADE
THE BLACK STAR PASSES (S3) Fantasy 1953; Ace F-346; 06701;
ISLANDS OF SPACE (N) Fantasy 1956; Ace M-143;
INVADERS FROM THE INFINITE (N) Fantasy 1961; Gnome 1961; Ace M-154;
ALL =THE JOHN W. CAMPBELL ANTHOLOGY (3N) Dday 1973

AARN MUNRO SERIES
THE MIGHTIEST MACHINE (N) Hadley 1947; Ace F-364; 53151;
THE INCREDIBLE PLANET (N) Fantasy 1949;

THE BEST OF JOHN W. CAMPBELL (C12) SFBC 1976; BB 24960;
CLOAK OF AESIR (S7) Shasta 1952; Lanc 75-333; Hyperion 1975;
THE MOON IS HELL (N+1) Fantasy 1950; Fantasy GSFL1; Ace 53870;
THE PLANETEERS (S5) Ace G+585, 1966;
THE ULTIMATE WEAPON (N) Ace F+585, 1966; 84331;
WHO GOES THERE? (C7) Shasta 1948;
WHO GOES THERE AND OTHER STORIES (C6) Dell D150, 1955;
THE SPACE BEYOND (C3) Prmd M3742, 1976;

CAPEK, KAREL (partial listing)

THE ABSOLUTE AT LARGE (N) Macmil 1927; Hyperion 1975; Garland 1976;
R.U.R. (Play) Dday 1923; Poc 46605, 1973; Wash Sq 46293;
WAR WITH THE NEWTS (N) Putnam 1939; Bant A1292; FC46; QC250; Berk S1404; 3168; Gregg 1976;

CAPON, PAUL

THE WORLD AT BAY (JN) Winston 1954;
LOST, A MOON (JN) Bobbs-M 1956;

CARPENTIER, ALEJO

WAR OF TIME (C5) Knopf 1970; (Marginal)

CARPENTER, ELMER J.

MOONSPIN (N) Flagship 92-715, 1967;

CARR, JOHN DICKSON - Also CARTER DICKSON

THE BURNING COURT (N) Harper 1937; Pop 28; Bant 1207; J2706; Award A459X; A771S;
THE DEVIL IN VELVET (N) Harper 1951; Bant A1009; F2052; S3637;
FEAR IS THE SAME (N) (as Dickson) Harper 1957;
FIRE BURN (N) Bant A1847, 1959; S3638; Award AD 1483;

CARR, JOHN F.

THE OPHIDIAN CONSPIRACY (N) Major 3055, 1976; 055;
THE PAIN GAIN (N) Major 3154, 1977;

CARR, ROBERT S.

BEYOND INFINITY (C4) Fantasy 1951; Dell 781;

CARR, TERRY WITH T. WHITE = NORMAN EDWARDS

INVASION FROM 2500 (N) (as Edwards) Monarch 453, 1964;
WARLORD OF KOR (N) Ace F+177, 1963;
CIRQUE (N) Bobbs-M 1977; Crest 23556,1978;(fc 5/78)
THE LIGHT AT THE END OF THE UNIVERSE (C15) Pyramid A 3982, 1977;

CARRIGAN, RICHARD AND NANCY

THE SIREN STARS (N) Prmd T2446, 1971;

CARROLL, GLADYS HASTY

MAN ON THE MOUNTAIN (N) Little - B 1969; Pop 1433;

CARTER, ANGELA

HEROES & VILLAINS (N) S&S 1970; Pocket 77492;
THE WAR OF DREAMS (N) HBJ 1974; Bard 31948;
THE PASSION OF NEW EVE (N) H-B-J 1977;

CARTER, LIN

THONGOR
THE WIZARD OF LEMURIA (N) Ace F-326, 1965;
=+THONGOR AND THE WIZARD OF LEMURIA (N) Berk X1777, 1969; N3042;
THONGOR OF LEMURIA (N) Ace F-383, 1966;
=+THONGOR AND THE DRAGON CITY (N) Berk X1799, 1970; N3068; 3572;
THONGOR AGAINST THE GODS (N) PBL 52-586, 1967;
THONGOR IN THE CITY OF MAGICIANS (N) PBL 53-655, 1968;

THONGOR FIGHTS THE PIRATES OF TARAKUS (N) Berk X1861, 1970; 3147;
THONGOR AT THE END OF TIME (N) PBL 53-780, 1970;

CALLISTO

JANDAR OF CALLISTO (N) Dell 4182, 1972; 14182;
BLACK LEGION OF CALLISTO (N) Dell 0925, 1972;
SKY PIRATES OF CALLISTO (N) Dell 8050, 1973;
MAD EMPRESS OF CALLISTO (N) Dell 6143, 1975;
MIND WIZARD OF CALLISTO (N) Dell 5600, 1975;
LANKAR OF CALLISTO (N) Dell 4648, 1975;
YLANA OF CALLISTO (N) Dell 14244, 1977;
RENEGADE OF CALLISTO (N) Dell 14377, 1978;(fc 8/78)

GREEN STAR

UNDER THE GREEN STAR (N) DAW 30, 1972; UY1185;
WHEN THE GREEN STAR CALLS (N) DAW 62, 1973; UY1267;
BY THE LIGHT OF THE GREEN STAR (N) DAW 110, 1974; UY1268;
AS THE GREEN STAR RISES (N) DAW 138, 1975;
IN THE GREEN STAR'S GLOW (N) DAW 180, 1976;

ZARKON-LORD OF THE UNKNOWN

THE NEMESIS OF EVIL (N) Dday 1975; Pop 04185;
INVISIBLE DEATH (N) Dday 1975; Pop 04256;(fc 7/78)
THE VOLCANO OGRE (N) Dday 1976;

GONDWANE

GIANT OF WORLD'S END (N) Belm B50-853, 1969;
THE WARRIOR OF WORLD'S END (N) DAW 125, 1974; UY1321;
THE ENCHANTRESS OF WORLD'S END (N) DAW 150, 1975;
THE IMMORTAL OF WORLD'S END (N) Daw 210, 1976;
THE BARBARIAN OF WORLD'S END (N) DAW 243, 1977;

HISTORY OF THE GREAT IMPERIUM

OUTWORLDER (N) Lanc 74-722, 1971;
THE MAN WITHOUT A PLANET (N) Ace G+606, 1966;
STAR ROGUE (N) Lanc 74-649, 1970;

BEYOND THE GATES OF DREAM (C7) Belm B60-1032, 1969; B-T 40-145; LB519DK
THE BLACK STAR (N) Dell 0932, 1973;
THE CITY OUTSIDE THE WORLD (N) Berk 3549, 1977;
DESTINATION SATURN (N) (See also D. Wolkheim co-author)
THE FLAME OF IRIDAR (N) Belm B50+759, 1967;
LOST WORLD OF TIME (N) Sig P4068, 1969;
THE MAN WHO LOVED MARS (N) GM T2690, 1973;
THE PURLOINED PLANET (N) Belm B60+1010, 1969; BT +50787;
THE QUEST OF THE KADJI (N) Belm B95-2146, 1971;
THE STAR MAGICIANS (N) Ace G+588, 1966;
THE THIEF OF THOTH (N) Belm B50+809, 1968; B-T 50+244;
TIME WAR (N) Dell 8625, 1974;
TOWER AT THE EDGE OF TIME (N) Belm B50-804, 1968; BT40-126; Towr 43-321;
TOWER OF THE MEDUSA (N) Ace+42900, 1969
THE VALLEY WHERE TIME STOOD STILL (N) Dday 1974; Pop 344;
WIZARD OF ZAO (N) Daw 293, 1978;

CARTMILL, CLEVE

THE SPACE SCAVENGERS (N) Major 3013, 1975;

CARVER, JEFFREY

SEAS OF ERNATHE (N) Laser 34, 1976;

CASEWIT, CURTIS W.

THE PEACEMAKERS (N) Avalon 1960; M-B 60-321,

CASTLE, J. LLOYD

SATELLITE E ONE (N) Dodd-M 1954; SFBC; Bant A1766;
VANGUARD TO VENUS (N) Dodd-M 1957; SFBC;

CHALKER, JACK L. QUEST FOR THE WELL OF SOULS 1978

A JUNGLE OF STARS (N) BB25457, 1976;
MIDNIGHT AT THE WELL OF SOULS (N) BBDR 25768, 1977;
THE WEB OF THE CHOZEN (N) BBDR 27376, 1978;

CHAMBERS, ROBERT W. (partial listing)

THE KING IN YELLOW (C10) Neely 1895; Ace M-132; Dover (C) 22500; Ace 44481;
THE MAKER OF MOONS (C8) Putnam 1896;
THE MAKER OF MOONS (S) Shroud 1954; Fantasy House F H 4 1974;

CHANDLER, A. BERTRAM

JOHN GRIMES & THE RIM WORLDS
INTO THE ALTERNATE UNIVERSE (N) Ace M + 107, 1964; + 114512;
CONTRABAND FROM OTHERSPACE (N) Ace G + 609, 1967;
THE ROAD TO THE RIM (N) Ace H + 29, 1967; +73100;
SPARTAN PLANET (N) Dell 8174, 1969;
THE RIM GODS (N) Ace +72400, 1969;
ALTERNATE ORBITS (N) Ace + 13783, 1971;
THE DARK DIMENSIONS (N) Ace + 13783, 1971;
TO PRIME THE PUMP (N) Curtis 7116, 1971;
THE INHERITORS (N) Ace + 37062, 1972 +37063
THE GATEWAY TO NEVER (N) Ace + 37062, 1972;+37063
THE HARD WAY UP (N) Ace + 31755, 1972; +73100;
THE BIG BLACK MARK (N) DAW 139, 1975; 1355;
STAR COURIER (N) DAW 234, 1977;
THE WAY BACK (N) Daw 273, 1978;
TO KEEP THE SHIP (N) Daw 295, 1978;

OTHER RIM WORLDS STORIES
THE RIM OF SPACE (N) Avalon 1961; Ace F + 133;
RENDEZVOUS ON A LOST WORLD (N) Ace F + 117, 1961; + 15890;
BEYOND THE GALACTIC RIM (S4) Ace F + 237, 1963;
THE SHIP FROM OUTSIDE (N) Ace F + 237, 1963;
CATCH THE STAR WINDS (N + 1) Lancer 74-533, 1969;

EMPRESS
EMPRESS OF OUTER SPACE (N) Ace M + 129, 1965;

SPACE MERCENARIES (N) Ace M + 133, 1965;
NEBULA ALERT (N) Ace G + 632, 1967;

THE ALTERNATE MARTIANS (N) Ace M + 129, 1965;
BRING BACK YESTERDAY (N) Ace D + 517, 1961;
THE COILS OF TIME (N) Ace M + 107, 1964; + 114512;
GLORY PLANET (N) Avalon 1964;
THE HAMELIN PLAGUE (N) Monarch 390, 1963;
THE SEA BEASTS (N) Curtis 7135, 1971;

CHANT, JOY

RED MOON AND BLACK MOUNTAIN (N) BB 2178, 1971; SFBC; 23611, Dutton 1976;
THE GREY MANE OF MORNING (N) Allen & Unwin 1977;

CHAPMAN, D.D. & TARZAN, DELORIS LEHMAN

RED TIDE (N) Ace 71160, 1975;

CHARBONNEAU, LOUIS

BARRIER WORLD (N) Lanc 74-687, 1970;
CORPUS EARTHLING (N) Zenith ZB-40, 1960;
DOWN TO EARTH (N) Bant F3442, 1967;
EMBRYO (N) Warn 86-004, 1976;
NO PLACE ON EARTH (N) Dday 1958; SFBC; Crst S342;
PSYCHEDELIC - 40 (N) Bant F2929, 1964;
THE SENSITIVES (N) Bant H3759, 1968; (from script by Deane Romeno)
THE SENTINEL STARS (N) Bant J2686, 1963;

CHARNAS, SUZY McKEE

WALK TO THE END OF THE WORLD (N) BB 23788, 1974; BBDR 25661

CHASE, ADAM = P. FAIRMAN AND M. LESSER

CHERRYH, C. J.

MORGAINE SERIES
GATE OF IVREL (N) DAW 188, 1976; 1375;
WELL OF SHIUAN (N) Daw 284;

THE FADED SUN: KESRITH (N) SFBC 1978;
HUNTER OF WORLDS (N) SFBC 1977; DAW 252
BROTHERS OF EARTH (N) SFBC 1976; DAW 212

CHESTER, WILLIAM L.

KIOGA SERIES
HAWK OF THE WILDERNESS (N) Harper 1936; Ace G-586, 1966;
KIOGA OF THE WILDERNESS (N) DAW 209, 1976;
ONE AGAINST THE WILDERNESS (N) DAW 228, 1977;
KIOGA OF THE UNKNOWN LAND (N) Daw 290, 1978;

CHESTERTON, G. K. (Partial Listing)

THE MAN WHO WAS THURSDAY (N) Dodd-M 1908; Capricorn CAP 27, 1960; BB 2305; Sheed & Ward 1975;

CHILSON, ROBERT

AS THE CURTAIN FALLS (N) DAW 98, 1974;
THE STAR-CROWNED KINGS (N) DAW 161, 1975;
THE SHORES OF KANSAS (N) Pop 358, 1976;

CHRISTOPHER, JOHN = CHRISTOPHER SAM YOUD

TRIPODS SERIES
THE PRINCE IN WAITING (JN) Macmil 1970; Coll;
BEYOND THE BURNING LANDS (JN) Macmil 1971; Coll;
THE SWORD OF THE SPIRITS (JN) Macmil 1972; Coll 4264;

WILL PARKER SERIES
THE WHITE MOUNTAINS (JN) Macmil 1967; Coll 4271;
THE CITY OF GOLD AND LEAD (JN) Macmil 1967; Coll 4270;
THE POOL OF FIRE (JN) Macmil 1968; Coll 4272;

OTHER JUVENILE NOVELS
THE GUARDIANS (JN) Macmil 1970; Coll 4268;
WILD JACK (JN) Macmil 1974;
THE LOTUS CAVES (JN) Macmil 1969; Coll 4269;

THE LITTLE PEOPLE (N) S&S 1966; SFBC; Avon V2243;
THE LONG WINTER (N) S&S 1962; SFBC; Crst d612; GM R2001; T2323;
PENDULUM (N) S&S 1968; SFBC; Lanc 75-080;
PLANET IN PERIL (N) Avon T371, 1959;
THE POSSESSORS (N) S&S 1964; SFBC; Avon S230;
NO BLADE OF GRASS (N) S&S 1957; SFBC; Poc 1183; Avon S288; V2398; E23903;
THE RAGGED EDGE (N) S&S 1965; SFBC; Sig P3124;
SWEENEY'S ISLAND (N) S&S 1964; Cres R1029;
THE TWENTY-SECOND CENTURY (C20) Lanc 74-811, 1962;

CLAGETT, JOHN

A WORLD UNKNOWN (N) Pop 275, 1975;
THE ORANGE R (N) Pop 04225, 1978;

CLARK, CURT = DONALD WESTLAKE

ANARCHAOS (N) Ace F-421, 1967;

CLARK, RONALD

THE BOMB THAT FAILED (N) Morrow 1969;
QUEEN VICTORIA'S BOMB (N) Morrow 1968;

CLARKE, ARTHUR C.

ONMIBUS COLLECTIONS (reprints of novels and stories)
ACROSS THE SEA OF STARS (B. + D. +C18) Harcourt 1959; SFBC;
FROM THE OCEAN, FROM THE STARS (A. + C. +C24) H-B-W 1961; SFBC;
THE NINE BILLION NAMES OF GOD (C21) Harcourt 1967; HPL 50; Sig Y5949;
PRELUDE TO MARS (E. + F. +C16) H-B-W. 1965; SFBC;

AGAINST THE FALL OF NIGHT (N) Gnome 1953; Perm 310; Prmd G554; F754; S1703; N 2281;
A. =+ THE CITY AND THE STARS (N) Harcourt-B 1956; SFBC; Sig S1464; D1858; Y6452;

B. CHILDHOOD'S END (N) BBHC 1953; BB 33; 398K; U2111; U5066; 1558; SFBC; BB 24937;
C. THE DEEP RANGE (N) Harcourt-B 1957; Sig S1583; D2528; Harcourt HPL 36; Y5995;
DOLPHIN ISLAND (JN) H-R-W 1963; Berk F1495; S1914;
D. EARTHLIGHT (N) BBHC 1955; BB97; 249; F698; U2824; 1560; 2752; 22752; 24888; 25193;
EXPEDITION TO EARTH (C11) BBHC 1953; BB 52; 472K; U2112; 1559; 2751; 22751; 24849; 25587;
A FALL OF MOONDUST (N) H-B-W 1961; Dell 2463; HPL 46; Sig Y5814; W 7322;
GLIDE PATH (N) Harcourt-B 1963; Dell 2919; (Not S. F.)
IMPERIAL EARTH (N) H-B-J 1976; SFBC; BB 25232;
ISLANDS IN THE SKY (JN) Winston 1952; Sig S1769; KD 510; T4895; Q5521;
THE LION OF COMARRE & AGAINST THE FALL OF NIGHT (2N) H-B-W 1968; SFBC; HPL 56;
E. PRELUDE TO SPACE (N) Galx 3, 1951; Gnome 1954; BB 68; (=) Lanc 75172; BB 25113;
=MASTER OF SPACE (N) Lanc 72-610, 1961
=THE SPACE DREAMERS (N) LANC 74-524, 1969
RENDEZVOUS WITH RAMA (N) H-B-J 1973; SFBC; BB 24175; 25346;
F. SANDS OF MARS (N) Gnome 1952; SFBC; Poc 989; Perm M4149; HPL 53; Sig Y5754; W7486;
2001: A SPACE ODYSSEY (N) NAL 1968; SFBC; Sig Q3580; Y5224; E6625;
THE OTHER SIDE OF THE SKY (C24) Harcourt-B 1958; Sig S1729; D2433; Q5553;
REACH FOR TOMORROW (C12) BBHC 1956; BB 135; U2110; 1561; 2753; 22753; 25037;
TALES FROM THE WHITE HART (C15) BB 186, 1957; 539; U2113; 1562; HBW 1970; BB 2754; 24165;
TALES OF TEN WORLDS (C15) Harcourt-B 1962; Dell 8467, 1964; HPL 47; Sig Q5452;
THE WIND FROM THE SUN (C19) H-B-J, 1973; SFBC; Sig Q5581;

CLARKSON, HELEN = ?

THE LAST DAY (N) Dodd Mead 1959;

CLAYTON, JO

DIADEM FOR THE STARS (N) DAW 235, 1977;
LAMARCHOS (N) DAW 275, 1978;

CLEMENT, HAL = HARRY C. STUBBS

SERIES
MISSION OF GRAVITY (N) Dday 1954; Galaxy 33; SFBC; Prmd F786; X2063; N3479; BBDR 27092; Gregg 1978;
STAR LIGHT (N) BB 2361, 1971; BBDR 27358;

CLOSE TO CRITICAL (N) BB U2215, 1964; 1949; 24508;
CYCLE OF FIRE (N) BBHC 1957; BB 200; 1948; 70007; 24368;
ICEWORLD (N) Gnome 1953; Lanc 75-128; 75422; BBDR 25805; 27092;
NATIVES OF SPACE (N) BB U2235, 1965; 1950;
NEEDLE (N) Dday 1950; SFBC; Avon S255; Lanc 74-557; 75-385; Avon E28555;
=FROM OUTER SPACE (N) Avon T175, 1957; G1168;
OCEAN ON TOP (N) DAW 57, 1973;
RANGER BOYS IN SPACE (JN) Page 1956;
SMALL CHANGES (C9) Dday 1969
=SPACE LASH (C9) Dell 8039, 1969;
THROUGH THE EYE OF A NEEDLE (N) BBDR 25850;

CLIFTON, MARK

EIGHT KEYS TO EDEN (N) Dday 1960; SFBC; BB F639;
THEY'D RATHER BE RIGHT (N) (with F. Riley) Gnome 1957;
=THE FOREVER MACHINE (N) Galaxy 35, 1959;
WHEN THEY COME FROM SPACE (N) Dday 1962; SFBC; M-B 40-105; 50-341

CLINE, LINDA

THE MIRACLE SEASON (N) Berk/Put 1976; Berk 3447;

CLINGERMAN, MILDRED

A CUPFUL OF SPACE (C16) BB 519K, 1961;

CLINTON, JEFF

KANE'S ODYSSEY (N) Laser 16, 1976;

CLOW, MARTHA deMAY

STARBREED (N) BB 1857, 1970;

COBLENTZ, STANTON A.

AFTER 12,000 YEARS (N) FPCI 1950; Garland 1975;
THE BLUE BARBARIANS (N) Avalon 1958;
THE CRIMSON CAPSULE (N) Avalon 1967;
=THE ANIMAL PEOPLE (N) Belm 75-2038, 1970
THE DAY THE WORLD STOPPED (N) Avalon 1968;
HIDDEN WORLD (N) Avalon 1957; Air SF6,
=IN CAVERNS BELOW (N) Garland 1975;
THE ISLAND PEOPLE (N) Belm 75-2180, 1971;
INTO PLUTONIAN DEPTHS (N) Avon 281, 1950
THE LAST OF THE GREAT RACE (N) Arcadia 1964;
THE LIZARD LORDS (N) Avalon 1964;
LORD OF TRANERICA (N) Avalon 1966;
LOST COMET (N) Arcadia 1964;
THE MOON PEOPLE (N) Avalon 1964; Belm 75-2024, 1970;
NEXT DOOR TO THE SUN (N) Avalon 1960;
THE PLANET OF YOUTH (N) FPCI 1952;
THE RUNAWAY WORLD (N) Avalon 1961;
THE SUNKEN WORLD (N) FPCI 1949;
UNDER THE TRIPLE SUNS (N) Fantasy 1955;
WHEN THE BIRDS FLY SOUTH (N) Wings 1945;
THE WONDER STICK (N) Cosmopolitan 1929;

COGSWELL, THEODORE R.

THE THIRD EYE (C16) Belm B50-840, 1968;
THE WALL AROUNG THE WORLD (C10) Prmd F-703, 1962; N3278;
SEE STAR TREK SERIES;

COHEN, BARNEY

THE NIGHT OF THE TOY DRAGONS (N) Berk 3452, 1977;

COLE, BURT

THE FUNCO FILE (N) Dday 1969; SFBC; Avon N313;

COLE, EVERETT B.

THE PHILOSOPHICAL CORPS (N) Gnome 1962;

COLEMAN, JAMES NELSON

THE NULL FREQUENCY IMPULSER (N) Berk X1660, 1969;
SEEKER FROM THE STARS (N) Berk X1438, 1967;

COLLIER, JOHN

FANCIES AND GOODNIGHTS (C50) Dday 1951; Bant A1106; F1703; SC 91; N4614;
THE JOHN COLLIER READER (C49) Knopf 1972
=THE BEST OF JOHN COLLIER (C47+2) Poc 80076, 1975;
HIS MONKEY WIFE (N) Appleton 1931; Dday 1957; Dolphin C30; Poc 78873;

COLLINS, HUNT see EVAN HUNTER

COLLINS, MICHAEL = DENNIS LYNDS

THE PLANETS OF DEATH (N) Berk S1872, 1970;
LUKAN WAR (N) Belm B60-1023, 1969

COMPTON, D. G.

CHRONOCULES (N) Ace 10480, 1970;
FAREWELL, EARTH'S BLISS (N) Ace 22830, 1971;
THE MISSIONARIES (N) Ace 53570, 1972;
THE QUALITY OF MERCY (N) Ace 69540, 1970;
THE SILENT MULTITUDE (N) Ace 76385, 1970;
THE STEEL CROCODILE (N) Ace 78575, 1970; Gregg 1976;
SYNTHAJOY (N) Ace H-96, 1968; Gregg 1977;
THE UNSLEEPING EYE (N) DAW 102, 1974;

CONEY, MICHAEL G.

FRIENDS COME IN BOXES (N) DAW 56, 1973;
THE HERO OF DOWNWAYS (N) DAW 70, 1973;
THE JAWS THAT BITE, THE CLAWS THAT CATCH (N) DAW 144, 1975;
MIRROR IMAGE (N) DAW 31, 1972;
MONITOR FOUND IN ORBIT (C9) DAW 120, 1974;
RAX (N) DAW 170, 1975;
SYZYGY (N) BB 03056, 1973;

CONNER, MICHAEL

I AM NOT THE OTHER HOUDINI (N) Harper 1978; (fc 6/78)

CONQUEST, ROBERT

A WORLD OF DIFFERENCE (N) BB U2213, 1964

CONWAY, GERARD F. also Wallace Moore

MINDSHIP (N) DAW 90, 1973;
THE MIDNIGHT DANCERS (N) Ace 52975, 1971;
SEE BALZAN SERIES

CONRAD, EARL

THE DAVINCI MACHINE (S16) Fleet 1969; Curt 7105, 1971;

CONVERTITO, BILL

THE ROMBELLA SHUTTLE (N) Major 3160, 1977;

COOK, GLEN

THE HEIRS OF BABYLON (N) Sig Q5299, 1972;

COOMBS, CHARLES IRA

THE MYSTERY OF SATELLITE (JN) Westminister 1958; Tempo T9;

COON, HORACE C.

43,000 YEARS LATER (N) Sig 1534, 1958;

COOPER, EDMUND ALSO RICHARD AVERY

ALL FOOL'S DAY (N) Walker 1966; Berk X1469;
THE CLOUD WALKER (N) BB 3209, 1973;
DEADLY IMAGE (N) BB260, 1958; 01577;
A FAR SUNSET (N) Walker 1967; Berk X1607; Ace 22819;
FIVE TO TWELVE (N) Putnam 1969; SFBC; Berk X1768;
THE FIREBIRD (in Double Phoenix) BB 2420, 1971;
GENDER GENOCIDE (N) Ace 27905, 1972;
KRONK (N) Putnam 1971; Berk S2068;
THE LAST CONTINENT (N) Dell 4655, 1969;
NEWS FROM ELSEWHERE (C8) Berk X1696, 1969;
THE OVERMAN CULTURE (N) Putnam 1972; SFBC; Berk S2421; Z3155;
PRISONER OF FIRE (N) Walker 1976;
SEAHORSE IN THE SKY (N) Putnam 1969; SFBC; Berk S1997; Ace 75655;
SEED OF LIGHT (N) BB 327, 1959; 1681;
THE SLAVES OF HEAVEN (N) Putnam 1974; SFBC; Berk N2792;
THE TENTH PLANET (N) Putnam 1973; Berk N2711;
TOMORROW'S GIFT (C10) BB 279K, 1958;
TRANSIT (N) Lanc 74-758, 1964; 73-690; 75-204; Ace 82206;
SEE EXPENDIBLE SERIES;

COOPER, HUGHES

SEXMAX (N) PBL 64-174, 1969;

COOPER, LOUISE

THE BOOK OF PARADOX (N) Delacourte 1973; Dell 3343

COOPER, PARLEY J.

THE FEMINISTS (N) Pinn P014-N, 1971
THE CROP (C) Manor 1976;

COPPEL, ALFRED -ALSO ROBERT CHAM GILMAN

SERIES
THE REBEL OF RHADA (JN) (as Gilman) H-B-W 1968; Ace 71065;
THE NAVIGATOR OF RHADA (JN) (as Gilman) H-B-W 1969;
THE STARKAHN OF RHADA (JN) H-B-W 1970

DARK DECEMBER (N) G-M S989, 1960; T2315;

CORDELL, ALEXANDER

IF YOU BELIEVE THE SOLDIERS (N) Dday 1974;

COREY, PAUL

THE PLANET OF THE BLIND (N) PBL 63-147, 1969;

CORLETT, WILLIAM

THE DARK SIDE OF THE MOON (N) Bradbury 1977;
THE LAND BEYOND (N) Bradbury 1976;
RETURN TO THE GATE (N) Bradbury 1977;

CORLEY, EDWIN

THE JESUS FACTOR (N) Stein & Day 1970; PBL 66-680;
SARGASSO (N) Dday 1977 BC Dell 17575;

CORREY, LEE = G HARRY STINE

CONTRABAND ROCKET (N) Ace D+147, 1956;
STARSHIP THROUGH SPACE (JN) Holt 1954;
ROCKET MAN (JN) Holt 1955

COULSON, JUANITA

SPACE TRAP (N) Lasr 20, 1976;
UNTO THE LAST GENERATION (N) Lasr 11, 1975;
THE SINGING STONES (N) Ace H+77, 1968;
CRISIS ON CHEIRON (N) Ace H+27, 1967;

COULSON, ROBERT "BUCK"

JOE KARNS SERIES
NOW YOU SEE HIM/IT/THEM (N) (with G. DeWeese) Dday 1976;
CHARLES FORT NEVER MENTIONED WOMBATS (N) (with G. DeWeese) Dday 1977;

GATES OF THE UNIVERSE (N) (with G DeWeese) Laser 4, 1975;
TO RENEW THE AGES (N) Laser 26, 1976;

COVER, ARTHUR BYRON

THE PLATYPUS OF DOOM AND OTHER NIHILISTS (S4) Warn 88-079, 1976;
AUTUMN ANGELS (N) Prmd V3787, 1975;
THE SOUND OF WINTER (N) Prmd V4017, 1976;

COWPER, RICHARD = JOHN MIDDLETON MURRAY

BREAKTHROUGH (N) BB 01653, 1969;
CLONE (N) Dday 1973; SFBC; Avon 20453;
KULDESAK (N) Dday 1972;
PHOENIX (N) BB 1856, 1970; SFBC;
THE TWILIGHT OF BRIAREUS (N) Day 1974; SFBC; DAW 158;

CRANE, ROBERT = BERNARD GLEMSER

HERO'S WALK (N) BBHC 1954; BB71;

CRAWFORD, MARION

KHALED (N) Macmil 1891; BBAF 2446, 1971;

CREASEY, JOHN (partial listing)

DR. PALFREY & Z5 (some are not Science Fiction)
THE BLIGHT (N) Walker 1968; Lancer 74-623;
THE CHILDREN OF HATE
DEATH IN THE RISING SUN (N) Walker 1976; probably not sf
DARK HARVEST;
THE DAWN OF DARKNESS;
THE DEPTHS (N) Walker 1967; Berkley X1613;
THE DROUGHT (N) Walker 1967;
THE FAMINE (N) Walker 1967; Lancer 74-652;
THE FIRE;
THE FLOOD (N) Walker 1969; Lancer 74-675;
THE HOUSE OF THE BEARS (N) Walker 1975; probably no sf
THE HOUNDS OF VENGEANCE;
THE INFERNO (N) Walker 1965; Berkley X1627;
THE INSULATORS (N) Walker 1973; Manor 12311;
THE KILLERS OF INNOCENCE (N) Walker 1971; Award AN 1067;
THE LEGION OF THE LOST; (N) Walker 1974;
THE LEAGUE OF LIGHT;
THE MAN WHO SHOOK THE WORLD;
THE MISTS OF FEAR;
THE PLAGUE OF SILENCE (N) Walker 1968; Lancer 74-602;
THE PROFIT OF FIRE;
THE OASIS (N) Walker 1972;
SHADOW OF DOOM;
SONS OF SATAN;
THE SLEEP (N) Walker 1968; Lancer 74-759;
THE SMOG (N) Walker 1971; Award AN1028;
THE TOUCH OF DEATH (N) Walker 1969; Lancer 75-237;
THE TERROR (N) Walker 1966; Berkley X1639;
THE THUNDER MAKER (N) Walker 1976;
THE UNBEGOTTEN (N) Walker 1972 Manor 12310;
THE VOICELESS ONES (N) Walker 1974;
THE WINGS OF PEACE;

CRICHTON, MICHAEL -ALSO JOHN LANGE

THE ANDROMEDIA STRAIN (N) Knopf 1969; Dell 0199;
THE TERMINAL MAN (N) Knopf 1972; Bant X7545; 10065;
WESTWORLD (N) Bant Q3441, 1974;
EATERS OF THE DEAD (N) Knopf 1976; Bant; 10237;

CRISTABEL -CHRISTINE ABRAHAMSEN

THE CRUACHAN AND THE KILLANE (N) Curt 7093, 1970;
THE GOLDEN OLIVE (N) Curt 9146, 1972;
MANALACOR OF VELTAKIN (N) Curt 7092, 1970;
THE MORTAL IMMORTALS (N) Walker 1971;

CROSS, JOHN KEIR

THE ANGRY PLANET (N) Coward McCann 1946;
THE RED JOURNEY BACK (N) Coward McCann 1954;
THE OTHER PASSENGER (C18) Lipp 1946; (C9) BB 480K

CROSSEN, KENDELL FOSTER -ALSO RICHARD FOSTER

ONCE UPON A STAR (N) Holt 1953;
THE REST MUST DIE (N) (as Foster) G-M s853, 1959;
YEAR OF CONSENT (N) Dell 32, 1954;

CROWLEY, JOHN

BEASTS (N) Dday 1976; SFBC; Ban 11102
THE DEEP (N) Dday 1975; Berk D3163

CULLEN, SEAMUS

ASTRA AND FLONDRIX (N) Pantheon pb 1976;

CUMMINGS, M.A.

EXILE AND OTHER TALES OF FANTASY (C14) Flagship 864, 1968;

CUMMINGS, RAY

MATTER SPACE & TIME
THE GIRL IN THE GOLDEN ATOM (N) Harper 1923; Hyperion 1975;
PRINCESS OF THE ATOM (N) Avon FN 1, 1950;
THE MAN WHO MASTERED TIME (N) McClurg 1929; Burt 1930; Ace D+173, 1956;
THE SHADOW GIRL (N) Ace D-535 1962;
THE EXILE OF TIME (N) Avalon 1964; Ace F-343

HALJAN SERIES
BRIGANDS OF THE MOON (N) McClurg 1931; Ace D-324, 1958;
WANDL THE INVADER (N) Ace D+497, 1961;

TAMA SERIES
TAMA OF THE LIGHT COUNTRY (N) Ace F-363, 1965;
TAMA, PRINCESS OF MERCURY (N) Ace F-406, 1966;

BEYOND THE STARS (N) Ace F-248, 1963;
BEYOND THE VANISHING POINT (N) Ace D+331, 1958;
A BRAND NEW WORLD (N) Ace F-313, 1964; 07840;

EXPLORERS INTO INFINITY (N) Avalon 1965;
THE INSECT INVASION (N) Avalon 1967;
THE SEA GIRL (N) McClurg 1930; Burt 1932;
TARRANO THE CONQUEROR (N) McClurg 1930; Burt 1931; Garland 1976;

DAGMAR, PETER

ALIEN SKIES (N) Arcadia 1967
SANDS OF TIME (N) Arcadia 1967;

DAIN, ALEX

THE BAIN OF KANTHOS (N) Ace + 42800, 1959;

DALEY, BRIAN

THE DOOMFARERS OF CORAMONDE (N) BBDR 25708, 1977

DALLAS, PAUL V.

THE LOST PLANET (JN) WINSTON 1956;

DALMAS, JOHN

THE YNGLING (N) Prmd T2466, 1971;

DANIEL, TERRY C.

THE SPACE MACHINE (N) Lennox Hill 1971

DANN, JACK

STARHIKER (N) H&R 1977;

DARNAY, ARSEN

A HOSTAGE FOR HINTERLAND (N) BB 25306, 1976;

DAVENTRY, LEONARD

CLAUS COMAN
A MAN OF DOUBLE DEED (N) Dday 1965; SFBC; Berk X1491;
REFLECTIONS IN A MIRAGE & THE TICKING IS IN YOUR HEAD (2N) Dday 1969
=& REFLECTIONS IN A MIRAGE (N) Curtis 7061, 1970;
=&THE TICKING IS IN YOUR HEAD (N) Curtis 7065, 1970;

THE TWENTY—ONE BILLIONTH PARADOX (N) Dday 1971;

DAVINCI, LEONARDO & ROBERT PAYNE

THE DELUGE (N) Twayne 1954; Lion 233;

DAVIDSON, AVRAM A.

CLASH OF THE STAR—KINGS (N) Ace G+576, 1966;
THE ENEMY OF MY ENEMY (N) Berk X1341, 1966;

THE ENQUIRES OF DOCTOR ESZTERHAZY (N) Warn 76-981, 1975;
THE ISLAND UNDER THE EARTH (N) Ace 37425, 1969;
JOYLEG (N) (see W. Moore Co-Author)
THE KAR-CHEE REIGN (N) Ace G+574, 1966;
MASTERS OF THE MAZE (N) Prmd R1208, 1965; Manor 12439;
MUTINY IN SPACE (N) Prmd R1069, 1964; X2079; N3376;
OR ALL THE SEAS WITH OYSTERS (C17) Berk F639, 1962; Poc 80806;
THE PHOENIX AND THE MIRROR (N) Dday 1969; Ace 66100;
PEREGRINE: PRIMUS (N) Walker 1971; Ace 65950
THE REDWARD EDWARD PAPERS (C6) Dday 1978; (fc 7/78)
ROGUE DRAGON (N) Ace F-353, 1965;
RORK (N) Berk F1146, 1965; Manor 15227;
STRANGE SEAS AND SHORES (C18) Dday 1971;
URSUS OF ULTIMA THULE (N) Avon 17657, 1973;
WHAT STRANGE STARS AND SKIES (C14) Ace F-330, 1965;

DAVIDSON, MICHAEL

THE KARMA MACHINE (N) Pop 248, 1975; 3202;

DAVIES, L.P. = LESLIE PURNELL DAVIES

THE ALIEN (N) Dday 1971;
THE ARTIFICIAL MAN (N) Dday 1967; SFBC; Scholastic T1248;
DIMENSION A (N) Dday 1969; Dell 1957;
GENESIS TWO (N) Dday 1971; Play 16139;
THE PAPER DOLLS (N) Dday 1966; Sig P3027; Q4866;
PSYCHOGEIST (N) Dday 1967; SFBC; Tower 44-115;
STRANGER TO TOWN (N) Dday 1969;
TWILIGHT JOURNEY (N) Dday 1968; SFBC;
WHAT DID I DO TOMORROW (N) Dday 1973;
WHO IS LEWIS PINDER (N) Dday 1965; Sig P3375; (Borderline)

DE CAMP, L. SPRAGUE

HAROLD SHEA (WITH F. PRATT)

THE INCOMPLETE ENCHANTER (N) Holt 1942; Prime 1950; Prmd G-530; G-723; X1928;
THE CASTLE OF IRON (N) Gnome 1950; Prmd F722, 1962;
BOTH = THE COMPLETE ENCHANTER (2N) SFBC; 1976; BB 24638;
WALL OF SERPENTS (N) Avalon 1960;

VIAGENS

THE CONTINENT MAKERS AND OTHER TALES OF THE VIAGENS (S8) Twayne 1953; Sig Q4825;
COSMIC MANHUNT (N) Ace D+61, 1954;
= THE QUEEN OF ZAMBA (N) Dale 006, 1978;
THE SEARCH FOR ZEI (N) Avalon 1962; Ace F+249;
THE HAND OF ZEI (N) Avalon 1963; Ace F+249;
THE TOWER OF ZANID (N) Avalon 1963; Air SF2; M-B 75-467;
ROGUE QUEEN (N) Dday 1951; SFBC; Dell 600; Ace F-333; Sig Q5256; W8097;
THE VIRGIN AND THE WHEELS (2N) Pop 362, 1976; (2nd novel not in series)
THE HOSTAGE OF ZIR (N) Berk/Put 1978;

NOVARIA
THE GOBLIN TOWER (N) Prmd T1927, 1968;
THE CLOCKS OF IRAZ (N) Prmd T2584, 1971;
THE FALLIBLE FIEND (N) Sig Q5370, 1973

THE BEST OF L SPRAGUE DE CAMP (C18) SFBC 1978; BBDR 25474;
THE CARNELIAN CUBE (N) (with F. Pratt) Gnome 1948; Lanc 73-662; 74676
DIVIDE AND RULE (N+1) Fantasy 1948; Lanc 72-768;
GENUS HOMO (N) (with P.S. Miller) Fantasy 1950; Berk G536;
THE GLORY THAT WAS (N) Avalon 1960; PBL 63-542;
A GUN FOR DINOSAUR (C14) Dday 1963; SFBC; Curt 9018;
LAND OF UNREASON (N) (see F. Pratt co-author);
LEST DARKNESS FALL (N) Holt 1941; Prime 1949; Galx 24; Prmd F817; X2056;BB 24139; 24847;
THE RELUCTANT SHAMAN (C7) Prmd T2347, 1970;
SOLOMON'S STONE (N) Avalon 1956;
TALES FROM GAVAGAN'S BAR (S23)(with F. Pratt) Twayne 1953; Owlswick 1977;
THE TRITONIAN RING (N+3) Twayne 1953; (N) PBL 53-618; 64-696; BBDR 25803; Owlswick 1977;
THE UNDESIRED PRINCESS (N+1) FPCI 1951;
THE WHEELS OF IF (C7) Shasta 1949; Berk S1893;
SEE ALSO R.E. HOWARD — CONAN SERIES

DEE, ROGER = ROGER D. AYCOCK

AN EARTH GONE MAD (N) Ace D+84, 1954;

DEFORD, MIRIAM ALLEN

XENOGENESIS (C16) BB 1546, 1969;
ELSEWHERE, ELSEWHEN, ELSEHOW (C18) Walker 1971;

DEFONTENAY, C. I.

STAR: PSI CASSIOPEIA (N) (French 1854); DAW 167, 1975; Gregg 1976;

DEIGHTON, LEN

BILLION DOLLAR BRAIN (N) Putnam 1966; Dell 0583; Berk Z 2149

DELILLO, DON

RATNER'S STAR (N) Knopf 1976;

DELANY, SAMUEL R.

TOROMON
CAPTIVES OF THE FLAME (N) Ace F+199, 1963;
=+OUT OF THE DEAD CITY (N) Ace 22643, 1977;
THE TOWERS OF TORON (N) Ace F+261, 1964; rev. Ace 81945;
CITY OF A THOUSAND SUNS (N) Ace F-322, 1965; 10718;
ALL (rev) = THE FALL OF THE TOWERS (3N) Ace 22640, 1970; Gregg 1977;

BABEL -17 (N) Ace F-388, 1966; 04590; Gregg 1976; Ace 04595;
THE BALLAD OF BETA - 2 (N) Ace M+121, 1965; 04722; +20571; Gregg 1977;
DHALGREN (N) Bant Y8554, 1975; Gregg 1977;

DRIFTGLASS (C10) SFBC 1971; Sig 04834; W7415; Gregg 1977;
THE EINSTEIN INTERSECTION (N) Ace F-427, 1967; 19680; Garland 1976;
EMPIRE STAR (N) Ace M+139, 1966; +20571; Gregg 1977;
THE JEWELS OF APTOR (N) Ace F+173, 1962; G-706; 39021; Gregg 1976;
NOVA (N) Dday 1968; SFBC; Bant H4738; T2243; 10031; Gregg 1977;
TRITON (N) Bant Y2567, 1976; Gregg 1977;

DEL MARTIA, ASTON = JOHN RUSSEL FEARN

DEL REY, LESTER also PHILLIP ST. JOHN; also ERIC VAN LHIN: WITH FRED POHL = EDSON MCCANN

SERIES
STEP TO THE STARS (JN) Winston 1954; PBL 52-955;
MISSION TO THE MOON (JN) Winston 1956;
MOON OF MUTINY (JN) H-R-W 1961; Sig KP536; Q5539; BBDR 27119

JUVENILE NOVELS With Paul Fairman uncredited co-author (See Note 1)
PRISONERS OF SPACE (JN) Westminster 1968;
THE RUNAWAY ROBOT (JN) Westminster 1965; SBS TX863;
TUNNEL THROUGH TIME (N) Westminster 1966; SBS TX1065;

OTHER JUVENILE NOVELS
ATTACK FROM ATLANTIS (JN) WINSTON 1953; Tempo 5306; 5682; BBDR 27448;
BATTLE ON MERCURY (JN) (as Van Lhin) Winston 1953;
THE INFINITE WORLDS OF MAYBE (JN) Holt 1966;
MAROONED ON MARS (JN) Winston 1952; PBL 52-415;
THE MYSTERIOUS PLANET (JN) Winston 1952 (as Wright); BBDR 27121(as del Rey);
OUTPOST OF JUPITER (JN) H-R-W 1963; BBDR 27120
ROCKET FROM INFINITY (JN) Holt 1966;
ROCKET JOCKEY (JN) (as St. John) Winston 1954;
ROCKETS TO NOWHERE (JN) (as St. John) Winston 1954;

AND SOME WERE HUMAN (C12) Prime 1948; (C8) BB 552
DAY OF THE GIANTS (N) Avalon 1959; Air SF 5;
THE EARLY DEL REY (C24) Dday 1975; SFBC;
=& THE EARLY DEL REY VOL 1 (C12) BB 25063, 1976;
=& THE EARLY DEL REY VOL 2 (C12) BB 25111, 1976;
THE ELEVENTH COMMANDMENT (N) Regency RB 113, 1962; (rev) BB 2068; 23987;
GODS AND GOLEMS (C5) BB 3087, 1973;
MORTALS AND MONSTERS (C12) BB U2236, 1965;
NERVES (N) BBHC 1956; BB 151; U2344; 2069; 23789; rev. BB 24995;
POLICE YOUR PLANET, (N) (as Van Lhin) Avalon 1956; BB 24465;
PSTALEMATE (N) Putnam 1971; Berk N2292;
ROBOTS AND CHANGELINGS (C11) BB 246, 1957;
THE SKY IS FALLING & BADGE OF INFAMY (2N) Magabook 1, 1963; Ace +79690
WEEPING MAY TARRY (N) (with R. F. Jones) Pinn 40-215-5; 1978;

NOVELS WITH PAUL FAIRMAN uncredited co-author
THE SCHEME OF THINGS (N) Belmont B50-682, 1966;
SIEGE PERILOUS (N) Lancer 73-468, 1966;
=THE MAN WITHOUT A PLANET(N) Lancer 74-538, 1969;

with FRED POHL AS EDSON MCCANN
PREFERRED RISK (N) S&S 1955; Dell R114

DENAERDE, STEFAN

OPERATION SURVIVAL EARTH (N) Poc 80840, 1977;

DENNIS, NIGEL

CARDS OF IDENTITY (N) Vanguard 1955; Sig P2432,

DERMOT, VERN

PLANET FINDERS (N) Lennox Hill 1971; Manor 12499;

DERLETH, AUGUST - WEIRD & HORROR FICTION MOSTLY

HARRIGAN'S FILE (C17) Arkham 1975;

DETZLER, DIANE ALSO ADAM LUKENS, ALSO JORGE DE REYNA

ALIEN WORLD (N) (as Lukens) Avalon 1963;
CONQUEST OF LIFE (N) (as Lukens) Avalon 1960;
EEVALU (N) (as Lukens) Avalon 1963;
THE GLASS CAGE (N) (as Lukens); Avalon 1962;
THE PLANET OF FEAR (N) Avalon 1968;
THE RETURN OF THE STARSHIPS (N) (as de Reyna) Avalon 1968;
THE SEA PEOPLE (N) (as Lukens) Avalon 1959;
SONS OF THE WOLF (N) (as Lukens) Avalon 1961;
THE WORLD WITHIN (N) (as Lukens) Avalon 1962;

DEVET, CHARLES V.

COSMIC CHECKMATE (N) (with K. McClean) Ace F+149, 1962;
SPECIAL FEATURE (N) Avon 24562, 1975;

DEWEESE, GENE

JEREMY CASE (N) Laser 36, 1976;
NOW YOU SEE IT/HIM/THEM (N) (with R. Coulson) Dday 1975;
CHARLES FORT NEVER MENTIONED WOMBATS (N) (with R. Coulson)Dday 1977;
GATES OF THE UNIVERSE (N) (with R. Coulson) Laser 4, 1975;

DEXTER, WILLIAM = W. T. PRITCHARD

CHILDREN OF THE VOID (N) PBL 52-357, 1966;
WORLD IN ECLIPSE (N) PBL 52-338, 1966;

DIBELL, ANSEN = ?

PURSUIT OF SCREAMER (N) Daw 296, 1978;(fc 7/78)

DICK, PHILLIP K.

THE BEST OF PHILLIP K DICK (C19) BBDR 25359, 1977;
THE BOOK OF PHILLIP K. DICK (C9) DAW 44, 1973;
CLANS OF THE ALPHANE MOON (N) Ace F-309, 1964; 11036;
COSMIC PUPPETS (N) Ace D+249, 1957;
COUNTER CLOCK WORLD (N) Berk X1372, 1967; N2568;
THE CRACK IN SPACE (N) Ace F-377, 1966; 12126;

DEUS IRAE (N) (with Zelazny) Dday 1976; Dell 11838;
DO ANDROIDS DREAM OF ELECTRIC SHEEP (N) Dday 1968; Sig T3800; T4758;
DR. BLOODMONEY OR HOW WE GOT ALONG AFTER THE BOMB (N) Ace F-377, 1965; 15670; Gregg 1977;
DR. FUTURITY (N) Ace D+421, 1960; +15697;
EYE IN THE SKY (N) Ace D-211, 1956; H-39; 22385;
FLOW MY TEARS, THE POLICEMAN SAID (N) Dday 1974; DAW 146; UW 1266;
GALACTIC POT HEALER (N) Berk X1705, 1969; SFBC; N2569;
THE GAME-PLAYERS OF TITAN (N) Ace F-251, 1963; 27310;
THE GANYMEDE TAKEOVER (N) (with R. Nelson) Ace G-637, 1967; 27346;
THE MAN IN THE HIGH CASTLE (N) Putnam 1963; SFBC; Pop SP250; 60-2289; Berk Z2543;
THE MAN WHO JAPED (N) Ace D+193, 1956; 51910;
MARTIAN TIME-SLIP (N) BB U2191, 1964; 25244;
A MAZE OF DEATH (N) Dday 1970; PBL 64-636; Bant 10740;
NOW WAIT FOR LAST YEAR (N) Dday 1967; M-B 60-352; Manor 12-214; 12410;
OUR FRIENDS FROM FROLIX-8 (N) Ace 64400, 1970; SFBC;
THE PENULTIMATE TRUTH (N) Belm 92-603, 1964; Leis 285NK;
THE PRESERVING MACHINE (C15) Ace 67800, 1969; SFBC; Ace 67801;
A SCANNER DARKLEY (N) Dday 1977; SFBC; BBDR 26064;
THE SIMULACRA (N) Ace F-301, 1964; 76701;
SOLAR LOTTERY (N) Ace D+103, 1955; D-340; G-718; 77410; Gregg 1978;
THE THREE STIGMATA OF PALMER ELDRITCH (N) Dday 1965; SFBC; M-B 60-240; 75-399; 12296; Bant 10586;
TIME OUT OF JOINT (N) Lipp 1959; Belm 92-618, 1965; BT 51143;
UBIK (N) Dday 1969; SFBC; Dell 9200; Bant 10402;
THE UNTELEPORTED MAN (N) Ace G+602, 1966; +15697;
THE VARIABLE MAN (C5) Ace D-261, 1956; 86050;
VULCAN'S HAMMER (N)(Ace D+457, 1960; 86608;
WE CAN BUILD YOU (N) DAW 14, 1972; UY1164;
THE WORLD JONES MADE (N) Ace D+150, 1956; F-429; 90951;
THE ZAP GUN (N) Prmd R1569, 1967; Dell 19907;(fc 8/78)

DICKINSON, PETER

THE GREEN GENE (N) Pantheon 1973; DAW 174;
KING & JOKER (N) Pantheon 1976; Avon 35006
THE POISON ORACLE (N) Pantheon 1974;
THE WEATHERMONGER (N) Little-B 1968; DAW 104;
THE BLUE HAWK (N) Little Brown 1976; BBDR 25759;

DICKSON, GORDON R.

CHILDE CYCLE
THE GENETIC GENERAL (N) Ace D+449, 1960; F-426;
=+ DORSAI (N) DAW 181, 1976; UE1342;
SOLDIER ASK NOT (N) Dell 8090, 1967; DAW 172; UE1339;
TACTICS OF MISTAKE (N) Dday 1971; DAW 9; UW 1279;
NECROMANCER (N) Dday 1962; SFBC; (rev)Daw 274;
= NO ROOM FOR MAN (N) Mfad MB50-179, 1963; 50-329; Manor 75-482; 95-367
LAST TWO + DORSAI = THREE TO DORSAI (3N) SFBC 1975;

ROBBY HOENIG
SECRET UNDER THE SEA (JN) Holt 1960; SBS TX 959
SECRET UNDER ANTARCTICA (JN) Holt 1963;
SECRET UNDER THE CARIBBEAN (JN) Holt 1964;

ALIEN ART (JN) Dutton 1973; Ace 01684;
ALIEN FROM ARCTURUS (N) Ace D+139, 1956;
THE ALIEN WAY (N) Bant F2941, 1965; N6658; War 84-552;
ANCIENT MY ENEMY (C9) Dday 1974; SFBC; DAW 190;
DANGER HUMAN (C13) Dday 1970;
= THE BOOK OF GORDON R. DICKSON (C13) DAW 55, 1973;
DELUSION WORLD (N) Ace F+119, 1961;
THE FAR CALL (N) Dial 1978;
GORDON R. DICKSON'S SF BEST (C9) Dell 13181, 1978;
THE DRAGON AND THE GEORGE (N) SFBC 1976; BB 25361;
GREMLINS GO HOME (JN) (with Bova) St Martins 1974;
HOUR OF THE HORDE (N) Putnam 1970; Berk S1957;
MANKIND ON THE RUN (N) Ace D+164, 1956;
MISSION TO UNIVERSE (N) Berk F1147, 1965; (rev.) BBDR 25703;
MUTANTS (C12) Macmil 1970; Collier 1954;
NAKED TO THE STARS (N) Prmd F682, 1961; Lanc 74-667; (rev.)DAW 227;
NONE BUT MAN (N) Dday 1969; Prmd T2428; N3328; DAW 266;
THE OUTPOSTER (N) Lipp 1972; Manr 95249; 12-392;
THE PRITCHER MASS (N) Dday 1972; DAW 69; UY1236;
THE R MASTER (N) Lipp 1973; SFBC; DAW 137;
SLEEPWALKERS WORLD (N) Lipp 1971; DAW 28; UY1192;
SPACE PAW (JN) Putnam 1969; Berk S1715; Z3083;
THE SPACE SWIMMERS (N) Berk X1371, 1967;
SPACE WINNERS (JN) Holt 1965;
SPACIAL DELIVERY (N) Ace F+119, 1961;
THE STAR ROAD (C9) Dday 1973; SFBC; DAW 116;
TIME TO TELEPORT (N) Ace D+449, 1960;
WOLFLING (N) Dell 9633, 1969; 19633;
TIME STORM (N) St Martins 1977; SFBC;

DISCH, THOMAS

THE EARLY S. F. STORIES OF THOMAS DISCH (C15) Gregg 1977; (= Mankind Under The Leash & 102 H-Bombs)
CAMP CONCENTRATION (N) Dday 1969; Avon V2348; 3392;
ECHO ROUND HIS BONES (N) Berk X1349, 1967;
FUN WITH YOUR NEW HEAD (C17) Dday 1971; SFBC; Sig T4913;
THE GENOCIDES (N) Berk F1170, 1965; Gregg 1978;
GETTING INTO DEATH (C16) Knopf 1976; Pocket 80926;
MANKIND UNDER THE LEASH (N) Ace G+597, 1966;
ONE HUNDRED AND TWO H-BOMBS (C14) Berk S2044, 1971;
344 (N) Avon 18176, 1974;
THE PRISONER (N) (tv tie-in- borderline) Ace 67900, 1969;

DIXON, ROGER

NOAH II (N) Ace 58250, 1970;

DOCTOROW, E. L.

RAGTIME (N) Random 1975; (marginal)
BIG AS LIFE (N) S&S 1966;

DOLAN, MIKE

SANTANA MORNING (C17) Pow PP 1008-N, 1970;

DOLINSKY, MIKE

MIND ONE (N) Dell 5648, 1972

DONIS, MILES

THE FALL OF NEW YORK (N) McKay 1971 (Marginal)

DONALDSON, STEPHEN R.

CHRONICLES OF THOMAS COVENANT THE UNBELIEVER

LORD FOUL'S BANE (N) SFBC 1977; Holt 1977; BBDR 25716;(fc 8/78)
THE ILLEARTH WAR (N) Holt 1977; SFBC;
THE POWER THAT PRESERVES (N) Holt 1977; SFBC;

DOW DELL, DEL

WARLORD OF GHANDOR(N) DAW 253, 1977;

DOYLE, ARTHUR CONAN

PROFESSOR CHALLENGER SERIES

THE LOST WORLD (N) Doran 1912; Perm 279; Prmd PR-15; G514; F713; Berk F1162;
THE POISON BELT (N) Doran 1913; Macmil 1964; Berk F1203;

THE MARACOT DEEP (C4) Dday 1929; Norton 1968; Belm 75-2056;

DOZOIS, GARDNER

THE VISIBLE MAN (C12) Berk 03595, 1977
NIGHTMARE BLUE (N) (with G. Effinger) Berk 02819, 1975;
STRANGERS (N) Berk-Put 1978;

DREIFUS, KURT

THE OTHER SIDE OF THE UNIVERSE (N) Twayne 1961;

DREYFUSS, ERNST

THE UNFROZEN (N) Towr T-060-11, 1970;

DUDLEY, ROY

GALACTIC GAMBIT (N) Lennox HIll, 1972;

DUBOIS, THEODORA

SOLUTION T-15, (N) Dday 1951; SFBC;

DUKE, MADELAINE

THIS BUSINESS OF BOMFOG (N) Dday 1969; Curt 7077;
CLARET, SANDWITCHES AND SIN (N) Dday 1966; Curt 6050;

DU MAURIER, DAPHNE

THE HOUSE ON THE STRAND (N) Dday 1969; Avon W212;

DUNCAN, BRUCE

MIRROR IMAGE (N) BELM B60+081, 1968;

DUNCAN, DAVID

THE MADRONE TREE (N) MacMil 1949; BC;
BEYOND EDEN (N) BB HC 1955; BB102;
DARK DOMINION (N) BB HC 1954; BB56;
OCCAM'S RAZOR (N) BB HC 1957; BB230;
THE SHADE OF TIME (N) Random 1946;

DUNN, J. ALLAN

THE TREASURE OF ATLANTIS (N) Centaur 1971; Centaur pb;

DUNSANY, LORD = EDWARD J.M.D. PLUNKETT (Partial Listing)

THE CHARWOMAN'S SHADOW (N) Putnam 1926; BBAF 3085, 1973; 23085; BBDR 27090;
BEYOND THE FIELDS WE KNOW (C51+8A) BBAF 2599, 1972; 2884;
DON RODRIGUEZ: CHRONICLES OF SHADOW VALLEY (S12) Putnam 1922; BBAF 2244, 1971;
THE KING OF ELFLAND'S DAUGHTER (N) Putnam 1924; BBAF 1628, 1969; 23517; 25523;
AT THE EDGE OF THE WORLD (C30) BBAF 1879, 1970;
OVER THE HILLS AND FAR AWAY (C37) BBAF 23886, 1974;
TALES OF THREE HEMISPHERES (C14) Owlswick 1976;
THE FOOD OF DEATH (C51) Newcastle F102, 1974;

DURRELL, LAWRENCE

TUNC (N) Dutton 1968; Poc 78012;
NUNQUAM (N) Dutton 1970, Poc 78072;

DVORKIN, DAVID

THE CHILDREN OF SHINY MOUNTAIN (N) Pocket 80954, 1977;

DYE, CHARLES

PRISONER IN THE SKULL (N) Abelard 1952; Major 3027;

E

ECKERT, ALLAN W.

THE HAB THEORY (N) Little-Brown 1976; Pop 8597;

ECKSTROM, JACK DENNIS

THE TIME OF THE HEDRONS (N) Avalon 1968

EDDISON, E. R.

ZIMIAMVIAN

A FISH DINNER IN MEMISON (N) Dutton 1941; BB U7064, 1968; 2032; BBDR 27222;
THE MEZENTIAN GATE (N) (Brit 1958; BBAF 1578, 1969; BBDR 27221;
MISTRESS OF MISTRESSES (N) Dutton 1935; BB U7063, 1968; BBDR 27220;

STYRBIORN THE STRONG (N) Boni 1926; (Borderline)
THE WORM OUROBOROS (N) Boni 1926; Dutton 1952; Xanadu pb 1962; BB U7061; 2001; 22001; 24309; BBDR 27122;

EDMONDSON, G. C. = J.M.G.O. EDMONDSON Y COTTON

THE ALUMINIUM MAN (N) Berk N2737, 1975;
CHAPAYECA (N) Dday 1971;
=BLUE FACE (N) DAW 17, 1972
THE SHIP THAT SAILED THE TIME STREAM (N) Ace M+109, 1965; 76094;
STRANGER THAN YOU THINK (S7) Ace M+109, 1965;
T. H. E. M. (N) Dday 1974;

EDSON, J. T.

BUNDUKI (N) DAW 201, 1976;

EDWARDS, NORMAN =TED WHITE & TERRY CARR

EDWARDS,PETER

TERMINUS (N) St Martins 1976;

EHRLICH, MAX

THE BIG EYE (N) Dday 1949; BC; Pop 273; Bant A1860;
THE EDICT (N) SFBC 1971; BANT N 7161
THE REINCARNATION OF PETER PROUD (N) Bobbs-M 1974; Mystery Guild 1975; Bant X6444;

EFFINGER, GEORGE ALEC

DEATH IN FLORENCE (N) Dday 1978;
IRRATIONAL NUMBERS (C8) Dday 1976;
MIXED FEELINGS (C11) H&R 1974;
NIGHTMARE BLUE (N) (See G. Dozois co-author)
RELATIVES (N) H&R 1973; Dell 7353, 1976;
THOSE GENTLE VOICES (N) Warn 86-113, 1976;
WHAT ENTROPY MEANS TO ME (N) Dday 1972; Sig Q5504;
See Planet of the Apes Series

EINSTEIN, CHARLES

THE DAY NEW YORK WENT DRY (N) GM K1446, 1964;

EISENBERG, LARRY

THE BEST LAID SCHEMES (C21) Macmil 1971; Coll 1977;
THE VILLA OF THE FERROMONTE (N) S&S 1974;

EKLUND, GORDON

ALL TIMES POSSIBLE (N) DAW 108, 1974;
BEYOND THE RESURRECTION (N) Dday 1973;
DANCE OF THE APOCALYPSE (N) Laser 46, 1976;
THE ECLIPSE OF DAWN (N) Ace 18630; 1971;
FALLING TOWARD FOREVER(N) Laser 10, 1975;
THE GRAYSPACE BEAST (N) Dday 1976; Pocket 81390;
INHERITORS OF EARTH (N) (from idea by P. Anderson) Chilton 1974; Prmd V4068;
SERVING IN TIME (N) Laser 6, 1975;
A TRACE OF DREAMS (N) Ace 82070, 1972;

ELDER, MICHAEL

THE ALIEN EARTH (N) Pinn P43N, 1971; P829;
FLIGHT TO TERROR (N) Pinn P219, 1973;
NOWHERE ON EARTH (N) Pinn P157, 1973;
PARADISE IS NOT ENOUGH (N) Pinn P034N, 1971;

ELGIN, SUZETTE HADEN

COYOTE JONES SERIES

THE COMMUNIPATHS (N) Ace +11560, 1970;
FURTHEST (N) Ace 25950, 1971;
AT THE 7TH LEVEL (N) DAW 10, 1972;

ELIAS, ALBERT J

THE BOWMAN TEST (N) Dell 10787, 1977;

ELLIN, STANLEY

THE BLESSINGTON METHOD (C10) BB 24531, 1975;

ELLIOTT, BRUCE

ASYLUM EARTH (N) Belm B50-819, 1968;
THE RIVIT IN GRANDFATHER'S NECK (N) Curt 7101, 1971;

ELLIOTT, H. CHANDLER

REPRIEVE FROM PAPADISE (N) GNOME 1955;

ELLIS, CHARLES

THE SECOND CRASH (N) S&S 1973; BB 24052

ELLISON, HARLAN

ALONE AGAINST TOMORROW (C20) Macmil 1971; SFBC; Coll 1978;
APPROACHING OBLIVION (C11) Walker 1974; SFBC; Signet Y6848; W7718
THE BEAST THAT SHOUTED LOVE AT THE HEART OF THE WORLD (C15) Avon V2300, 1969; SFBC; Sig Y5870; W7235;

DEATHBIRD STORIES (C19) H&R 1975; Dell 1737;
DOOMSMAN (N) Belm B50+779, 1967; B-T 50+244;
ELLISON WONDERLAND (C16) PBL 52-149; 1962; Sig Y6041; W7717;
=EARTHMAN GO HOME (C16) PBL 52-508, 1965; 53-727;
FROM THE LAND OF FEAR (C11) Belm B60-069, 1967; B-T 50-529; 50750;
I HAVE NO MOUTH AND I MUST SCREAM (C7) Prmd X1611, 1967; T2638; N3521;
LOVE AIN'T NOTHING BUT SEX MISSPELLED (C22) Trident 1968; (C15) Prmd M3798;
THE MAN WITH NINE LIVES (N) Ace D+413, 1959;
NO DOORS, NO WINDOWS (C16) Prmd A3799, 1975;
OVER THE EDGE (C15) Belm 75-1091, 1970; BT 50282;
PAINGOD AND OTHER DELUSIONS (C7) Prmd R1270, 1965; X1991 (C8) V3646;
PHOENIX WITHOUT ASHES (N) (see E. Bryant - coauthor)
STRANGE WINE (?) Harper 1978; (fc /78)
A TOUCH OF INFINITY (C6) Ace D+413, 1959;

ELY, DAVID

SECONDS (N) Pantheon 1963; Signet D2507;

EMTSEN, MIKHAIL

WORLD SOUL (N) (with E. Parnov) Macmil 1978;

ENDORE, GUY S.

METHINKS THE LADY (N) Duell Sloan 1945;
=THE FURIES IN HER BODY (N) Avon 323, 1951;
=NIGHTMARE (N) Dell D183, 1957;
THE WEREWOLF OF PARIS (N) Farrar-Rinehart 1933; Poc 97; Avon 354; Ace K-160; Poc 80584;

ENGLAND, GEORGE ALLAN (Partial Listing)

DARKNESS AND DAWN (N) Avalon 1964;
BEYOND THE GREAT OBLIVION (N) Avalon 1965;
THE PEOPLE OF THE ABYSS (N) Avalon 1966;
OUT OF THE ABYSS (N) Avalon 1967;
THE AFTERGLOW (N) Avalon 1967;
ALL = DARKNESS AND DAWN (N) Small Maynard 1914; Hyperion 1975; HC & PB;

ENGLE, ELOISE

COUNTDOWN FOR CINDY (N) Hammond 1962; Bant J2753;

ENGH, M. J.

ARSLAN (N) Warn 86-104, 1976;

ENSTROM, ROBERT

ENCOUNTER PROGRAM (N) Dday 1977; SFBC;

ERNSTING, WALTER

THE DAY THE GODS DIED (N) Bantam X2060, 1976;

ESHBACH, LLOYD ARTHUR

TYRANT OF TIME (C9) Fantasy 1955;

EVANS, E. EVERRETT

GEORGE HANLON SERIES

MAN OF MANY MINDS (N) Fantasy 1953; Pyramid G458; X1891;
ALIEN MINDS (N) Fantasy 1955;

FOOD FOR DEMONS (C9) Krueger Dawn Press 1958?; Shroud 1971;(C5) Fantasy House pb;
THE PLANET MAPPERS (JN) Dodd-Mead 1955;

EVANS, LAWRENCE WATT-
THE SEVEN ALTARS OF DUSARRA 81

F

FAIRMAN, PAUL W. Also IVAR JORGENSEN; with M. LESSER = ADAM CHASE

See Also L.DEL REY co-author- Note 1. See Also Note 2.

CITY UNDER THE SEA (N) Pyramid R1162, 1965;
THE DOOMSDAY EXHIBIT (N) Lancer 74-782, 1971;
THE FORGETFUL ROBOT (C15) Holt 1968;
I, THE MACHINE (N) Lancer 73-735, 1968; Lode B5011;
REST IN AGONY (N) (as I. Jorgensen) Monarch 362, 1963; Lancer 74-905;
=THE DIABOLIST (N) Lancer 75-411, 1973;
TEN FROM INFINITY (N) (As I. Jorgensen) Monarch 297, 1963;
=THE DEADLY SKY (N) Pinnacle 023, 1970;
=TEN DEADLY MEN (N) Pinn 817, 1975;
THE WORLD GRABBERS (N) Moanarch 471, 1964;
WHOM THE GODS WOULD SLAY (N) (as I. Jorgensen) Belm B 50-849, 1968;
THE GOLDEN APE (N) (as Chase) Avalon 1959;

FANTHORPE, ROBERT LIONEL

FANTHORPE WROTE UNDER ALL OR MOST OF THE PEN NAMES LISTED BELOW ALTHOUGH SOME WERE USED BY OTHERS AS WELL. THE SAME WORK OFTEN APPEARED WITH ANOTHER PEN NAME OR TITLE OR BOTH.

AS FANTHORPE

ALIEN FROM THE STARS (N) Arcadia 1968;
ASTEROID MAN (N) Arcadia 1967;
HAND OF DOOM (N) Arcadia 1968;
HYPERSPACE (N) Arcadia 1966; (As Fanhope)
SPACE FURY (N) Arcadia 1968;

AS LEO BRETT

EXIT HUMANITY (N) Arcadia 1965;
POWER SPHERE (N) Arcadia 1968;
THE ALIEN ONES (N) Arcadia 1969; Towr T-060-1;
MIND FORCE (N) Lennox Hill 1971;

AS BRON FANE

BLUE JUGGERNAUT (N) Arcadia 1965;
SOMEWHERE OUT THERE (N) Arcadia 1965;

AS MARSTON JOHNS

SPACE VOID (N) Arcadia 1965
BEYOND TIME (N) Arcadia 1966;
THE VENUS VENTURE (N) Arcadia 1965;

AS LIONEL ROBERTS

THE IN WORLD (N) Arcadia 1968;

AS ROBERT LIONEL

TIME ECHO (N) ARCADIA 1964; M-B 60-459;
THE FACE OF X (N) Arcadia 1965;

AS JOHN E. MULLER

CRIMSON PLANET (N) Arcadia 1966;
URANIUM 235 (N) Arcadia 1967;
DAY OF THE BEASTS (N) Arcadia 1966; M-B 75-407;
FORBIDDEN PLANET (N) Arcadia 1965;
MOON ROCKET (N) Arcadia 1967;
THE MAN FROM BEYOND (N) Arcadia 1969;
SURVIVAL PROJECT (N) Arcadia 1968;

AS MEL JAY

ORBIT ONE (N) Arcadia 1966; M-B 60-447, 1970;

AS TREVOR THORPE

LIGHTNING WORLD (N) Arcadia 1964;

AS PEL TORRO

BEYOND THE BARRIER OF SPACE (N) Tower 43-268, 1969;
EXILED IN SPACE (N) Arcadia 1968;
FROZEN PLANET (N) Arcadia 1967;
GALAXY 666 (N) Arcadia 1968; Towr 42-185; Leis LB 259;
THE LAST ASTRONAUT (N) Towr 43-247; 1969;
MAN OF METAL (N) Lennox Hill 1970;

AS KARL ZEIGFREID

BARRIER 346 (N) Arcadia 1966;
NO WAY BACK (N) Arcadia 1968;
RADAR ALERT (N) Arcadia 1968;
WORLD OF THE FUTURE (N) Arcadia 1964;
ZERO MINUS X (N) Arcadia 1965;

IN ADDITION THE FOLLOWING VEGA PAPERBACK BOOKS MAY BE BY FANTHORPE. SOME ARE REPRINTS OF THE TITLES LISTED ABOVE

ZEIGFREID - WALK THROUGH TOMORROW (N) Vega VSF 1, 1963;
FANTHORPE - SPACE FURY (N) Vega VSF 2, 1963;
MULLER - THE DAY THE WORLD DIED (N) Vega VSF 3, no date
ZEIGFREID - RADAR ALERT (N) Vega VSF 4, no date
MULLER - IN THE BEGINNING (N) Vega VSF 6, no date
BARTON - THE PLANET SEEKERS (N) Vega VSF 7, no date;

MULLER - SPECIAL MISSION (N) Vega VSF 8, no date
FANE - SUSPENSION (N) Vega VSF 9, no date;
TORRO - THE RETURN (N) Vega VSF 10, no date;
MULLER - THE VENUS VENTURE (N) VSF 11, no date
ZEIGFREID - PROJECTION INFINITY (N) Vega VSF 12, no date
BECHER - A TICKET TO NOWHERE (N) Vega VSF 13, 1966
CRUMLEY - STAR TRAIL (N) Vega VSF 14, 1966;

FARCA, MARIE C.

COMPLEX MAN (N) Dday 1973;
EARTH (N) Dday 1972;

FARLEY, RALPH MILNE =ROGER SHERMAN HOAR

MYLES CABOT SERIES

THE RADIO MAN (N) FPCI 1948;
=AN EARTHMAN ON VENUS (N) Avon 285, 1950;
THE RADIO BEASTS (N) Ace F-304, 1964; 70301;
THE RADIO PLANET (N) Ace F-312, 1964; 70320;

THE HIDDEN UNIVERSE (N+1) FPCI 1950;
THE OMNIBUS OF TIME (C14) FPCI 1950;
STRANGE WORLDS (2N) FPCI 1952
=HIDDEN UNIVERSE + RADIO MAN

FARMER, PHILIP JOSE' Also KILGORE TROUT

RIVERWORLD SERIES

TO YOUR SCATTERED BODIES GO (N) Putnam 1971; Berk S2057; 2333; D1375;
THE FABULOUS RIVERBOAT (N) Putnam 1971; Berk 2329; Z2808;
THE DARK DESIGN (N) Berk/Put 1977;
THE MAGIC LABYRINTH (N) Berk/Put 1978;

TIER WORLD SERIES

THE MAKER OF UNIVERSES (N) Ace F-367, 1965; Garland 1976; Ace 51621;
THE GATES OF CREATION (N) Ace F-412, 1966; Ace 27387;
A PRIVATE COSMOS (N) Ace G-724, 1968; 67952;
BEHIND THE WALLS OF TERRA (N) Ace 71135, 1970; 05360;
THE LAVALITE WORLD (N) Ace 47420, 1977;

HERALD CHILDE

THE IMAGE OF THE BEAST (N) Essex 108, 1968;
BLOWN (N) Essex 20138, 1969;

OPAR

HADON OF ANCIENT OPAR (N) DAW 100, 1974; UW1241;
FLIGHT TO OPAR (N) DAW 197, 1976;

DOC CALIBAN & LORD GRANDRITH SERIES

A FEAST UNKNOWN (N) Essex 121, 1969; Fokker 1975;
LORD OF THE TREES (N) Ace +51375, 1970;
THE MAD GOBLIN (N) Ace +51375, 1970

BIOGRAPHY

TARZAN ALIVE (B) Dday 1972; Pop 427; 8547;

DOC SAVAGE: HIS APOCALYPTIC LIFE (B) Dday 1973; Bant Q8834;

THE ADVENTURES OF THE PEERLESS PEER (N) Aspen 1974; Dell 0042, 1976;

THE ALLEY GOD (C3) BB F588, 1962;

THE BOOK OF PHILIP JOSE' FARMER (C16) DAW 63, 1973;

CACHE FROM OUTER SPACE (N) Ace F+165, 1962;

THE CELESTIAL BLUEPRINT (C4) Ace F+165, 1962;

DARE (N) BB U2193, 1965;

DOWN IN THE BLACK GANG (C8) SFBC 1971; Sig T4805;

FLESH (N) Galx 277, 1960; Dday 1968; Sig T3861; T5097; Y6767

THE GATE OF TIME (N) Belm B50-717, 1966; 75-2016;

GREEN ODYSSEY (N) BBHC 1956; BB210; U2345; Gregg 1978;

INSIDE OUTSIDE (N) BB U2192, 1964; Avon E 22830;

IRONCASTLE (N) DAW 187, 1976 (completed from story by Rosny)

JESUS ON MARS (N) Pinn (fc 1978)

LORD TYGER (N) Dday 1970; Sig Q5096;

THE LOVERS (N) BB 507K, 1961; 2762;

NIGHT OF LIGHT (N) Berk F1248, 1966; S2249; Garland 1976; Berk 03366;

THE OTHER LOG OF PHILEAS FOGG (N) DAW 48, 1973;

STRANGE RELATIONS (C5)BB 391K, 1960; Avon E 20578;

THE STONE GOD AWAKENS (N) Ace 78650, 1970;

TIMES LAST GIFT (N) BB 2468, 1972; (rev)BBDR 25843;

TONGUES OF THE MOON (N) Prmd R1055, 1964; T2260; Jove 04595;(fc 7/78)

TRAITOR TO THE LIVING (N) BB 23613, 1973; BBDR 27446;

VENUS ON THE HALF-SHELL (N) (as Trout) Dell 6149, 1975;

THE WIND WHALES OF ISHMAEL (N) Ace 89237, 1971;

A WOMAN A DAY (N) Galx 291, 1960;

=THE DAY OF TIMESTOP (N) Lanc 73-715, 1968;

=TIMESTOP (N) Lanc 74-616, 1970

LOVE SONG (N) Brandon 6134, 1970; (not SF)

FIRE AND THE NIGHT (N) Regeancy RB 118, 1962; (Not SF)

FARREN, MICK

THE TEXTS OF FESTIVAL (N) Avon 27011, 1975

FAST, HOWARD

THE EDGE OF TOMORROW (C7) Bant A2254, 1961; F3309;

THE GENERAL ZAPPED AN ANGEL (C9) Morrow 1969; Ace 27910; 27911;

THE HUNTER AND THE TRAP (2N) Dial 1967;

A TOUCH OF INFINITY (C13) Morrow 1973; HALL 1974; DAW 124;

ALL = TIME AND THE RIDDLE (C31) Ward Ritchie 1975;

FAST JONATHAN (Son of HOWARD FAST)

THE SECRETS OF SYNCHRONICITY (N) Sig W7556, 1977;

MORTAL GODS (N) Harper 1978;

FAST, JULIUS

THE LEAGUE OF GREY-EYED WOMEN (N) Lipp 1970; Prmd N2574;

FAUCETTE, JOHN

THE AGE OF RUIN (N) Ace H+103, 1968; +11360;
CROWN OF INFINITY (N) H+51, 1968; +12375;
SEIGE OF EARTH (N) Unibook pb 1971; Belm B95-2194;
THE WARRIORS OF TERRA (N) Belm B75-2002, 1970;

FEARING, KENNETH

LONELIEST GIRL IN THE WORLD (N) Harcourt-B 1951;

FEARN, JOHN RUSSELL Also THORNTON AYRE; Also DENNIS CLIVE; Also ASTRON DEL MARTIA; Also VARGO STATTEN

ONE AGAINST TIME (N) (as del Martia) PBL 63-270, 1970;
*NOTE: Others used these psuedonyms and this may not be by Fearn.
VALLEY OF PRETENDERS (S) (as Clive) Columbia 2, about 1940;
THE VOICE COMMANDS (S) (as Clive) Columbia 5 About 1940;

FEDERBUSH, ARNOLD

THE MAN WHO LIVED IN INNER SPACE (N) Houghton-M 1973; Bant Q8794;

FERRO, ROBERT

THE OTHERS (N) Scrib 1977;

FIEDLER, LESLIE A

THE MESSENGERS WILL COME NO MORE (N) Stein & Day 1974;

FINDLAY, TIMOTHY

THE BUTTERFLY PLAGUE (N) Viking 1969; Bant N5364;

FINNEY, CHARLES G.

THE CIRCUS OF DR. LAO (N) Viking 1935; Bant F2755; Avon E 30239;
THE GHOSTS OF MANACLE (C8) Prmd R1042, 1964;
THE UNHOLY CITY (N) Vanguard 1937; Prmd X1818;

FINNEY, JACK =WALTER BRADEN FINNEY

THE BODY SNATCHERS (N) Dell 42, 1955; 0674, 1967; Gregg 1976;
=INVASION OF THE BODY SNATCHERS (N) Dell B204, 1961; Awrd AN 1125; AD 1594;
I LOVE GALESBURG IN THE SPRINGTIME (C10) S&S 1963;
THE NIGHT PEOPLE (N) Dday 1977;
THE THIRD LEVEL (C12) Rinehart 1956; SFBC; Dell D-274;
TIME AND AGAIN (N) S&S 1970; PBL 66-651; 78592; Warn 78-636;
THE WOODROW WILSON DIME (N) S&S 1968;

FISHER, JAMES P.

THE GREAT BRAIN ROBBERY (N) Belm B75-2072, 1970;

FISHER, LOU

SUNSTOP 8 (N) Dell 12622, 1978;

FITZGIBBON, CONSTANTINE

WHEN THE KISSING HAD TO STOP (N) Norton 1960; Bant F2255; Arlington 1973;
THE IRON HOOP (N) Knopf 1949;
THE GOLDEN AGE (JN) Norton 1975;

FLAGG, FRANCIS =HENRY GEORGE WEISS

THE NIGHT PEOPLE (S) FPCI pb 1947;

FLANAGAN, RICHARD

THE HUNTING VARIETY (N) Putnam 1973; (Marginal)

FLINT, HOMER EON

THE DEVOLUTIONIST AND THE EMANCIPATRIX (2N) Ace F-355, 1965;
THE LORD OF DEATH AND THE QUEEN OF LIFE (2N) Ace F-345, 1965;
THE BLIND SPOT (N) (See A.Hall co-author)

FONTANA, DOROTHY C

THE QUESTOR TAPES (N) BB 24236, 1974; Aeonion Press 1976;

FONTENAY, C. L.

THE DAY THE OCEANS OVERFLOWED (N) Monarch 443, 1964;
REBELS OF THE RED PLANET (N) Ace F+113, 1961;
TWICE UPON A TIME (N) Ace D+266, 1958;

FOREMAN, RUSSELL

THE RINGWAY VIRUS (N) Little-Brown 1977;

FORREST, MARYANN

HERE (N) Coward McCann 1970;

FOSTER, ALAN DEAN

FLINX
THE TAR—AIYM KRANG (N) BB 2547, 1972; 24085;
ORPHAN STAR (N) BBDR 25507, 1977;
BLOODHYPE (N) BB 3163, 1973; BBDR 25845;
THE END OF THE MATTER (N) BBDR 25861, 1977

ICERIGGER (N) BB 23836, 1974; 25176;
DARK STAR (N) BB 24267, 1974; 24693;
LUANA (N) BB 23793, 1974;
MIDWORLD (N) SFBC 1975; BB 25364;
SPLINTER OF THE MIND'S EYE (N) Del Rey 1978; BBDR 26062; (Star Wars 2)
WITH FRIENDS LIKE THESE (C12) BBDR 25701, 1977;
See Also Star Trek Series
THE MAN WHO USED THE UNIVERSE 83
THE BLACK HOLE

FOSTER, M. A.

THE GAME PLAYERS OF ZAN (N) DAW 236, 1977
THE WARRIORS OF DAWN (N) DAW 135, 1975; UW1291;

FOX, GARDNER F. Also BART SOMERS; SIMON MAJORS

KOTHAR - BARBARIAN SWORDSMAN (N) Belm B60-1003, 1969; Leis LB 146 SK
KOTHAR OF THE MAGIC SWORD (2N) Belm B60-1043, 1969;
KOTHAR AND THE DEMON QUEEN (N) Tower T-075-2, 1969; Leis LB 147 SK;
KOTHAR AND THE CONJURERS CURSE (N) Belm B75-2051, 1970;
KOTHAR AND THE WIZARD SLAYER (N) Belm B75-2080, 1970;

KYRICK: WARLOCK WARRIOR (N) Leis LB 252 NK, 1975;
KYRICK FIGHTS THE DEMON WORLD (N) Leis LB 284 NK, 1975;
KYRICK AND WIZARD'S SWORD (N) Leis LB 333 ZK, 1976;
KYRICK AND THE LOST QUEEN (N) Leis LB 420 ZK, 1976;

WARRIOR OF LLARN (N) Ace F-307, 1964;
THIEF OF LLARN (N) Ace F-399, 1966;

AS BART SOMERS

BEYOND THE BLACK ENIGMA (N) PBL 52-848, 1965; 53-785; 62-718;
ABANDON GALAXY (N) PBL 52-430, 1967;

ARSENAL OF MIRACLES (N) Ace F+299, 1964;
CONEHEAD (N) Ace 11658, 1973;
THE DRUID STONE (N) (as Majors) PBL 52-488, 1967; 63-359;
ESCAPE ACROSS THE COSMOS (N) PBL 52-273, 1964; 52-635;
THE HUNTER OUT OF TIME (N) Ace F-354, 1965;

FRANCOIS, YVES REGIS

THE CTZ PARADIGM (N) DDay 1975;

FRANK, PAT =HARRY HART

ALAS BABYLON (N) Lipp 1959; Bant F2054; HP70; Sp 4841; N6991; Q8581; 2923;
FORBIDDEN AREA (N) Lipp 1956; SFBC; Bant A1553;
MR. ADAM (N) Lipp 1946; Poc 498; 2498;

FRANKE, HERBERT W.

THE MIND NET (N) DAW 123, 1974;
THE ORCHID CAGE (N) DAW 79, 1973;
ZONE NULL (N) Seabury 1974;

FRANKLIN, JAY =JOHN FRANKLIN CARTER

THE RAT RACE (N) FPCI 1950; FPCI pb; Galx 10;

FRAYN, MICHAEL

THE TIN MEN (N) Viking 1965; Ace 81290;
A VERY PRIVATE LIFE (N) Viking 1968; Dell 9303, 1969;
SWEET DREAMS (N) Viking 1974; BB 24326;

FRAZEE, STEVE

THE SKY BLOCK (N) Rinehart 1953; Lion LL3; Prmd PG13;

FREE, COLIN

THE SOFT KILL (N) Berk 2459, 1973;

FREEDMAN, NANCY

THE IMMORTALS (N) St. Martins 1976;
JOSHUA, SON OF NONE (N) Delacorte 1973; Dell 4344;

FRETLAND, DON J.

OLEANDRE SERIES
THE PERSIMMION SQEUENCE (N) Apollo 117, 1971;
WINDS OF HELIOPOLIS (N) Apollo 149, 1972;
THE OLEANDRE SOLUTION (N) Apollo ?

FRIEDBERG, GERTRUDE

THE REVOLVING BOY (N) Dday 1966; Ace H-58;

FRIEDELL, EGON

RETURN OF THE TIME MACHINE (N) DAW 22, 1972;

FRIEL, ARTHUR O.

THE KING OF NO-MAN'S LAND (N) Harper 1924;
THE PATHLESS TRAIL (N) Centaur pb 1969;
TIGER RIVER (N) Harper 1923; Centaur pb 1971;

FRIEND, OSCAR J.

THE KID FROM MARS (JN) Fell 1949;
THE STAR MEN (N) Avalon 1963;

FRITCH, CHARLES E.

CRAZY MIXED-UP PLANET (C14) Pow PP197, 1969;
HORSES ASTEROID (C13) Pow PP 1004, 1970;

FUNNELL, AUGUSTINE

BRANDY JACK (N) Laser 39, 1976;
REBELS OF MERKA (N) Laser 48, 1976;

FYFE, H. B.

D-99 (N) Prmd F-794, 1962;

G

GALLICO, PAUL

THE FOOLISH IMMORTALS (N) Dday 1953 (Borderline)
THE MAN WHO WAS MAGIC (JN) Dday 1966;
THE ABANDONED (N) Knopf 1950; Avon W311; 31013; (marginal)

GALLUN, RAMOND Z. Also WILLIAM CALLAHAN

THE EDEN CYCLE (N) BB 24255, 1974;
PEOPLE MINUS X (N) S&S 1957; Ace D+291;
THE PLANET STRAPPERS (N) Prmd G-658, 1961;
THE MACHINE THAT THOUGHT (S) (as Callahan) Columbia 3, about 1940;

GALOUYE, DANIEL F.

DARK UNIVERSE (N) Bant J2266, 1961; S5734; Gregg 1976;
THE INFINITE MAN (N) Bant N7130, 1973;
LORDS OF THE PSYCHON (N) Bant J2555, 1963;
A SCOURGE OF SCREAMERS (N) Bant F3585, 1968;
SIMULACRON - 3 (N) Bant J2797, 1964;

GANTZ, KENNETH F.

NOT IN SOLITUDE (N) Dday 1959; SFBC; Berk Y582;

GARDNER, JOHN

GRENDEL (N) Knopf 1971; BB2876;

GARDNER, RICHARD

MANDRILL (N) Poc 80047, 1975;

GARNER, ALAN

SERIES
THE WEIRDSTONE OF BRISINGAMEN (JN) Watts 1961; Ace G-570; Walck 1969;Ace 87935;
THE MOON OF GOMRATH (JN) Walck 1967; Ace G-753;

ELIDOR (JN) Walck 1967; Ace 20275;
RED SHIFT (JN) Macmil 1973;

GARNET, WILLIAM

DOWN BOUND TRAIN (N) Dday 1973, Popular 204;

GARNETT, DAV = DAVID S. GARNETT

MIRROR IN THE SKY (N) Berk X1743, 1969;
THE STAR SEEKERS (N) Berk S1956, 1971;

GARRETT, RANDALL Also DARREL T. LANGART

With L. JANIFER = MARK PHILLIPS
With R. SILVERBERG = ROBERT RANDALL

MALONE SERIES (AS PHILLIPS)
BRAIN TWISTER (N) Pyramid F-783, 1962;
THE IMPOSSIBLES (N) Pyramid F-875, 1963; X1299;
SUPERMIND (N) Pyramid F-909, 1963;

ANYTHING YOU CAN DO (N) (as Langart) Dday 1963; SFBC; (as Garrett) Lancer 74-532
DAWNING LIGHT (N) (as Randall) Gnome 1958;
PAGAN PASSIONS (N) Galaxy 263, 1959 (with Larry M. Harris (L. Janifer)
THE SHROUDED PLANET (N) (as Randall) Gnome 1957;
TOO MANY MAGICIANS (N) Dday 1967; Curtis 7022;
UNWISE CHILD (N) Dday 1962; SFBC;

GARSON, PAUL

THE GREAT QUILL (N) Dday 1973;

GARTH, WILL (See Note 3.)

DR. CYCLOPS (N) Phoenix 1940; Bookfinger 1974; Centaur PB 1976;

GARY, ROMAIN

THE GASP (N) Putnam 1973; Pocket 78419;
THE ENCHANTERS (N) Putnam 1975;

GARVIN, RICHARD with EDMOND G. ADDEO

THE FORTEC CONSPIRACY (N) Sherbourne 1968; Sig T3832, 1969;
THE TALBOTT AGREEMENT (N) Sherbourne 1968; Awrd AS 569, 1969; AN1135;

GASKELL, JANE = JANE DENVIL LYNCH

ATLANTIS SERIES

THE SERPENT (N) PBL 55-693, 1968; 64-451;
= & THE SERPENT (N) St Martins 1977;
= & THE DRAGON (N) St Martins 1977;
ATLAN (N) PBL 55-738, 1968; 64-452; St Martin's 1978;
THE CITY (N) PBL 64-019, 1968; 64-450; St. Martin's 1978;

A SWEET SWEET SUMMER (N) St. Martins 1973;

GAT, DIMITRI V.

THE SHEPHERD IS MY LORD (N) Dday 1971;

GAWRON, JEAN MARK

ALGORITHM (N) Berk 03751, 1978;
AN APOLOGY FOR RAIN (N) Dday 1974;

GAYLE, HENRY K

SPAWN OF THE VORTEX (N) Comet 1957;

GENTRY, CURT

THE LAST DAYS of the GREAT STATE of CALIFORNIA (N) Putnam 1968; BB1725; 2483; 24342;

GEORGE, PETER Also PETER BRYANT

COMMANDER - 1 (N) Delacorte 1965; Dell 1430, 1966;
DR. STRANGELOVE (N) Bant F2679, 1964; S3856;
RED ALERT (N) (as Bryant) Ace D350, 1959; D-551; F-210;

GERNSBACH, HUGO

RALPH 124c 41+ (N) Stratford 1925; Fell 1950; Crst s226;
ULTIMATE WORLD (N) Walker 1971; Avon E 26179;

GERROLD, DAVID

DEATHBEAST (N) Pop 04245, 1978;(fc 7/78)
MOONSTAR ODYSSEY (N) Signet W7372, 1977;
THE MAN WHO FOLDED HIMSELF (N) Random 1973; SFBC; Pop 546;
SPACE SKIMMER (N) BB 2644, 1972;
WHEN HARLIE WAS ONE (N) SFBC 1972; BB 2885; 24390;
WITH A FINGER IN MY I (C9) BB 2645, 1972;
YESTERDAY'S CHILDREN (N) Dell 9780, 1972;
THE FLYING SORCERERS (N) (with L. Niven) BB 2331, 1971; BBDR 25307;
See Also PLANET OF THE APES Series

GERSON, NOEL B.

DOUBLE VISION (N) Dday 1972; Popular 452;

GESTON, MARK S.

THE DAY STAR (N) DAW 6, 1972;
LORDS OF THE STARSHIP (N) Ace G-673, 1967;
OUT OF THE MOUTH OF THE DRAGON (N) Ace 64460, 1969;
THE SIEGE OF WONDER (N) Dday 1976; DAW 258;

GIESY, JOHN ULRICH

JASON CROFT SERIES
PALOS OF THE DOGSTAR PACK (N) Avalon 1965;
THE MOUTHPIECE OF ZITU (N) Avalon 1966;
JASON, SON OF JASON (N) Avalon 1966;

GILLMAN, ROBERT CHAM =ALFRED COPPEL

GILBERT, STEPHEN

RATMAN'S NOTEBOOKS (N) Viking 1969; Lancer 75-142;
=WILLARD (N) Lancer 75-189, 1971(movie tie-in);

GILLON DIANA & MEIR

THE UNSLEEP (N) BB F571, 1962;

GILFORD, C. B.

THE LIQUID MAN (N) Lanc 74-560, 1969;

GILLIATT, PENELOPE

ONE BY ONE (N) Atheneum 1965;

GILMORE, ANTHONE =HARRY BATES + D. W. HALL

SPACE HAWK (S5) Greenberg 1952;

GILMOUR, WILLIAM

LOST ON JUPITER (N) House of Greystoke 1962;
TARZAN AND THE LIGHTNING MAN (N) House of Greystoke 1963;
BACK TO THE EARTH'S CORE (N) House of Greystoke 1971;

GLASBY, JOHN

PROJECT JOVE (N) Ave +68310, 1971;

GLUT, DONALD F.

SPAWN (N) Laser 43, 1976;

GLYNN, A. A.

PLAN FOR CONQUEST (N) Arcadia, 1970; Vega SF5;

GODWIN, PARKE

MASTERS OF SOLITUDE (with M. Kaye) (N) Dday 1978; (fc 7/78)

GODWIN, TOM

THE SPACE BARBARIANS (N) Prmd R993, 1964;
THE SURVIVORS (N) Gnome 1958;
=SPACE PRISON (N) Prmd G-480, 1960; F-774;
BEYOND ANOTHER SUN (N) Curt 7129, 1971;

GOLD, H. L.

THE OLD DIE RICH (C12) Crown 1955;

GOLDIN, STEPHEN married to KATHLEEN SKY

ASSAULT ON THE GODS (N) Dday 1977;
CARAVAN (N) Laser 8, 1975;
FINISH LINE (N) Laser 45, 1976;
HERDS (N) Laser 2, 1975;
MINDFLIGHT (N) Crest 13980, 1978;
SCAVENGER HUNT (N) Laser 25, 1975;
SEE ALSO E. E. 'DOC' SMITH CO-AUTHOR:

GOLDING, MORTON J.

NIGHTMARE (N) Dell 6422, 1970;

GOLDING, WILLIAM THE SPIRE 1966

THE INHERITORS (N) H-B-W 1962; Poc GC 787;

GOLDMAN, WILLIAM

THE PRINCESS BRIDE (N) H-B-J 1973; BB 24255; 25483;

GORDON, REX = S. B. HOUGH

FIRST ON MARS (N) Ace D-233, 1957; Avon E 28084;
FIRST THROUGH TIME (N) Ace F-174, 1962;
FIRST TO THE STARS (N) Ace D-405, 1959;
UTOPIA MINUS X (N) Ace F-416, 1966;
THE YELLOW FRACTION (N) Ace 94350, 1969;

GORDON, STUART

TIME STORY (N) DAW 47, 1973;
ONE-EYE (N) DAW 76, 1973;
TWO-EYES (N) DAW 122, 1974;
THREE-EYES (N) DAW 171, 1975;

GOTSCHALK, FELIX C.

GROWING UP IN TIER 3000 (N) Ace 30420, 1975;

GOTLIEB, PHYLLIS

O MASTER CALIBAN (N) H&R 1976;
SUNBURST (N) GM K1488, 1964; Berk 03622;

GOULART, RON

AFTER THINGS FELL APART (N) Ace 00950, 1970; Gregg 1977; Ace 00951;
BROKE DOWN ENGINE (C13) Macmil 1971; Coll 2074,
CALLING DR PATCHWORK (N) DAW 283, 1978;
CHALLENGERS OF THE UNKNOWN (N) Dell 11377, 1977;
THE CHAMELEON CORPS (C11) Macmil 1972; Coll 2075, 1973;
CLOCKWORKS PIRATES (N) Ace+11182, 1971;
CRACKPOT (N) Dday 1977;
DEATH CELL (N) Beagle 95-111, 1971;
THE ENORMOUS HOURGLASS (N) Award AQ1510, 1976;
THE FIRE-EATER (N) Ace 28860, 1970;
FLUX (N) DAW 107, 1974;
GADGET MAN (N) Dday 1971; WPBL 65-879, 1972;
GHOST BREAKER (C9) Ace+11182, 1971;
HAWKSHAW (N) Dday 1972; Awrd AN1202, 1974;
THE HELLHOUND PROJECT (N) Dday 1975;
NUTZENBOLTS AND MORE TROUBLES WITH MACHNES (C11) Macmil 1975;
ODD JOB #101 (C7) Scrib 1975;
PLUNDER (N) Beagle 95-210, 1972;
SHAGGY PLANET (N) Lanc 75420, 1972;
SPACEHAWK INC. (N) DAW 132, 1974;
THE SWORD SWALLOWER (N) Dday 1968; Dell 8442,
A TALENT FOR THE INVISIBLE (N) DAW 37, 1973;
THE TIN ANGEL (N) DAW 80, 1973;
WHAT'S BECOME OF SCREWLOOSE (C10) Scrib 1971; DAW 60,
WHEN THE WAKER SLEEPS (N) DAW 175, 1975;
A WHIFF OF MADNESS (N) DAW 207, 1976;
WILDSMITH (N) Ace 88872, 1972;
NEMO (N) Berk 3395, 1977;
THE EMPEROR OF THE LAST DAYS (N) Pop 3201, 1977;
THE PANCHRONICON PLOT (N) DAW 231, 1977;

QUEST OF THE GYPSY (N) Pyramid A4034, 1976; (Weird Heroes #3)
EYE OF THE VULTURE (N) Jove 04293, 1977; (Weird Heroes 7

See Also VAMPIRELLA Series

GRANT, C. L.

THE RAVENS OF THE MOON (N) Dday 1978;
THE SHADOW OF ALPHA (N) Berk Z3143, 1976;
ASCENSION (N) Berk 03412, 1977;

GRAVES, ROBERT

WATCH THE NORTH WIND RISE (N) Creative Age 1949; Avon V2075; V2296;
HERCULES, MY SHIPMATE (N) Creative Age 1945; Universal UL 19; Prmd R1346;

GRAY, CURME

MURDER IN MILLENNIUM VI (N) Shasta 1952;

GRAZIER, JAMES

RUNTS OF 61 CYGNI C (N) Belm B75-2062, 1970;

GREEN, JOSEPH L.

CONSCIENCE INTERPLANETARY (N) Dday 1973; DAW 131;
THE LOAFERS OF REFUGE (N) BB U2233, 1965;
THE MIND BEHIND THE EYE (N) DAW 2, 1972;
THE HORDE (N) Laser 27, 1976;

GREEN, I. G.

TIME BEYOND TIME (N) Belm B75-2164, 1971;

GREEN, MARTIN

THE EARTH AGAIN REDEEMED: A Metaphysical Metaphor in 22 Tableaux (N) Basic 1977;

GREEN, ROLAND

WANDOR'S RIDE (N) Avon 16600, 1973; 27441;
WANDOR'S JOURNEY (N) Avon 24372, 1975;

GREENFIELD, IRVING A.

THE ANCIENT OF DAYS (N) Avon 14860, 1973;
THE FACE OF HIM (N) Manor 15202, 1976;
JULIUS CAESAR IS ALIVE AND WELL (N) Manor 19160, 1977;
THE OTHERS (N) Lancer 74-994, 1969; Manor 12490;
THE STARS WILL JUDGE (N) Dell 8504, 1974;
= STAR TRIALS (N) Manor 15276, 1977;
WATERS OF DEATH (N) Lancer 73-672, 1967; 74-655;

GRINNELL, DAVID See D. WOLLHEIM

GROVES, J.W.

SHELLBREAK (N) PBL 63-293, 1970;

GUIN, WYMAN

LIVING WAY OUT (C7) Avon S298, 1967;
THE STANDING JOY (N)Avon N2314, 1970;

GUNN, JAMES

THE END OF DREAMS (C3) Scrib 1975; SFBC;
BREAKING POINT (C8) Walker 1972; DAW 73,
THE BURNING (C3) Dell 0861, 1972;
FUTURE IMPERFECT (C10) Bant J2717, 1964;
THE IMMORTALS (N) Bant J2484, 1962; H3915;
THE JOY MAKERS (N) Bant A2219, 1961; S5953;
KAMPUS (N) Bant 2693, 1977;
THE LISTENERS (N) Scribners 1972; SFBC; Sig Y6160; W8037;
THE MAGICIANS (N) Scribners 1976;
SOME DREAMS ARE NIGHTMARES (C4) Scribners 1974;
STARBRIDGE (N) (see J. Williamson- coauthor)
STATION IN SPACE (C5) Bant A1825, 1958;
THIS FORTRESS WORLD (N) Gnome 1955; Ace D+223;
THE WITCHING HOUR (C3) Dell 9605, 1970;

GUTTERAGE, LINDSAY

COLD WAR IN A COUNTRY GARDEN (N) Putnam 1971; Pocket 77623;
KILLER PINE (N) Putnam 1973; Berkley N2545;

HADLEY, ARTHUR T.

THE JOY WAGON (N) Viking 1956; Berk G466;

HADLEY, FRANKLIN = RUSS WINTERBOTHAM

HAGGARD, H. RIDER (Partial Listing)

SHE (N) Lovell 1887; Dell 339, 1949; 1339; Lanc 72-614; 72-925; Prmd 1403; Hart 1976;
AYESHA: THE RETURN OF SHE (N) Dday 1905; Lanc 74-899; Newcastle F-113;
SHE & THE RETURN OF SHE (2N) Lanc 78692, 1972;
SHE AND ALLAN ( ) Newcastle F105, 1975;

ALLAN QUARTERMAIN (N) Harper 1887; Royal Giant +18, 1953; BB X743,
PEOPLE OF THE MIST (N) Longmans 1894;BBAF 23660, 1973; 23927; BBDR 25787;
CLEOPATRA (N) Longmans 1927; Poc 7025, 1963;
KING SOLOMON'S MINES (N) Lovell 1886; Dell 433, Royal Giant +18; BB X733;
WHEN THE WORLD SHOOK (N) BBDR 27359, 1978;
WISDOM'S DAUGHTER (N) BBDR 27428, 1978;
HEART OF THE WORLD ( ) Newcastle F105, 1976;
THE SAGA OF ERIC BRIGHTEYES ( ) Newcastle F101, 1974;
THE WORLD'S DESIRE (N) (with A. Lang) Harper 1890; BBAF 2467, 1972; BBDR 27218;

HAHN, STEVE

MINDWIPE (N) Laser 51, 1976;

HAIBLUM, ISIDORE

THE RETURN (N) Dell 7395, 1973; 17395;
TRANSFER TO YESTERDAY (N) BB 23418, 1973;
THE TSADDIK OF THE SEVEN WONDERS (N) BB 2445, 1971;
THE WILK ARE AMONG US (N) DdAY 1975;
INTERWORLD (N) Dell 12285, 1977;

HALDEMAN, JOE -Also ROBERT GRAHAM

ALL MY SINS REMEMBERED (N) St Martins 1977;
THE FOREVER WAR (N) St. Martins 1975; BB 24767; 25798;
MINDBRIDGE (N) St. Martins 1976; SFBC; BB; Avon 33605;
WAR YEAR (N) Holt 1972; Poc 81400; (not SF- war adventure)
See ATTAR THE MERMAN Series
See Listing of STAR TREK titles

HALL, AUSTIN

THE BLIND SPOT (N) (with H.E. Flint) Prime 1951; Ace G-547; 06731;
PEOPLE OF THE COMET (N) Griffin 1948;
THE SPOT OF LIFE (N) Ace F-318, 1964;

HALL, JOHN RYDER See WILLIAM ROTSLER

HAMILTON, EDMUND Also BRETT STERLING

Married to LEIGH BRACKETT

STARWOLF
THE WEAPON FROM BEYOND (N) Ace G-639, 1967
THE CLOSED WORLDS (N) Ace G-701, 1968;
WORLD OF THE STARWOLVES (N) Ace G-766, 1968;

INTERSTELLAR PATROL
CRASHING SUNS (S5) Ace F-319, 1965;
OUTSIDE THE UNIVERSE (N) Ace F-271, 1964;

JOHN GORDON SERIES
THE STAR KINGS (N) Fell 1949; (=); PBL 53-538; 64-472; Warn 76-942;
=BEYOND THE MOON (N) Signet 812, 1950;
RETURN TO THE STARS (N) Lancer 74-612, 1970;

BATTLE FOR THE STARS (N) Torquil 1961; SFBC; PBL 52-311; 52-609;
THE BEST OF EDMUND HAMILTON (C21) SFBC 1977; BBDR 25900;
CITY AT WORLD'S END (N) Fell 1951; Galx 18; Crst s184; S494; L758; M2026; P2625;
DOOMSTAR (N) Belm B50-657, 1966; B50-857;
FUGITIVE OF THE STARS (N) Ace M+111, 1965;
THE HAUNTED STARS (N) Torquil 1960; SFBC; Prmd F-698;
THE HORROR ON THE ASTEROID (C6) (British 1936) Gregg 1975;
THE STAR OF LIFE (N) Torquil 1959; SFBC; Crst s329;
THE SUN SMASHER (N) Ace D+351, 1959;
THE VALLEY OF CREATION (N) Lanc 72-721, 1964; 73-577; Lode B 5006;
WHAT'S IT LIKE OUT THERE (C12) Ace 88065, 1974;
A YANK AT VALHALLA (N) Ace +93900, 1973;

CAPTAIN FUTURE SERIES (FROM PULPS)
DANGER PLANET (as Sterling) (N) Pop 2335, 1967;
THE MAGICIAN OF MARS (N) Pop 2450, 1970;
CAPTAIN FUTURE & THE SPACE EMPEROR (N) Pop 2457, 1970;
OUTLAW WORLD (N) Pop 2376, 1968;
QUEST BEYOND THE STARS (N) Pop 2389, 1968;
OUTLAWS OF THE MOON (N) Pop 2399, 1969;
THE COMET KINGS (N) Pop 2407, 1969;
PLANETS IN PERIL (N) Pop 2416, 1969;
CALLING CAPTAIN FUTURE (N) Pop 2421, 1969;
CAPTAIN FUTURE'S CHALLENGE (N) Pop 2430, 1969;
GALAXY MISSION (N) Pop 2437, 1969;

HANCOCK, NIEL

CIRCLE OF LIGHT
GREYFAX GRIMWALD (N) Pop 8595, 1977;
FARAGON FAIRINGAY (N) Pop 8616, 1977;
CALIX STAY (N) Pop 4047, 1977;
SQUARING THE CIRCLE (N) Pop 4089, 1977;

DRAGON WINTER (N) Pop 04191, 1978;

HANNA, W. C.

THE TANDAR SAGA (N) Arcadia 1964;

HARDING, LEE

FUTURE SANCTUARY (N) Laser 41, 1976;

HARNESS, CHARLES L.

FLIGHT INTO YESTERDAY (N) Bouregy + Curl 1953;
=THE PARADOX MEN (N) Ace D+118, 1955;
THE RING OF RITORNEL (N) Berk X1630; 1968;
THE ROSE (N+2) Berk X1648, 1969;
WOLFHEAD (N) Berk 03658, 1978;

HARRINGTON, ALAN

PARADISE - 1 (N) Little-B 1978;

HARRIS, BARBARA S.

WHO IS JULIA? (N) McKay 1972; Pop 170;

HARRISON, HARRY

JASON DIN ALT
DEATHWORLD (N) Bant A2160; F3890;
DEATHWORLD 2 (N) Bant F2838, 1964;
DEATHWORLD 3 (N) Dell 1849, 1968;
ALL = DEATHWORLD TRILOGY (3N) SFBC 1974; Berk T3071;

TRILOGY TO THE STARS
1 HOMEWORLD 1980 BANT
2 WHEELWORLD 1981 BANT

SLIPPERY JIM DI GRIZ
THE STAINLESS STEEL RAT (N) F-672, 1961; Walker 1970; Berk S2015;
THE STAINLESS STEEL RAT'S REVENGE (N) Walker 1970; Berk S2304;
THE STAINLESS STEEL RAT SAVES THE WORLD (N) Putnam 1972; Berk 2475;
All = THE ADVENTURES OF THE STAINLESS STEEL RAT (3N) SFBC 1977;

THE BEST OF HARRY HARRISON (C20) Poc 80525, 1976;
BILL, THE GALACTIC HERO (N) Dday 1965; Berk F1186; Avon E 25767;
CAPTIVE UNIVERSE (N) Putnam 1969; Berk X1725; Z3072;
THE DALETH EFFECT (N) Putnam 1970; Berk S1880; 03649;
THE LIFESHIP (N) (with G. Dickson) H&R 1976; Poc 81044;
MAKE ROOM, MAKE ROOM (N) Dday 1966, Berk X1416; 2390; = Soylent Green Movie
MAN FROM P. I. G. (JN) Avon ZS136, 1968;
THE MEN FROM P.I.G. AND R.O.B.O.T. (JS2) Atheneum 1978;
ONE STEP FROM EARTH (C9) Macmil 1970; SFBC; Coll 2090;
PLAGUE FROM SPACE (N) Dday 1965; Bant F3640;
=THE JUPITER LEGACY (N) Bant S5445, 1970;
PLANET OF THE DAMNED (N) Bant J2316, 1962; S5769;
PRIME NUMBER (C19) Berk S1857, 1970;
SPACESHIP MEDIC (JN) Dday 1970;
STARSMASHERS OF THE GALAXY RANGERS (N) Putnam 1973; Berk N2688;
STONEHENGE (N) (with Stover) Scrib 1972; Manor 15149;
THE TECHNICOLOR TIME MACHINE (N) Dday 1967; Berk X1640;
TUNNEL THROUGH THE DEEPS (N) Putnam 1972; Berk N2565;
TWO TALES AND EIGHT TOMORROWS (C10) Bant F3722, 1968;
WAR WITH THE ROBOTS (C8) Prmd F771, 1962; X1898;
THE CALIFORNIA ICEBERG (JN) Walker 1975;
SKYFALL (N) Atheneum 1977;

HARRISON, M. JOHN

THE CENTAURI DEVICE (N) Dday 1974;
THE COMMITTED MEN (N) Dday 1971;
THE PASTEL CITY (N) Dday 1972; Avon 19711; 29637;

HARRISON, WILLIAM

ROLLER BALL MURDER (S13) Morrow 1974;
= ROLLER BALL (S13) Warn 76-839; 1975;

HARTLEY, L. P.

FACIAL JUSTICE (N) Dday 1961; SFBC; Curt 7028;

HARTRIDGE, JON

BINARY DIVINE (N) Dday 1969; Play 16147;
EARTHJACKET (N) Walker 1970;

HASSE, HENRY

THE STARS WILL WAIT (N) Avalon 1968;

HASSLER, KENNETH

THE DREAM SQUAD (N) Lennox Hill 1970;
THE GLASS CAGE (N) Arcadia 1970;
A MESSAGE FROM EARTH (N) Lennox Hill 1970;
DESTINATION TERRA (N) Lennox Hill 1970;
INTERGALACTIC AGENT (N) Lennox Hill 1971;
THE MULTIPLE MAN (N) Lennox Hill 1972;

HATCH, GERALD = DAVE FOLEY

THE DAY THE EARTH FROZE (N) Monarch 354, 1963;

HAYES, RALPH

THE VISITING MOON (N) Lennox Hill 1971;

HEARD, H. F.

THE DOPPELGANGERS (N) Vanguard 1947; Ace M-142, 1966;

HEATH, PETER

ASSASSINS FROM TOMORROW (N) Lanc 73-631, 1967;
MEN WHO DIE TWICE (N) Lanc 73-783, 1968;
THE MIND BROTHERS (N) Lanc 73-600, 1967;

HEIM, MICHAEL

ASWAN (N) Knopf 1972; PBL 78-284

HEINE, WILLIAM C.

DEATH WIND (N) Prmd 3961, 1976;

HEINLEIN, ROBERT A.

JUVENILE NOVELS

BETWEEN PLANETS (JN) Scribner 1951; Scrib SL-67; Ace 05500; BBDR 26070;
CITIZEN OF THE GALAXY (JN) Scribner 1957; Ace 10600;
FARMER IN THE SKY (JN) Scribner 1950; Dell 2518; Ace 24375;
HAVE SPACE SUIT, WILL TRAVEL (JN) Scrib 1958; Ace 31800; BBDR 26071;
RED PLANET (JN) Scribner 1949; Scrib SL-100; Ace 71140; BBDR 26069;
ROCKET SHIP GALILEO (JN) Scribner 1947; Ace 73330; BBDR 26068;
THE ROLLING STONES (JN) Scribner 1952; Ace 73440; BBDR 26067;
SPACE CADET (JN) Scribner 1948; Ace 77730;
THE STAR BEAST (JN) Scribner 1954; Ace 78000; BBDR 26066;
STARMAN JONES (JN) Scribner 1953; Dell 8246; BB 24354;
TIME FOR THE STARS (JN) Scribner 1956; SFBC; Ace 81125; BBDR 26073;
TUNNEL IN THE SKY (JN) Scribner 1955; Ace 82660; BBDR 26065;

FUTURE HISTORY SERIES

THE MAN WHO SOLD THE MOON (S6) Shasta 1950; (S4) Sig 847; S1644; D2348; T4307;+
THE GREEN HILLS OF EARTH (S10) Shasta 1951; Sig 943; S1537; D2348; T3193;+
REVOLT IN 2100 (S3) Shasta 1953; Sig 1194; S1699; D2638; P3563; T4236; Q5340;+

FRIDAY N 1982 DEL REY

METHUSELAH'S CHILDREN (N) Gnome 1958; Sig 1752; D2191, D2621; T4226; Y6382;+
ALL (-1+1)=THE PAST THROUGH TOMORROW (S21) Putnam 1967; SFBC; Berk T2738;
UNIVERSE (S) Dell 36, 1951;
=+ORPHANS OF THE SKY (S2) Putnam 1964; SFBC; Sig D2618; P3344; Berk S1908; 03786;
TIME ENOUGH FOR LOVE (N) Putnam 1973; SFBC; BErk T2493; 03471;

ASSIGNMENT IN ETERNITY (C4) Fantasy 1953; Sig 1161; D2587; P3163; T3968; +
BEYOND THIS HORIZON (N) Fantasy 1948; G&D 1952; Sig 1891; D2539; P3907; T4211; +
THE DOOR INTO SUMMER (N) Dday 1957; SFBC; Sig S1639; D2443; T3750; Q5693;
DOUBLE STAR (N) Dday 1956; SFBC; Sig S1444; D2419; P3669; T5566; Gregg 1978;
FARNHAM'S FREEHOLD (N) Putnam 1964; SFBC; Sig T2704; Berk Z1981; D2095; 03568;
GLORY ROAD (N) Putnam 1963; SFBC; Avon V2102; V2202; Berk N1809; 03783;
I WILL FEAR NO EVIL (N) Putnam 1970; Berk Z2085; D2321; 03425;
THE MENACE FROM EARTH (C8) Gnome 1959; Sig D2105; T4306;
THE MOON IS A HARSH MISTRESS (N) Putnam 1966; Berk N1601; 03436;
PODKAYNE OF MARS (JN) Putnam 1963; Avon G1211; S335; Berk S1791; N2073; 03434;
THE PUPPET MASTERS (N) Dday 1951; SFBC; Sig 980; S1544; D2366; P2863; T3752;
SIXTH COLUMN (N) Gnome 1949;
=THE DAY AFTER TOMORROW (N) Sig 882, 1951; S1577; D2649; T4227;
STARSHIP TROOPERS (JN) Putnam 1959; Sig D1987; D2381; Berk S1560; 02605; 03787;
STRANGER IN A STRANGE LAND (N) Putnam 1961; SFBC; Avon V2056; V2191; Berk N1571; +
THREE BY HEINLEIN (3N) Dday 1965; SFBC;= PUPPET MASTER + WALDO & MAGIC INC.
THE UNPLEASANT PROFESSION OF JONATHAN HOAG (C6) Gnome 1959; (=) Berk N2822;
= 6 X H (C6) Prmd G642; F910; X2023; V3635;
WALDO AND MAGIC INC (2N) Dday 1950; (=); Prmd F859; X1286; S1758; Sig T3690;
=WALDO: GENIUS IN ORBIT (2N) Avon T-261, 1958;
THE WORLDS OF ROBERT A HEINLEIN (C5) Ace F-375, 1966; 91501;

HENDERSON, ZENNA

THE PEOPLE
PILGRIMAGE: THE BOOK OF THE PEOPLE (N) Dday 1961; Avon G1185; S243; V2312; 297173;
THE PEOPLE: NO DIFFERENT FLESH (S6) Dday 1967; Avon S328; V2344; 29165;

THE ANYTHING BOX (C14) Dday 1965; Avon V2264; 34579;
HOLDING WONDER (C20) Dday 1971; Avon N445, 24737;

HENDRICKSON, WALTER B. JR.

CLASS G-ZERO (N) Major 3110, 1976;

HENSLEY, J. L.

THE BLACK ROADS (N) Laser 17, 1976;

HERBERT, FRANK

ARRAKIS
DUNE (N) Chilton 1965; Ace N-3; SFBC; Ace 17263; Berk T2706;
DUNE MESSIAH (N) Putnam 1969; Berk N1847; Z2601; D2952; SFBC;
CHILDREN OF DUNE (N) Putnam 1976; SFBC; Berk 3310;

JORG X MCKIE SERIES GOD EMPORER OF DUNE 1983
WHIPPING STAR (N) Putnam 1970; Berk S1909; N2824; (rev) 3504;
THE DOSADI EXPERIMENT (N) Berk/Put 1977;

THE BOOK OF FRANK HERBERT (C10) Daw 39, 1973; UW1301;
DESTINATION VOID (N) Berk F1249, 1966; S1864;
THE DRAGON IN THE SEA (N) Dday 1956; SFBC; (=); Avon S290; V2330; (=)
=21ST CENTURY SUB (N) Avon T-146, 1956; G1092;
=UNDER PRESSURE (N) BB 23835, 1974; 24494; 25597;
THE EYES OF HEISENBERG (N) Berk F1283, 1966; S1865; N2810;
THE GODMAKERS (N) Putnam 1972; Berk N2344;
THE GREEN BRAIN (N) Ace F-379, 1966; 30261;
THE HEAVEN MAKERS (N) Avon S319, 1968; (rev)BBDR 25304;
HELLSTROM'S HIVE (N) SFBC; 1973; Bant T8276;
THE SANTAROGA BARRIER (N) Berk S1615, 1968; 2811; Berk/Put 1977;
THE WORLDS OF FRANK HERBERT (C9) Ace 90925, 1971; Berk 3502;
SOUL CATCHER (N) (not S.F.)
THE JESUS INCIDENT BERK 1980

HERBERT, JAMES

THE FOG (N) Signet W6708, 1975;
THE RATS (N) Signet W6460, 1975;
THE SURVIVOR (N) Signet E7393, 1976;

HERSEY, JOHN

THE CHILD BUYER (N) Knopf 1960; Bant H2290; N4160;
MY PETITION FOR MORE SPACE (N) Knopf 1974; SFBC; Bant; 2270;
WHITE LOTUS (N) Knopf 1965; Bant Q3095;

HERSHMAN, MORRIS

SHAREWORLD (N) Walker 1972;
= THE CRASH OF 2086 (N) Major 3090, 1976;

HERZOG, ARTHUR

THE SWARM (N) S & S 1974; Sig J6351;
HEAT (N) S & S 1977

HEYWOOD, VICTOR D.

PRISON PLANET (N) Papillon OSF 503, 1974;

HICKEY, T. EARL

THE TIME CHARIOT (N) Avalon 1966;

HIGH, PHILIP E.

INVADER ON MY BACK (N) Ace H+85, 1968; +14280;
THE MAD METROPOLIS (N) Ace M+135, 1966;
NO TRUCE WITH TERRA (N) Ace F+275, 1964;
THE PRODIGAL SUN (N) Ace F-255, 1964;
REALITY FORBIDDEN (N) Ace G+609, 1967;
THESE SAVAGE FUTURIANS (N) Ace G+623, 1967;
THE TIME MERCENARIES (N) Ace H+59, 1968; +81150;
TWIN PLANETS (N) PBL 52-392, 1967;

HILL, DAVID C. and ALBERT FAY HILL

THE DEADLY MESSIAH (N) Avon 32466, 1977;

HILL, ERNEST

PITY ABOUT EARTH (N) Ace H+56, 1968;

HILL, JOHN

THE LONG SLEEP (N) Pop 325, 1975;

HILTON, JAMES

LOST HORIZON (N) Morrow 1933; Poc 1; 6100;

HJORTSBERG, WILLIAM

GRAY MATTERS (N) S&S 1971; Poc 78242;

HOBAN, RUSSELL

THE LION OF BOAZ-JACHIN AND JACHIN-BOAZ (N) Stew & Day 1973; Poc 78392;

HOCH, EDWARD D.

THE FELLOWSHIP OF THE HAND (N) Walker 1973;
THE TRANSVECTION MACHINE (N) Walker 1971; Poc 77640;

HODDER-WILLIAMS, CHRISTOPHER

CHAIN REACTION (N) Dday 1959;
THE EGG-SHAPED THING (N) Putnam 1967; SFBC;
THE MAIN EXPERIMENT (N) Putnam 1965; SFBC; BB U6049;
THE PRAYER MACHINE (N) St. Martin's 1977;

HODGSON, WILLIAM HOPE

THE BOATS OF THE GLEN CARRIG (N) (Brit 1907) BBAF 2145, 1971; Hyperion 1976;
CARNACKI, THE GHOST -FINDER ( ) Mycroft and Moran 1947;
THE DREAM OF X (N) (Condensation of the Night Land) DMG 1977;
THE GHOST PIRATES (N) (Brit 1909) Hyperion 1976;
DEEP WATERS ( ) Arkham 1967;
THE HOUSE ON THE BORDERLAND (N) (Brit 1908) Ace D-553, 1962; Freeway FP 2038; Hyperion 1976;
THE HOUSE ON THE BORDERLAND AND OTHER NOVELS (4N) Arkham 1946;
THE NIGHT LAND (N) (Brit 1912) Hyperion 1976;
=& THE NIGHT LAND I (N) BBAF 2669, 1972;
=& THE NIGHT LAND II (N) BBAF 2670, 1972;
OUT OF THE STORM (N) DMG 1975;

HOFFMAN, LEE

ALWAYS THE BLACK KNIGHT (N) Avon S417, 1970;
THE CAVES OF KARST (N) BB 1507, 1969;
TELEPOWER (N) Belm B50+779, 1967;
CHANGE SONG (N) Dday 1972;

HOGAN, JAMES P.

THE GENESIS MACHINE (N) Del Rey 1978; BBDR 27231;
INHERIT THE STARS (N) BBDR 25704, 1977;

HOLDEN, RICHARD

SNOW FURY (N) Dodd-M 1955; SFBC; Perm M3034;

HOLDSTOCK, ROBERT P.

EYE AMONG THE BLIND (N) Dday 1977;

HOLLAND, CECELIA

FLOATING WORLDS (N) Knopf 1976; Poc 80867;

HOLLY, J. HUNTER = JOAN C. HOLLY

THE DARK ENEMY (N) Avalon 1965;
THE DARK PLANET (N) Avalon 1962; M-B 75-426;
DEATH DOLLS OF LYRA (N) Manor 15290, 1977;
ENCOUNTER (N) Avalon 1959; Mon 240;
THE FLYING EYES (N) Mon 260, 1962;
THE GREEN PLANET (N) Avalon 1960; Mon 213;
THE GREY ALIENS (N) Avalon 1963;
KEEPER (N) Laser 22, 1976;
THE MIND TRADERS (N) Avalon 1966; M-B 60-291; 95304;
THE RUNNING MAN (N) Mon 342, 1963;
THE TIME TWISTERS (N) Avon G1231, 1964;
SHEPARD (N) Laser 55, 1977;

HOLMES, JOHN ERIC

MAHARS OF PELLUCIDAR (N) Ace 51590, 1976;

HOOVER, HAM.

THE DELIKON (N) Viking 1977;
THE RAINS OF ERIDAN (JN) Viking 1977;

HOSKINS, ROBERT

MASTER OF THE STARS (N) Laser 40; 1976;
THE SHATTERED PEOPLE (N) Dday 1975;
TO CONTROL THE STARS (N) BBDR 25253, 1977;
TOMORROW'S SON (N) Dday 1977;

HOWARD, HAYDEN

THE ESKIMO INVATION (N) BB U6122, 1967;

HOWARD, ROBERT E. (Partial Listing)

SOLOMON KANE
RED SHADOWS (S12+3P) Grant 1968; Grant 1971;
=& THE MOON OF SKULLS (S3) Centaur pb 1969;
=& THE HAND OF KANE (S4) Centaur pb 1970;
=& SOLOMON KANE (S7) Centaur pb 1971;

BRAN MAK MORN

BRAN MAK MORN (S8) Dell 0774, 1969;
=& WORMS OF THE EARTH (S7) Grant 1974; Zebra 126; 234;
=&+ TIGERS OF THE SEA (S4) Grant 1974; Zebra 119;
Series continued by Karl Edward Wagner

CONAN-INITIAL HARD COVERS "D" = De Camp; "N" = Nyberg

CONAN THE CONQUEROR (N) Gnome 1950; Ace D+36, 1954;
= THE HOUR OF THE DRAGON (N) Berk 3608, 1977; Berk/Put 197
THE SWORD OF CONAN (S4) Gnome 1952;
KING CONAN (S5) Gnome 1953;
THE COMING OF CONAN (S5+S3) Gnome 1953; (Conan and Kull stories);
CONAN THE BARBARIAN (S5) Gnome 1955;
TALES OF CONAN (S4) Gnome 1955; (with D);
THE RETURN OF CONAN (N) Gnome 1957; (by D & N);

CONAN-COMPLETE CHRONOLOGICAL SERIES "C" = Carter

CONAN (S7)(With C&D) Lanc 73-685, 1967; 74-958; 75-104; 78-744; Ace 11671;
CONAN OF CIMMERIA (S8) (with D) Lanc 75-072, 1969; 78-742; Ace 11672;
CONAN THE FREEBOOTER (S5) (with D) Lanc 74-963,1968; 75-119; Ace 11673;
CONAN THE WANDERER (S4) (with C&D) Lanc 74-976, 1968; 78-741; Ace 11674;
CONAN THE ADVENTURER (S4) (with D) Lanc 73-526, 1966; 75-102; 78-743; Ace 11675;
CONAN THE BUCCANEER (N) (by C&D) Lanc 75-181, 1971; Ace 11676;
CONAN THE WARRIOR (S3) Lanc 73-549, 1967; 75-148; 78-746; Ace 11677;
CONAN THE USURPER (S4) (with D) Lanc 73-599, 1967; 75-103; Ace 11678;
CONAN THE CONQUEROR (N) Lanc 73-572, 1967; 75-137; Ace 11679;
CONAN THE AVENGER (N) (by D&N) Lanc 73-780, 1968; 75-149; 78-747; Ace 11680;
CONAN OF AQUILONIA (S4) (by C&D) (NOT published by Lancer) Ace 11682, 1977;
CONAN OF THE ISLES (N) (by C&D) Lanc 73-800, 1968; 75-136; 78-745; Ace 11681;

BERKLEY REPRINTS OF ORIGINAL STORIES FROM PULPS

THE HOUR OF THE DRAGON (N) Berk 3608, 1977; Berk/Put 1977;
THE PEOPLE OF THE BLACK CIRCLE (S4) Berk 3609, 1977;
RED NAILS (N) Berk 3610, 1977;

QUALITY REPRINTS OF CONAN TALES

THE PEOPLE OF THE BLACK CIRCLE (N) DMG 1974;
THE TOWER OF THE ELEPHANT (S2) DMG 1975; (+The God in the Bowl)
A WITCH SHALL BE BORN (N) DMG 1975;
RED NAILS (N) DMG 1975;
ROUGES IN THE HOUSE (S2) DMG 1976; (+ The Frost Giants Daughter)
THE DEVIL IN IRON (S2) DMG 1976; G&D 1978;

ALMURIC (N) Ace F-305, 1964; 07150; DMG 1975; Berk 3483;
BLACK CANAAN (C) Berk 03711, 1978;
THE DARK MAN AND OTHERS (C15) Arkham 1963; Lanc 75-265;
=PIGEONS FROM HELL (C14) Zebra 189, 1976;
THE GREY GOD PASSES (S) Miller pb 1975;
KING KULL (S13) Lanc 73-650, 1967; 74-561; 75-371;
MARCHERS OF VALHALLA (C2) DMG 1972; (C3) DMG 1977; Berk 03702;
THE RETURN OF SKULLFACE (N) (with Ludoff) FAX 1977;

THE LOST VALLEY OF ISKANDER (C4) Fax 1975; Zebra 157;
SKULL-FACE AND OTHERS (C23) Arkham 1946;
SKULL FACE (N) Berk 03708, 1978;
THE SWORD WOMAN (C5) Zebra 261, 1977;
WOLFSHEAD (C7) Lanc 73-721, 1968; 75-299;

SELECTED NON—FANTASY TITLES
BRECKINRIDGE ELKINS (Western)
A GENT FROM BEAR CREEK (S14) Grant 1965; Grant 1975; Zebra 132;
THE PRIDE OF BEAR CREEK (S7) Grant 1966; Grant 1977;

BLACK VULMEA'S VENGEANCE (C3) Grant 1976; Zebra 244 (Pirate) Baronet 1978;
THE BOOK OF ROBERT E. HOWARD (C21) Zebra 163, 1976;
THE IRON MAN (C4) Grant 1976; Zebra 171;
THE INCREDIBLE ADVENTURES OF DENNIS DORGAN (S11) Fax 1975; Zebra 149
RED BLADES OF BLACK CATHAY (C3) (with Tevis Clyde Smith) Grant 1971; (Oriental)
SECOND BOOK OF ROBERT E HOWARD (C21) Zebra 183, 1976;
SON OF THE WHITE WOLF (C2) Fax 1977; Berk 03710;
THE SOWERS OF THE THUNDER (C4) DMG 1973; Zebra 113; DMG 1976;
SWORDS OF SHAHRAZAR (N) Fax 1976; Berk 03709;
THREE BLADED DOOM (N) Zebra 277, 1977; (El Borak- Adventure)
THE VULTURES (C2) Fictioneer 1973;
THE VULTURES OF WHAPETON (C4) Zebra 144, 1975;
See David C. Smith for additional Black Vulmea stories
See also Andrew J. Offutt - continuation of Cormac Mac Art series

POETRY
ALWAYS COMES EVENING (P66) Arkham 1958; Underwood Miller 1977;
BLACK DAWN (P1) Squires 1972;
ECHOES FROM AN IRON HARP (P) Grant 1972;
ETCHINGS IN IVORY (P6) Glenn Lord 1968;
ROAD TO ROME (P1) Squires 1972;
SINGERS IN THE SHADOWS (P20) Grant 1970; SF Graphics 1977;
SONG OF THE NAKED LANDS (P1) Squires 1973;

HOYLE, FRED

ANDROMEDA (with J. Elliot - Coauthor)
A FOR ANDROMEDA (N) H&R 1962; SFBC; Crst d773; R1205; Avon 23366;
ANDROMEDA BREAKTHROUGH (N) H&R 1964; SFBC; Crst R1080; T2357;

THE BLACK CLOUD (N) H&R 1957; SFBC; Sig S1673; D2202; P3384; T5486; Q6605;
ELEMENT 79 (C15) Nal 1967; SFBC; Sig P3463; Q5279;
OCTOBER THE FIRST IS TOO LATE (N) H&R 1966; SFBC; Crst R1155; T1434;
OSSIANS RIDE (N) H&R 1959; SFBC; Berk G495; X1506;

DICK WARBOYS (with Geoffrey Hoyle co-author)
ROCKETS IN URSA MAJOR (N) H&R 1969; SFBC; Crest T1648; P2514;
INTO DEEPEST SPACE (N) H&R 1974; SFBC; Signet Y6764;

OTHER NOVELS WITH GEOFFREY HOYLE Co-AUTHOR
THE INCANDESCENT ONES (N) H&R 1977; Sig 08062;
FIFTH PLANET (N) H&R 1963, SFBC; Crest d812; G-M T2243; M2873;
THE INFERNO (N) H&R 1973; SFBC;
THE MOLECULE MEN (2N) H&R 1971; SFBC;
SEVEN STEPS TO THE SUN (N) H&R 1970; Crest T1778;

HUBBARD, L. RON

DEATH'S DEPUTY (N) FPC1 1948; Leis LB5, 1970;
THE KINGSLAYER (N+2) FPCI 1949;
= SEVEN STEPS TO THE ARBITER (N+2) Major 3018, 1975;
BOTH =FROM DEATH TO THE STARS (2N) FPCI 1953;
FEAR & TYPEWRITER IN THE SKY (2N) Gnome 1951; Pop 4006;
=& FEAR (N) Galx 29, 1957;
FEAR & THE ULTIMATE ADVENTURE (2N) Berk S1811, 1970;
FINAL BLACKOUT (N) Hadley 1948; Leis LB32; Garland 1976;
RETURN TO TOMORROW (N) Ace S-66, 1954; Garland 1976;
SLAVES OF SLEEP (N) Shasta 1948; Lanc 73-573, 1967;
TRITON (N+1) FPCI 1949;
OLE DOC METHUSELAH (C7) Theta 1970; Daw 20, 1972;;

HUGHES, JAMES

ENDS (N) Knopf 1971;

HUGHES, RILEY

THE HILLS WERE LIARS (N) Bruce 1955; All Saints AS230;

HUGHES, RODNEY

THE DRAGON KEEPERS (N) Pop 524, 1974;

HUGHES, ZACH =HUGH ZACHARY

THE BOOK OF RACK THE HEALER (N) Awrd AN1149, 1973;
THE LEGEND OF MAIREE (N) BB 23888, 1974;
FOR TEXAS AND ZED (N) Pop 370, 1976;
THE ST. FRANCIS EFFECT (N) Berk K3111, 1976;
SEED OF THE GODS (N) Berk 2642, 1974;
THE STORK FACTOR (N) Berk N2781, 1975;
TIDE (N) Berk/Put 1974; Berkley N2813;
TIGER IN THE STARS (N) Laser 49, 1976;

HULL, E. MAYNE Married to A.E. VAN VOGT

PLANETS FOR SALE (N) Fell 1954; Book Co. of America 13, 1965; Tempo 5356; 12127;
SEE ALSO A. E. VAN VOGT, Coauthor;

HUNTER, EVAN = S. A. LOMBINO

ALSO HUNT COLLINS & RICHARD MARSTEN

DANGER DINOSAURS (JN) (as Marsten) Winston 1953;

FIND THE FEATHERED SERPENT (JN) Winston 1952;
ROCKET TO LUNA (JN) (as Marsten) Winston 1952;
TOMORROW'S WORLD (N) (as Collins) Avalon 1956;
= TOMORROW AND TOMORROW (N) (as Collins) Prmd G214, 1956; G654; R1170; X2250;

HUXLEY, ALDOUS

AFTER MANY A SUMMER DIES THE SWAN (N) Harper 1939; Avon 388; AT435; T75; VS1;
APE AND ESSENCE (N) Harper 1948; Bant A1793; HC262; SY4018;
BRAVE NEW WORLD (N) Dday 1932; Bant A1071; A1369; AC1 Hc206; SY4172; NY4802; Harper P3095;

HYNE, C. J. CUTLIFFE

THE LOST CONTINENT (N) Harper 1900; BB 2502; Train 1974; BB 22502; BBDR 27089;

J

JACKSON, BASIL

EPICENTER (N) Norton 1971; Berk N2258;
FLAMEOUT (N) Norton 1976;

JACKSON, SHIRLEY

HANGSAMAN (N) Ace K-185, 1964; 31705;
THE HAUNTING OF HILL HOUSE (N) Viking 1959; Pop K6; 60-8089; 1508;
THE LOTTERY (C26) Farrar-Straus 1949; Lion 14; Avon T449; S197; V529; Pop 300;
THE SUNDIAL (N) Farrar-Straus 1958; Ace K-166; H-96;
WE HAVE ALWAYS LIVED IN THE CASTLE (N) Viking 1962; Pop M2041; 60-2137; 60-8088;

JAKES, JOHN

BRAK

BRAK THE BARBARIAN (N) Avon S363, 1968; Tandem 167074; Poc 81278;
BRAK VS. THE MARK OF THE DEMONS (N) PBL 63-184, 1969; Poc 81371;
BRAK VS. THE SORCERESS (N) PBL 63-089, 1969; Poc 81372;
BRAK: WHEN THE IDOLS WALKED (N) Poc 81373; 1978;

II GALAXY

WHEN THE STAR KINGS DIE (N) Ace G-656, 1967; 88100; 88101;
THE PLANET WIZARD (N) Ace 67060, 1969; 67061;
TONIGHT WE STEAL THE STARS (N) Ace + 81680, 1969;

GAVIN BLACK

MASTER OF THE DARK GATE (N) Lanc 75113, 1970;
WITCH OF THE DARK GATE (N) Lanc 75415, 1972;

THE ASYLUM WORLD (N) PBL 63-236, 1969;
THE BEST OF JOHN JAKES (C10) DAW 244, 1977;
BLACK IN TIME (N) PBL 63-426, 1970;
THE HYBRID (N) PBL 63-049, 1969;
THE LAST MAGICIANS (N) Sig T3988, 1969;
MASK OF CHAOS (N) Ace +78400, 1970;
MENTION MY NAME IN ATLANTIS (N) DAW 25, 1972; UY 1196; UY 1261;
MONTE CRISTO 99 (N) Curt 7100, 1970;
ON WHEELS (N) PBL 75-123, 1973;
SIX GUN PLANET (N) PBL 63-313, 1970; Warn 84-721-6;(fc 8/78)
SECRETS OF STAR DEEP (JN) Westminister 1972;
TIME GATE (JN) Westminister 1969; Sig Y7889;
SEE PLANET OF THE APES SERIES;

JAMESON, MALCOLM

ATOMIC BOMB (N) Bond-Charteris pb 1945;
BULLARD OF THE SPACE PATROL (S7) World 1951; 1955;
TARNISHED UTOPIA (N) Galx 27, 1956;

JANIFER, LAURENCE MARK = LARRY MARK HARRIS

Also MARK PHILLIPS, With R. GARRETT - COAUTHOR
ANGELO DI STEFANO
TARGET: TERRA (N) (with S.J. Treibich) Ace H+91, 1968; 68660;
THE HIGH HEX (N) (with S. J. Treibich) Ace +72400, 1969;
THE WAGERED WORLD (N) (with S. J. Treibich) Ace +81680, 1969;
IMPOSSIBLE? (C16) Belm B50-810, 1968;
A PIECE OF MARTIN CANN (N) Belm B50-811, 1968;
POWER (N) Dell 8527, 1974;
SLAVE PLANET (N) Prmd F840, 1963;
SURVIVOR (N) Ace 79111, 1977
THE WONDER WAR (N) Prmd F963, 1964;
YOU SANE MEN (N) Lanc 72-789, 1965;
= BLOODWORLD (N) Lanc 73-752, 1968; Lode B5018;
PAGAN PASSIONS (N) See R. Garrett coauthor

JARRY, ALFRED

THE SUPERMALE (N) New Directions 1977;

JAVOR, F. A.

THE RIM–WORLD LEGACY (N) Sig P3183, 1967; Q5213; Y6814;

JEPPSON, J. O. (MARRIED TO I. ASIMOV)

THE SECOND EXPERIMENT (N) Hughton-M 1974; Crst 2-3005;

JETER, K. W.

THE DREAM FIELDS (N) Laser 33, 1976;
SEEKLIGHT (N) Laser 7, 1975;

JOHANNESSON, OLOF = ALFVEN HANNES

THE TALE OF THE GREAT COMPUTER (N) Coward-McCann 1968;
= THE END OF MAN (N) Award AX 448, 1969;

JOHNS, WILLY

THE FABULOUS JOURNEY OF HIERONYMUS MEEKER (N) Little-B 1954;

JONES, D. F. =DENNIS FELTHAM JONES

CHARLES FORBIN
COLOSSUS (N) Putnam 1967; SFBC; Berk X1455; S1840; Z3229;
THE FALL OF COLOSSUS (N) Putnam 1974; SFBC; Berk N2760;
COLOSSUS AND THE CRAB (N) Berk 3467, 1977;

DONT PICK THE FLOWERS (N) Walker, 1971;
=DENVER IS MISSING (N) Berk Z2509, 1974;
THE FLOATING ZOMBIE (N) Putnam 1974; SFBC; Berk Z2980;
IMPLOSION (N) Putnam 1968; SFBC; Berk S2150;

JONES, GUY PEARCE & CONSTANCE B.

PEABODY'S MERMAID (N) Random 1946; Pocket 503;

JONES, J. A.

BLUE LAB (N) Major 185, 1978;

JONES, LANGDON

EYE OF THE LENS (C5) Macmil 1972; Coll 2180;

JONES, NEIL R.

PROFESSOR JAMESON
THE PLANET OF THE DOUBLE SUN (S3) Ace F-420, 1967; Garland 1976;
THE SUNLESS WORLD (S3) Ace G-631, 1967;
SPACE WAR (S3) Ace G-650, 1967;
TWIN WORLDS (S3) Ace G-681, 1967;
DOOMSDAY ON AJIAT(S4) Ace G-719, 1968;

JONES, RAYMOND F.

PLANET OF LIGHT (JN) Winston 1953;
SON OF THE STARS (JN) Winston 1952;

THE ALIEN (N) Galx 6, 1951; Belm B50-708; LB444 ZK;
THE CYBERNETIC BRAINS (N) Avalon 1962; PBL 63-063;
THE KING OF EOLIM (N) Laser 12, 1975;
MOONBASE ONE (JN) Criterion 1971;
THE NON-STATISTICAL MAN (C4) Belm L92-588, 1964; B50-820;
RENAISSANCE (N) Gnome 1951;
= MAN OF TWO WORLDS (N) Prmd F941, 1963; T2413;
THE RIVER AND THE DREAM (N) Laser 54, 1977;
RENEGADES OF TIME (N) Laser 1, 1975;
THE SECRET PEOPLE (N) Avalon 1956;
= THE DEVIATES (N) Galx 242, 1959;

SYN (N) Belm B60-1018, 1969;
THIS ISLAND EARTH (N) Shasta 1952; SFBC;
THE TOYMAKER (C6) FPCI 1951;
WEEPING MAY TARRY (N) (with R. Del Rey) Pinn 40-215-5, 1978;
THE YEAR WHEN STARDUST FELL (JN) Winston 1958;

JONES, ROBERT

BLOODSPORT (N) S & S 1974; Dell 4398;

JOSEPH, M. K.

THE HOLE IN THE ZERO (N) Dutton 1968; Avon V2284;

JUDD, CYRIL See JUDITH MERRIL and CYRIL KORNBLUTH

KAMIN, NICK

EARTHRIM (N) Ace +66160, 1969;
THE HERROD MEN (N) Ace +13805, 1971;

KANE, GIL

BLACKMARK (N) (comic book form) Bant S5871, 1971;

KANGILASKI, JOAN

THE SEEKING SWORD (N) BB 25650, 1977;

KANTOR, MACKINLAY

IF THE SOUTH HAD WON THE CIVIL WAR (N) Bant A2241, 1961;

KAPP, COLIN

PATTERNS OF CHAOS (N) Awrd An1118, 1973; Ace 65390;
THE CHAOS WEAPON (N) BBDR 27115, 1977;
THE SURVIVAL GAME (N) BB 25192, 1976;
TRANSFINITE MAN (N) Berk F974, 1964;
THE WIZARD OF ANHARITTE (N) Awrd AN1156, 1973;

KARLINS, MARVIN

GOMORRAH (N) (with L. Andrews) Dday 1974;
THE LAST MAN IS OUT (N) Prentice-H 1969;

KARP, DAVID

ONE (N) Vanguard 1953;
=ESCAPE TO NOWHERE (N) Lion LL 10, 1955; Universal UL126;

KASTLE, HERBERT

THE REASSEMBLED MAN (N) G M L1494, 1964; 2041;

KATZ, JACK

THE FIRST KINGDOM (N) Poc Wallaby 79016, 1978; (stories in cartoon form)

KAVAN, ANNA = HELEN WOODS EDMONDS

ICE (N) Dday 1970; Pop 538;
HOUSE OF SLEEP (N) Dday 1947;
ASYLUM PIECE (C27) Dday 1946;
JULIA AND THE BAZOOKA (C15) Knopf 1975;

KAYE, MARVIN See GODWIN, PARKE

KEENE, DAY & PRUYN, LEONARD

WORLD WITHOUT WOMEN (N) G M s975, 1960; L1504;

KELLEAM, JOSEPH E.

HUNTERS OF SPACE (N) Avalon 1960;
THE LITTLE MEN (N) Avalon 1960;
OVERLORDS FROM SPACE (N) Ace D+173, 1956;
WHEN THE RED KING WOKE (N) Avalon 1966;

KELLER, DAVID H. (Partial Listing)

THE ETERNAL CONFLICT (N) Prime 1949;
THE HOMUNCULUS (N) Prime 1950;
LIFE EVERLASTING & (N+C10) Avalon Newark 1949; Hyperion 1975;
THE SIGN OF THE BURNING HART (S4) National Fantasy Fan 1948;
THE SOLITARY HUNTERS & THE ABYSS (2N) New Era 1948;
TALES FROM UNDERWOOD (C23) P&C 1952;
THE THOUGHT PROJECTOR (N) Stellar 2, 1930;

KELLEY, LEO P.

THE ACCIDENTAL EARTH (N) Belm B75-1088, 1970;
THE COINS OF MURPH (N) Berk S2069, 1971;
THE COUNTERFEITS (N) Belm B50-797, 1967;
THE EARTHTRIPPER (N) GM T2719, 1973;
MYTHMASTER (N) Dell 6216, 1973;
MINDMIX (N) GM T2549, 1972;
ODYSSEY TO EARTHDEATH (N) Belm B60-085, 1968;
TIME ROGUE (N) Lanc 74627, 1970;
TIME: 110100 (N) Walker 1972;

KELLY, ROBERT

THE SCORPIONS (N) Dday 1967;

KENNAWAY, JAMES = PEEBLES J. E.

THE MIND BENDERS (N) Atheneum 1963; Signet P2515;

KENYON, ERNEST M.

ROQUE GOLEN (N) Pop 4104, 1977;

KERN, GREGORY See E.C. TUBB & CAP KENNEDY SERIES

KERR, GEOFFREY

UNDER THE INFLUENCE (N) Lipp 1954; Berkley G518;

KERSH, GERALD

MEN WITHOUT BONES (C13) PBL 52-127, 1962;
NIGHTSHADE AND DAMNATION (C11) GM R1887, 1968;
ON AN ODD NOTE (C13) BB 268, 1958;
THE SECRET MASTERS (N) BBHC 1953; BB28;

KEYES, DANIEL

FLOWERS FOR ALGERNON (N) H—B—W 1966; Bant S3339;

KIMBERLY, GAIL

FLYER (N) Pop 8361, 1975;

KING, HAROLD;

PARADIGM RED (N) Bobbs-M 1975;

KING, VINCENT

ANOTHER END (N) BB 2109, 1971;
CANDY MAN (N) BB 2307, 1971;
LIGHT A LAST CANDLE (N) BB 1654, 1969;

KING, TAPPAN

NIGHTSHADE (N) (with B. Meacham) Prmd 4035, 1976; (Weird Heroes #4)

KIRST, HANS HELLMUT

THE SEVENTH DAY (N) Dday 1959; Ace K-110; Pyramid T1215;

KLEIN, GERARD

THE DAY BEFORE TOMORROW (N) DAW 11, 1972;
THE MOTE IN TIMES EYE (N) DAW 134, 1975;
THE OVERLORDS OF WAR (N) Dday 1973; SFBC; DAW 93; UW1313;
STARMASTERS' GAMBIT (N) DAW 68, 1973;

KLINE, OTIS ADELBERT

ROBERT GRANDON

PLANET OF PERIL (N) McClurg 1929, G&D 1930; Avalon 1961; Ace F-211;
PRINCE OF PERIL (N) McClurg 1930; Avalon 1962; Ace F-259;
THE PORT OF PERIL (N) Grandon 1949; Ace F-294;

MARS SERIES

THE SWORDSMAN OF MARS (N) Avalon 1960; Ace D-516; G-692;
THE OUTLAWS OF MARS (N) Avalon 1961; Ace D-531; G-693;

JAN SERIES

THE CALL OF THE SAVAGE (N) Clode 1937;
= JAN OF THE JUNGLE (N) Ace F-400, 1966;
JAN IN INDIA (N) Fictioneer 1, 1974;

THE BRIDE OF OSIRIS (N) Weinberg 1974;
THE MAN WHO LIMPED AND OTHER STORIES (S5) Saint Ent. (pb) 1946;
MAZA OF THE MOON (N) McClurg 1930; G&D 1931; Ace F-321;
TAM, SON OF THE TIGER (N) Avalon 1962;

KNIGHT, DAMON Married to KATE WILHELM

THE BEST OF DAMON KNIGHT (C22) SFBC 1976, Pocket 80699; Taplinger 1978;
A FOR ANYTHING (N) Berk F1136, 1965; Walker 1970; GM T 2545;
= THE PEOPLE MAKER (N) Zenith ZB-14, 1959;
ANALOGUE MEN (N) Berk F647, 1962;
= HELLS PAVEMENT (N) Lion LL13, 1955; GM T2416;
BEYOND THE BARRIER (N) Dday 1964; SFBC; Mfad 50-234; 60-444;
FAR OUT (C13) S&S 1961; SFBC; Berk F616;
THE FUTURIANS (NF) Crowell-Day 1977
IN DEEP (C8) Berk F760, 1963; Manor 75-444
MASTERS OF EVOLUTION (N) Ace D+375, 1959;
MIND SWITCH (N) Berk F1160, 1965;
= THE OTHER FOOT (N) MB 75-433, 1971;
OFF CENTER (C5) Ace M+113, 1965; Awrd AS 1071;
THE RITHIAN TERROR (N) Ace M+113, 1965; Awrd AS 1008; AN 1253;
THE SUN SABOTEURS (N) Ace F+108, 1961;
THREE NOVELS (C3) Dday 1967; SFBC; Berk S1706;
(RULE GOLDEN + NATURAL STATE + THE DYING MAN)
TOMORROW AND TOMORROW (C10) S&S 1973;
TURNING ON (C14) Dday 1966; Ace G-677;
WORLD WITHOUT CHILDREN & THE EARTH QUARTER (2N) Lanc 74-601, 1970;

KNOX, CALVIN M. See ROBERT SILVERBERG

KOCH, ERIC

THE LAST THING YOU'D WANT TO KNOW (N) Scrib 1976;

KOMATSU, SAKYO

JAPAN SINKS (N) H&R 1976;

KOONTZ, DEAN R.

AFTER THE LAST RACE (N) Atheneum 1974;
ANTI-MAN (N) PBL 63-384, 1970;
BEASTCHILD (N) Lanc 74719, 1970;
THE CRIMSON WITCH (N) Curt 7156, 1971;
THE DARK SYMPHONY (N) Lanc 74621, 1970;
THE DARKNESS IN MY SOUL (N) DAW 12, 1972;
DARK OF THE WOODS (N) Ace +13793, 1970;
DEMON SEED (N) Bant N7190, 1973; 10930;

THE FALL OF THE DREAM MACHINE (N) Ace +22600, 1969;
FEAR THAT MAN (N) Ace +23140, 1969;
THE FLESH IN THE FURNACE (N) Bant S6977, 1972;
THE HAUNTED EARTH (N) Lancer 75445, 1973;
HELL'S GATE (N) Lanc 74656, 1970;
NIGHTCHILLS (N) Atheneum 1976; Crest 3087;
NIGHTMARE JOURNEY (N) Berk/Put 1975; Berkley 2923;
SOFT COME THE DRAGONS (C8) Ace +13793, 1970;
STARBLOOD (N) Lanc 75-306, 1972;
STARQUEST (N) Ace H+70, 1968;
TIME THEIVES (N) Ace +00990, 1972;
THE VISION (N) Berk/Put 1977;
WARLOCK (N) Lanc 75386, 1972;
A WEREWOLF AMONG US (N) BB 3055, 1973;

KORNBLUTH, CYRIL M. WITH JUDITH MERRIL CYRIL JUDD

see MERRIL AND F. POHL - COAUTHORS

THE BEST OF C. M. KORNBLUTH (C19) SFBC; 1976; BB25461; Tap 1977;
THE EXPLORERS (C9) BB 86, 1954; F708, 1963;
THE MARCHING MORONS (C9) BB 303K, 1959; F760;
A MILE BEYOND THE MOON (C15) Dday 1958; SFBC; (C11) Mfad 40-100; 50-288; Manor 75-483; 12935;
NOT THIS AUGUST (N) Dday 1955; SFBC; Bant A1492;
THE SYNDIC (N) Dday 1953; SFBC; Bant 1317; Berk F1032; Avon E 20586;
TAKEOFF (N) Dday 1952; SFBC; Bant P15;
THIRTEEN O'CLOCK (C9) Dell 8731, 1970; (edited by Blish)

KOSINSKI, JERZY

BEING THERE (N) H B J 1971; Bantam Q7275;

KOTZWINKLE, WILLIAM

DOCTOR RAT (N) Knopf 1976; Ban 10382;

KRANTZ, E. KIRKER

THE CLOUDED MIRROR (N) Lennox Hill 1971;

KROPP, LLOYD

THE DRIFT (N) Dday 1969; Belm B95-2140;

KURLAND, MICHAEL

PLURIBUS (N) Dday 1975;
THE PRINCES OF EARTH (JN) Nelson 1978;
TOMORROW KNIGHT (N) DAW 183, 1976;
THE UNICORN GIRL (N) Prmd 1990, 1969; N3391;
THE WHENABOUTS OF BURR (N) DAW 157, 1975;
TRANSMISSION ERROR (N) Pyramid T2379, 1970; Jove 04514;

KURTZ, KATHERINE

DERYNI SERIES

DERYNI RISING (N) BBAF 1981, 1970; 24495; 25290;
DERYNI CHECKMATE (N) BBAF 2598, 1972; 24496; 25291; BBDR 27102;
HIGH DERYNI (N) BBAF 23485, 1973; 24497; 25626; BBDR 27113;
CAMBER OF CULDI (N) BBAF 24590, 1976;

KUTTNER, HENRY Also LEWIS PADGETT,

MARRIED TO C. L. MOORE WHO COLLABORATED ON MANY OTHER TITLES

With C. L. MOORE

BEYOND EARTH'S GATES (N) (as Padgett) Ace D+69, 1954;
EARTH'S LAST CITADEL (N) Ace F-306, 1964; 18111;
NO BOUNDARIES (C5) BBHC 1955; BB 122;

AHEAD OF TIME (C10) BBHC 1953; BB 30; U2341;
THE BEST OF HENRY KUTTNER (C17) SFBC 1975; BB 24415;
BYPASS TO OTHERNESS (C8) BB 497K, 1961;
THE CREATURE FROM BEYOND INFINITY (N) Pop 60-2355, 1968;
THE DARK WORLD (N) Ace F-327, 1965;
FURY (N) G&D 1950 (=); Lanc 75413;
= DESTINATION INFINITY (N) Avon T275, 1958; Garland 1976;
A GNOME THERE WAS (C11) (as Padgett) S&S 1950;
LINE TO TOMORROW (C7) (as Padgett) Bant 1251, 1954;
MUTANT (S5) (as Padgett) Gnome 1953; BB F724; U2859; Garland 1976;
RETURN TO OTHERNESS (C8) BB F619, 1962;
ROBOTS HAVE NO TAILS (S5) Gnome 1952 (as Padgett); Lanc 75464;
THE TIME AXIS (N) ACE F-356, 1965
TOMORROW AND TOMORROW & THE FAIRY CHESSMEN (2N) (as Padgett) Gnome 1951;
THE FAIRY CHESSMAN = CHESSBOARD PLANET (N) Galx 26, 1956;
THE MASK OF CIRCE (N) Ace 52075, 1971;
VALLEY OF THE FLAME (N) Ace F-297, 1964;
THE WELL OF THE WORLDS (N) Galx 17 (as Padgett) 1953; Ace F-344, 1965;

KYLE DAVID - See Doc Smith

L

LAFFERTY R. A.

APOCALYPSES (2N) Pinn 40-148, 1977;
ARRIVE AT EASTERWINE (N) Scrib 1971; BB3164,
THE DEVIL IS DEAD (N) Avon V2406, 1971; Gregg 1977;
THE FLAME IS GREEN (N) Walker, 1971; (S.F. ?)
DOES ANYONE ELSE HAVE ANYTHING FURTHER TO ADD (C17) Scrib 1974;
FOURTH MANSIONS (N) Ace 24590, 1969;
NINE HUNDRED GRANDMOTHERS (C21) Ace 58050, 1970;
NOT TO MENTION CAMELS (N) Bobbs-M 1976;
PAST MASTER (N) Ace H-54, 1968; Garland 1975; Ace 65301;
THE REEFS OF EARTH (N) Berk X1528, 1968; 03565;
SPACE CHANTEY (N) Ace H+56, 1968;
STRANGE DOINGS (C16) Scrib 1972; DAW 50,

LAKE, DAVID J.

DEXTRA SERIES

THE RIGHT HAND OF DEXTRA (N) DAW 239, 1977;
THE WILDINGS OF WESTRON (N) Daw 247, 1977;

THE GODS OF XUMA (N) Daw 279, 1978;
WALKERS ON THE SKY (N) DAW 223, 1976;

LAMPTON, CHRISTOPHER

CROSS OF EMPIRE (N) Laser 42, 1976;

LANCOUR, GENE = GENE FISHER

DIRSHAM, THE GODKILLER SERIES

THE LERIOS MECCA (N) Dday 1973;
SWORD FOR THE EMPIRE (N) Dday 1978;
THE WAR MACHINES OF KALINTH (N) Dday 1977;

LANDIS, ARTHUR H.

A WORLD CALLED CAMELOT (N) DAW 202, 1976;

LANG, ALLEN KIM

WILD AND OUTSIDE (N) Chilton 1966;

LANG, SIMON = DARLENE HARTMAN

ALL THE GODS OF EISERNON (N) Avon 15339, 1973;
THE ELLUVON GIFT (N) Avon 26518, 1975;

LANGART, DARREL T. See GARRETT, RANDALL

LANGE, JOHN =MICHAEL CRICHTON?

BINARY (N) Knopf 1972; Bant Q7613;

LANIER, STERLING E.

HIERO'S JOURNEY (N) Chilton 1973; Bant Q8534;
THE WAR FOR THE LOT (JN) Follett 1969;
THE PECULIAR EXPLOITS OF BRIGADIER FFELLOWS (S7) Walker 1972;

LASSWITZ, KURD

TWO PLANETS (N) (German 1897) Southern Ill Univ Press 1971; Pop 405,

LATHAM, PHILIP = R. S. RICHARDSON

FIVE AGAINST VENUS (JN) Winston 1953;
MISSING MEN OF SATURN (JN) Winston 1953;

LAUBENTHAL, SANDERS ANNE

EXCALIBER (N) BBAF 23416, 1973; 25635;

LAUMER, KEITH

RETIEF SERIES

ENVOY TO NEW WORLDS (S6) Ace F+223, 1963; 20730,
GALACTIC DIPLOMAT (S9) Dday 1965; Berk X1240;
RETIEF'S WAR (N) Dday 1966; Berk X1427;
RETIEF AND THE WARLORDS (N) Dday 1968; Berk X1800;
RETIEF: AMBASSADOR TO SPACE (S7) Dday 1969; Berk S1829;
RETIEF'S RANSOM (N) Putnam 1971; Berk S2138;
RETIEF OF THE C.D.T. (S5) Dday 1971;
RETIEF: EMISSARY TO THE STARS (S5) Dell 7425, 1975;

IMPERIUM SERIES

WORLDS OF THE IMPERIUM (N) Ace F+127, 1962; M-165, 91581; Berk 03466;
THE OTHER SIDE OF TIME (N) Berk F-1129, 1965; Walker 1971; Signet Q 5255;

O'LEARY SERIES

THE TIME BENDER (N) Berkley F-1185, 1966;
THE WORLD SHUFFLER (N) Putnam 1970; Berkley S1895;
THE SHAPE CHANGER (N) Putnam 1972; Berkley S2363;

ASSIGNMENT IN NOWHERE (N) Berk X1596, 1968;
THE BEST OF KEITH LAUMER (C9) Pocket 80310, 1976;
THE BIG SHOW (C6) Ace 06177, 1972;
BOLO: THE ANNALS OF THE DINOCHROME BRIGADE (S6) Berk/Put 1976; Berk 3450;
CATASTROPHE PLANET (N) Berk F1273, 1966;
THE DAY BEFORE FOREVER & THUNDERHEAD (2N) Dday 1968; Dell 1691;
DINOSAUR BEACH (N) Scrib 1971; DAW 21, UY 1174; UW1332;
EARTHBLOOD (N) (With R. G. Brown) Dday 1966; SFBC; Berk S1544;
GALACTIC ODYSSEY (N) Berk X1447, 1967;
THE GREAT TIME MACHINE HOAX (N) S&S 1964; Pock 50156; Award AN 1171; Ace 30256;
GREYLORN (C4) Berk X1514, 1968;
THE GLORY GAME (N) Dday 1973; Pop 526;
THE HOUSE IN NOVEMBER (N) Putnam 1970; SFBC; Berk S 1998;
THE INFINITE CAGE (N) Putnam 1972; Berkley N2582;
THE LONG TWILIGHT (N) Putnam 1969; Berk S1810; D3266;
ITS A MAD MAD MAD GALAXY (C5) Berk X1641, 1968;
THE MONITORS (N) Berk X1430, 1966;
NIGHT OF DELUSIONS (N) Putnam 1972; Berk N2497;
NINE BY LAUMER (C9) Dday 1067; Berk X1659;
ONCE THERE WAS A GIANT (C8) Dday 1971;
A PLAGUE OF DEMONS (N) Berk F1086, 1965; PBL 64-595; Warn 86001;
PLANET RUN (N) (with G. Dickson) Dday 1967; Berkley X1588;
THE STAR TREASURE (N) Putnam 1971; Berk S2025, Z3196;
TIMETRACKS (C5) BB 2575, 1972;
TIME TRAP (N) Putnam 1970; Berk S1871;
A TRACE OF MEMORY (N) Berk F-780, 1963; PBL 64-712; WPBL 65-712;
THE ULTIMAX MAN (N) St. Martin's, 1978; (fc 7/78)
THE UNDEFEATED (C4) Dell 9285, 1974;

SEE INVADERS T.V. SERIES;

LAURENS, MARSHALL

THE Z EFFECT (N) Poc 78357, 1974;

LEAHY, JOHN M.

DROME (N) FPCI 1952;

LEE, TANITH

SERIES

DON'T BITE THE SUN (N) DAW 184, 1976;
DRINKING SAPHIRE WINE (N) DAW 226, 1977;

BIRTHGRAVE SERIES

THE BIRTHGRAVE (N) DAW 154, 1975;
VAZKOR SON OF VAZKOR (N) Daw 272, 1978;
QUEST FOR THE WHITE WITCH (N) Daw 276, 1978;
THE DRAGON HORDE (N) FS&G, 1971;
THE STORM LORD (N) DAW 193, 1976; UJ1361;
VOLKHAVAAR (N) Daw 251, 1977;

COMPANIONS OF THE ROAD (JS2) Martins Press, 1977;
EAST OF MIDNIGHT (N) St. Martin's 1978;

LE GUIN, URSULA K.

EARTHSEA SERIES

A WIZARD OF EARTHSEA (JN) Parnassus 1968; Ace 90075; Bant T2168; 10135;
THE TOMBS OF ATUAN (JN) Atheneum 1971; Bantam T8318; 10132;
THE FARTHEST SHORE (JN) Atheneum 1972; Bantam T2126; 10131

CITY OF ILLUSIONS (N) Ace G-626, 1967; 10701; Garland 1976; Harper 1978;
THE DISPOSSESSED (N) H&R 1974; SFBC; Avon 24885;
THE LATHE OF HEAVEN (N) Scribners 1971; SFBC; Avon 14530; 25338;
THE LEFT HAND OF DARKNESS (N) Ace 47800, 1969; Walker 1969; SFBC; Ace 47802;
PLANET OF EXILE (N) Ace G+597, 1966; 66951; Garland 1976; H&R 1978;
ROCANNON'S WORLD (N) Ace G+574, 1966; 73291; Garland 1976; H&R 1977;
THE WINDS 12 QUARTERS (C17) H&R 1975; SFBC; Bant 2907;
THE WORD FOR WORLD IS FORREST (N) Berk/Put 1976; Berk D3279;

LEIBER, FRITZ

FAFHRD AND GRAY MOUSER

TWO SOUGHT ADVENTURE (S7) Gnome 1957;
=+ SWORDS AGAINST DEATH (S10) Ace 79150, 1970; Gregg 1977;
SWORDS AND DEVILTRY (S3) Ace 79170, 1970; Gregg 1977;
SWORDS IN THE MIST (S6) Ace H-90, 1968; 79180; Gregg 1977;
SWORDS AGAINST WIZARDRY (S4) Ace H-73, 1968; 79160; Gregg 1977;
THE SWORDS OF LANKHMAR (N) Ace H-38, 1968; 79220; Gregg 1977;
SWORDS AND ICE MAGIC (S8) Ace 79166, 1977; Gregg 1977;
=& RIME ISLE (N) Whispers Press 1977;

THE BEST OF FRITZ LEIBER (C22) SFBC 1974; BB 24256;
THE BIG TIME (N) Ace D+491, 1961; G-627; 06221; Gregg 1976;
THE BOOK OF FRITZ LEIBER (C10) DAW 87, 1974; UY1269;
CONJURE WIFE (N) Twayne 1953; Lion 179; (=); Award AX 341; AS680; AN1143; Gregg 1977; Ace 11686;
= BURN, WITCH BURN (N) Berk F-621, 1962;
DESTINY TIMES THREE (N) Galaxy 28, 1957; Dell +10564;(fc 8/78)
GATHER, DARKNESS (N) P&C 1950; G&D 1951; Berk F-679; Prmd X1976; BB 24585;
THE GREEN MILLENNIUM (N) Abelard 1953; Lion LL7; Ace +30300; 30301;
THE MIND SPIDER AND OTHER STORIES (C6) Ace D+491, 1961; 53330;
THE NIGHT OF THE WOLF (C4) BB U2254, 1966;
NIGHT MONSTERS (C4) Ace +30300, 1969;
NIGHTS BLACK AGENTS (C11) Arkham 1947; (C10) BB508K; Berk 03669;
OUR LADY OF DARKNESS (N) Berk/Put 1977; Berk 03660;
A PAIL OF AIR (C11) BB U2216, 1964;
THE SECOND BOOK OF FRITZ LEIBER (C13) DAW 164, 1975;
SHADOWS WITH EYES (C6) BB 577, 1962;
SHIPS TO THE STARS (C6) Ace F+285, 1964, 76110;
A SPECTER IS HAUNTING TEXAS (N) Walker 1969; SFBC; Bant S6733; Daw 278;
THE SILVER EGGHEADS (N) BB F-561, 1961; 1634;
TARZAN AND THE VALLEY OF GOLD (N) BB U6125, 1966; (authorized by E.R.B Inc.)
THE WANDERER (N) BB U6010, 1964; 1635; 2757; Walker 1970; BB 24907;
THE WORLDS OF FRITZ LEIBER (C22) Ace 91640, 1976;
YOU'RE ALL ALONE (C3) Ace 95146, 1972;
=& THE SINFUL ONES, Universal Giant G+5, 1953;

LEINSTER, MURRAY =WILL F. JENKINS

MED SERVICE

THE MUTANT WEAPON (N) Ace D+403, 1959; +66525;
THIS WORLD IS TABOO (N) Ace D-525, 1961;
DOCTOR TO THE STARS (S3) Prmd F987, 1964; T2367; Jove 04482;
S.O.S. FROM THREE WORLDS (S3) Ace G-647, 1967;

JOE KENMORE

SPACE PLATFORM (JN) Shasta 1953; Poc 920; Belm 92-625;
SPACE TUG (JN) Shasta 1953; Poc 1037; Belm B50-632; 50-846;
CITY ON THE MOON (JN) Avalon 1957; Ace D+277, 1958;

THE ALIENS (C5) Berk G410, 1960; F1139
THE BEST OF MURRAY LEINSTER (C) BBDR 25800; 1978;
THE BLACK GALAXY (N) Galx 20, 1954;
THE BRAIN-STEALERS (N) Ace D+79, 1954; 07690;
CHECKPOINT LAMBDA (N) Berk F1263, 1966;
COLONIAL SURVEY (N) Gnome 1956;
=THE PLANET EXPLORER (N) Avon T202, 1957;
CREATURES OF THE ABYSS (N) Berk G549, 1961;
THE DUPLICATORS (N) Ace F+275, 1964;
FIGHT FOR LIFE (N) Crestwood 'prize 10' nd. (1949)
THE FORGOTTEN PLANET (N) Gnome 1954; Ace D+146; D-146; D-528;

FOUR FROM PLANET 5 (N) GM s937, 1959; K1397;
GATEWAY TO ELSEWHERE (N) Ace D+53, 1954;
GET OFF MY WORLD (C3) Belm B50-676, 1966;
THE GREKS BRING GIFTS (N) Mfad 50-224, 1964; 50-418; Manor 95400;
INVADERS OF SPACE (N) Berk F1022, 1964;
THE LAST SPACESHIP (N) Fell 1949; SFBC; Galx 25;
MEN INTO SPACE (S6) Berk G461, 1960; (from T.V. series);
MINERS IN THE SKY (N) Avon G1310, 1967;
THE MONSTER FROM EARTH'S END (N) GM s832, 1959;
MONSTERS AND SUCH (C7) Avon T345, 1959;
MURDER MADNESS (N) Brewer Warren 1931; FPCI 1949; (Marginal);
THE MURDER OF THE U.S.A. (N) (as Jenkins) Crown 1946;
OPERATION OUTER SPACE (N) Fantasy 1954;Fantasy GSFL3; Sig S1346; T4106; Q5300;
OPERATION TERROR (N) Berk F694, 1962;
THE OTHER SIDE OF HERE (N) Ace D+94, 1955;
THE OTHER SIDE OF NOWHERE (N) Berk F918, 1964;
OUT OF THIS WORLD (S3) Avalon 1958;
THE PIRATES OF ZAN (N) Ace D+403, 1959; +66525;
SIDEWISE IN TIME (C6) Shasta 1950;
SPACE CAPTAIN (N) Ace M+135, 1966;
SPACE GYPSIES (N) Avon G1318, 1967;
TALENTS INCORPORATED (N) Avon G1120, 1962;
TIME TUNNEL (N) Prmd R1043, 1964;
TWISTS IN TIME (C7) Avon T389, 1960;
THE WAILING ASTEROID (N) Avon T483, 1961; G1306;
WAR WITH THE GIZMOS (N) GM s751, 1958;
TUNNEL THROUGH TIME (JN) Westminister 1966;
SEE ALSO LAND OF GIANTS SERIES
SEE ALSO TIME TUNNEL SERIES

LEM, STANISLAW

THE CYBERIAD (C15) Seabury 1974; Avon 27201;
THE FUTUROLOGICAL CONGRESS (N) Seabury 1974; Avon 28720;
THE INVESTIGATION (N) Seabury 1974; Avon 29314;
THE INVINCIBLE (N) Seabury 1973; Ace 37170;
MEMOIRS FOUND IN A BATHTUB (N) Seabury 1973; Avon 29959;
SOLARIS (N) Walker 1970; Berk S2101 D3380;
THE STAR DIARIES (N) Seabury 1976; Avon 35691;
MORTAL ENGINES (C14) Seabury 1977;

LENGYEL CORNEL

THE ATOM CLOCK (Play) FPCI 1951; (pb)

LEONARD, GEORGE

BEYOND CONTROL (N) Macmil 1975;

LEOURIER, CHRISTIAN

THE MOUNTAINS OF THE SUN (N) Berk N 2570, 1974;

LESSER, MILTON =STEPHEN MARLOWE WITH P.W. FAIRMAN = ADAM CHASE

THE GOLDEN APE (N) (as Chase) Avalon 1959;
EARTHBOUND (JN) Winston 1952;
RECRUIT FOR ANDROMEDA (N) Ace D+358, 1959;
SECRET OF THE BLACK PLANET (S2) Belm 92-631, 1965; 75-1045;
SPACEMEN GO HOME (JN) H-R-W 1961;
STADIUM BEYOND THE STARS (JN) Winston 1960;
THE STAR SEEKERS (JN) Winston 1953;

LESSING, DORIS

THE MEMOIRS OF A SURVIVOR (N) Knopf 1975; Bant 2494;

LEVENE, MALCOLM

CARDER'S PARADISE (N) Walker 1969;

LEVIE, REX DEAN

THE INSECT WARRIORS (N) Ace F-334, 1965;

LEVIN, IRA

THIS PERFECT DAY (N) Random 1970; Crst P1536; X2638;
ROSEMARY'S BABY (N) Random 1967; Dell 7509;
THE STEPFORD WIVES (N) Random 1972; Crst P1876;

LEVY, DAVID

THE GODS OF FOXCROFT (N) Arbor 1970; Poc 77384;

LEWIN, LEONARD C.

TRIAGE (N) Dial 1972; Warn 76-186;

LEWIS, C. S. (Partial Listing)

DR. RANSOM SERIES Science Fiction and Christian propaganda
OUT OF THE SILENT PLANET (N) Macmil 1943; Avon 195; T127; T410; Coll AS207; 8688;
PERELANDRA(N) Macmil 1944; Avon 27, 1950; T157; G404; Coll AS183; 8690;
THAT HIDEOUS STRENGTH (N) Macmil 1946; (=) Coll BS 58V; 8692;
= THE TORTURED PLANET (N) Avon T211, 1958;

THE DARK TOWER AND OTHER STORIES (C6) HBJ 1977;

LEWIS, IRWIN

THE DAY NEW YORK TREMBLED (N) Avon G1315, 1967;
THE DAY THEY INVADED NEW YORK (N) Avon G1227, 1964;

LICHTENBERG, JACQUELIN

HOUSE OF ZEOR (N) Dday 1974; Poc 80937;
UNTO ZEOR, FOREVER (N) Dday 1978;

LIEBSCHER, WALT

ALIEN CARNIVAL (C4) Fantasy House FH-1, 1974;(pb)

LIGHTNER, ALICE M.

SERIES
THE ROCK OF THREE PLANETS (JN) Putnam 1963;
THE PLANET POACHERS (JN) Putnam 1965;
THE DAY OF THE DRONES (JN) Norton 1969; Bant S5567; 10057;
DOCTOR TO THE GALAXY (JN) Norton 1965;
THE GALACTIC TROUBADOURS (JN) Norton 1965;
GODS OR DEMONS (JN) Four winds Press 1973;
THE SPACE GYPSIES (JN) McGraw-H 1974;
SPACE ARK (JN) Putnam 1968;
THE SPACE OLYMPICS (JN) Norton 1967; Temp 5336;
THE SPACE PLAGUE (JN) Norton 1966;
STAR CIRCUS (JN) Dutton 1977;
STAR DOG (JN) McGraw-H 1973;
THE THURSDAY TOADS (JN) MCGRAW-H 1971;

LINDSAY, DAVID (Partial Listing)

A VOYAGE TO ARCTURUS (N) (Brit 1920) Macmil 1963; BBAF 73010; 3208; 23208; 24681; Gregg 1977; BBDR 25844;

LIONEL, ROBERT SEE FANTHORPE, ROBERT

LIVINGSTON, HAROLD

THE CLIMACTICON (N) BB 406K, 1960;

LJOKA, DAN

SHELTER (N) Manor 95-252, 1973; 12474;

LLOYD, JOHN URI

ETIDORPHA: ON THE END OF EARTH (N) Lloyd 1895; Sun 1975; Poc 81867;

LOCKLEY, RONALD

SEAL WOMAN (N) Avon 30478, 1977;

LONDON, JACK (Partial Listing)

BEFORE ADAM (N) Macmil 1906; 1962; Bantam H5460; Ace 05330;
THE IRON HEEL (N) Macmil 1907; 1948; Arcadia 1950;
STAR ROVER (N) Macmil 1915; 1963;
THE SCIENCE FICTION OF JACK LONDON (C11) Gregg 1975;

LONG, FRANK BELKNAP

AND OTHERS SHALL BE BORN (N) Belmont B50+809, 1968;
THE HORROR FROM THE HILLS (N) Arkham 1963;
=+ODD SCIENCE FICTION (N+2) Belmont L92-600, 1964;
THE HOUNDS OF TINDALOS (C21) Arkham 1946;
=& THE HOUNDS OF TINDALOS (C9) Belmont L92-569, 1963;
=& THE DARK BEASTS (C9) Belmont L92-579, 1963;
THE DEMONS OF THE UPPER AIR (C) Squires 1969;

IT WAS THE DAY OF THE ROBOT (N) Belm 90-277, 1963;
THE EARLY LONG (C17) Dday 1975;
JOHN CARSTAIRS: SPACE DETECTIVE (S6) Fell 1949;
JOURNEY INTO DARKNESS (N) Belm B50-757, 1967;
LEST EARTH BE CONQUERED (N) Belm B50-726, 1966;
= THE ANDROIDS (N) Tower T060-3, 1969;
MARS IS MY DESTINATION (N) Prmd F-742, 1962;
THE MARTIAN VISITORS (N) Avalon 1964;
THE MATING CENTER (N) Chariot 162, 1961;
MISSION TO A STAR (N) Avalon 1964;
SPACE STATION #1 (N) Ace D+242, 1957; D-544, 1962;
RIM OF THE UNKNOWN (C23) Arkham 1972;
MONSTER FROM OUT OF TIME (N) Pop 2474, 1970;
SURVIVAL WORLD (N) Lanc 74750, 1971;
THE THREE FACES OF TIME (N) Towr 43-251, 1969;
THIS STRANGE TOMORROW (N) Belm B50-663, 1966;
THREE STEPS SPACEWARD (N) Avalon 1963;
WOMAN FROM ANOTHER PLANET (N) Chariot CB 123, 1960;

LONG, CHARLES R.

THE ETERNAL MAN (N) Avalon 1957;
THE INFINITE BRAIN (N) Avalon 1964;

LONGO, CHRIS

THE LAST GENE (N) Major 3117, 1976;

LOOMIS, NOEL

CITY OF GLASS (N) Columbia pb 1955;

LORY, ROBERT

THE EYES OF BOLSK (N) Ace +77710, 1969;
A HARVEST OF HOODWINKS (C12) Ace +52180, 1970;
IDENTITY SEVEN (N) DAW 95, 1974;
MASTER OF THE ETRAX (N) Dell 5523, 1970;
MASTERS OF THE LAMP (N) Ace +52180, 1970;
THE THIRTEEN BRACELETS (N) Ace 80680, 1974;
THE VEILED WORLD (N) Ace +31755, 1972;

LOVECRAFT, H.P. -WEIRD & HORROR FICTION ONLY

LOVELACE, DELOS W.

KING KONG (N) G & D 1933; Bant F3093; G & D 1976; Ace 44470;
(from idea by Edgar Wallace and Merian C. Cooper)

LOWNDES, ROBERT

BELIEVERS WORLD (N) Avalon 1961;

THE DUPLICATED MAN (N) (see J. Blish - coauthor)
MYSTERY OF THE THIRD MINE (JN) Winston 1953;
THE PUZZLE PLANET (N) Ace D+485, 1961;

LUCAS, GEORGE

STAR WARS (N) BB 26061, 1976; SFBC; BBDR 26079; (Movie Tie-in) Del Rey 1977;

LUDWIG, EDWARD W.

THE MASK OF JON CULON (N) Lenox Hill 1970;

LUKENS, ADAM SEE DETZER, DIANE

LUMLEY, BRIAN (Horror Fiction)

THE BURROWERS BENEATH (N) DAW 91, 1974;
THE TRANSITION OF TITUS CROW (N) DAW 151, 1975;

LUNDWALL, SAM J.

ALICE'S WORLD (N) Ace +58880, 1971;
BERNHARD THE CONQUEROR (N) DAW 58, 1973;
NO TIME FOR HEROS (N) Ace +58880, 1971;
2018 A.D. OR THE KING KONG BLUES (N) DAW 142, 1975;

LUPOFF, RICHARD

THE CRACK IN THE SKY (N) Dell 5419, 1976;
INTO THE AETHER (N) Dell 3830, 1974;
ONE MILLION CENTURIES (N) Lanc 74-892, 1967;
SACRED LOCOMOTIVE FLIES (N) Beagle 95143; 1971;
SANDWORLD (N) Berk Z3116, 1976;
THE TRIUNE MAN (N) Berk/Put 1976; Berk 3360;
LISA KANE (JN) Bobbs-M 1976;
SWORD OF THE DEMON (N) Harper 1977; Avon 37911;
SPACE WAR BLUES (N) Dell 16292, 1978;

LUTHER, RAY SEE SELLINGS, ARTHUR

LYLE, PETER

ROLIND OF MERU (N) Avon 32581, 1977;

LYMINGTON, JOHN

THE NOWHERE PLACE (N) Dday 1971;
THE COMING OF THE STRANGERS (N) M-B 75-423; 1971;
FROOMB (N) Dday 1966; SFBC; M-B 60-287; 75-355;
THE GREY ONES (N) M-B 60-401; 1969; 60-461; Manor +19180;
NIGHT OF THE BIG HEAT (N) Dutton 1960; M-B 60-384;
THE NIGHT SPIDERS (N) Dday 1965; Curtis 7006;
THE SCREAMING FACE (N) M-B 60-436; 1970;
THE SLEEP EATERS (N) M-B 75-224, 1969; 75-456;

THE STAR WITCHES (N) M-B 60-445, 1970;
A SWORD ABOVE THE NIGHT (N) M-B 75-398, 1971; Manor +19180;
TEN MILLION YEARS TO FRIDAY (N) Dday 1970; Lancer 74-741;

LYNDON, BARRE and JIMMY SANGSTER

THE MAN WHO COULD CHEAT DEATH (N) Avon T362, 1959; (movie tie-in)

McALLISTER, BRUCE

HUMANITY PRIME (N) Ace 34900, 1971;

MACAPP C. C. = CARROLL M. CAPPS

BUMSIDER (N) Lanc 75421, 1972;
OMHA ABIDES (N) PBL 52-649, 1968;
PRISONERS OF THE SKY (N) Lanc 74-587, 1969;
RECALL NOT EARTH (N) Dell 7281, 1970;
SECRET OF THE SUNLESS WORLD (N) (as Capps) Dell 7663, 1969;
SUBB (N) PBL 64-532, 1971;
WORLDS OF THE WALL (N) Avon V2308, 1969;

McCAFFREY, ANNE

DRAGONRIDERS OF PERN
DRAGONFLIGHT (N) BBU6124, 1968; Walker 1969; BB 2246; 23443; 24776;
DRAGONQUEST (N) Walker 1970; BB 2245; 23444; 24777;
A TIME WHEN (S) NESFA 1975;
DRAGONSONG (JN) Atheneum 1976; Bant 10300;
DRAGONSINGER (JN) Atheneum 1977;
THE WHITE DRAGON (N) Del Rey 1978; BBDR 25373;(fc 7/78)

DECISION AT DOONA (N) BB1576, 1969; 24416;
DINOSAUR PLANET (N) BBDR 27245, 1978; SFBC;
RESTOREE (N) BB U6108, 1967; BBDR 25744;
THE SHIP WHO SANG (S6) BB 1881, 1969; Walker 1969; BB 24823;
TO RIDE PEGASUS (N) BB 23417, 1973; BBDR 27357;
GET OFF THE UNICORN (C14) BBDR 25666, 1977;

McCANN, EDSON = LESTER DEL REY & FRED POHL

McCLARY, THOMAS CALVERT

THREE THOUSAND YEARS (N) Fantasy 1954; Ace D+176;
REBIRTH (N) Bart 6, 1944; Hyperion 1976;

MacCONNELL, COLUM

TARK AND THE GOLDEN TIDE (N) Leisure 470 Dk, 1977;

McDANIEL, DAVID

THE ARSENAL OUT OF TIME (N) Ace G-667, 1967;

MACDONALD, GEORGE

EVENOR (N) BBAF 2874, 1972;
LILITH (N) Dodd Mead 1895; Dutton 1925; BBAF 1711; 23528;
PHANTASTES (N) (Brit 1858); BBAF 1902, 1970;
VISIONARY NOVELS OF GEORGE MAC DONALD (2N) Noonday 1954;(Lilith + Phantastes)

MACDONALD, JOHN D.

BALLROOM OF THE SKIES (N) Greenberg 1952; GM R1993; T2380; P3252; 13852;
THE GIRL, THE GOLD WATCH AND EVERYTHING (N) GM s1259, 1962; k1513; d1792;
WINE OF THE DREAMERS (N) Greenberg 1951; (=); GM R1994; R2400; P 3263; 13876;
= PLANET OF THE DREAMERS (N) Poc 943, 1953;

McELROY, JOSEPH

PLUS (N) Knopf 1977; Knopf pb;

MACHEN, ARTHUR (partial listing)

THE THREE IMPOSTERS (N) Roberts Bros. 1890; BBAF 2643, 1972;
THE GREAT GOD PAN (N) Fantasy House FH-3, 1974;

MC HUGH, VINCENT

I AM THINKING OF MY DARLING (N) S&S 1943; Sig 778;

McINNES, GRAHAM

LOST ISLAND (N) World 1954;Sig S1215,

McINTOSH, J. T. = JAMES MURDOCH MACGREGOR

BORN LEADER (N) Dday 1954; SFBC;
= WORLDS APART (N) Avon T249, 1958;
THE FITTEST (N) Dday 1955; SFBC;
= RULE OF THE PAGBEASTS (N) Crst 150, 1956;
FLIGHT FROM REBIRTH (N) Avon V2411, 1971; 3970;
THE MILLION CITIES (N) Prmd F898, 1963;
ONE IN 300 (N) Dday 1954; SFBC; Ace D+113;
RULER OF THE WORLD (N) Laser 24, 1976;
SIX GATES FROM LIMBO (N) Avon V2274, 1969;
SNOW WHITE AND THE GIANTS (N) Avon S347, 1968;
THE SUICIDERS (N) Avon 17889, 1973;
TRANSMIGRATION (N) Avon V2375, 1970; 3640;
200 YEARS TO CHRISTMAS (N) Ace F+113, 1961;
WORLD OUT OF MIND (N) Dday 1953; SFBC; Perm M3027;

McINTYRE, VONDA N.

DREAM SNAKE (N) HOUGHTON-M 1978; SFBC;
THE EXILE WAITING (N) SFBC 1975; GM P3456;

MACISAAC, FRED (partial listing)

THE HOTHOUSE WORLD (N) Avalon 1965;

MACKELWORTH, R. W.

THE DIABOLS (N) PBL 63-110, 1969;
STARFLIGHT 3000 (N) BB 2774, 1972;
TILTANGLE (N) BB 1940, 1970;

McKENNA, RICHARD

CASEY AGONISTES AND OTHER F & SF (C5) Harper 1973; Ace 09227;

McKENNEY, KENNETH

THE MOONCHILD (N) S&S 1978;
THE PLANTS (N) Putnam 1976; Bant 2976;

MACKENROTH, NANCY J.

THE TREES OF ZHARKA (N) Pop 639, 1975;

McKILLIP, PATRICIA A.

THE HED SERIES

THE RIDDLE MASTER OF HED (N) Atheneum 1977; BBDR 27467;
HEIR OF SEA AND FIRE (N) Atheneum 1977;

THE FORGOTTEN BEASTS OF ELD (N) Atheneum 1974; Avon 25502;
THE HOUSE ON PARCHMENT STREET (JN) Atheneum 1973;
THE NIGHT GIFT (JN) Atheneum 1976;
THE THROME OF THE ERRIL OF SHERRILL (JN) Atheneum 1973;

McLAUGHLIN, DEAN

DOME WORLD (N) Prmd F763, 1962; T2492;
THE FURY FROM EARTH (N) Prmd F923, 1963; T2542;
HAWK AMONG THE SPARROWS (C3) Scrib 1976;
THE MAN WHO WANTED STARS (N) Lanc 73-441, 1965; Magnum 74-949;

MACLEAN, KATHERINE

MISSING MAN (N) Putnam 1976; SFBC; Berk 03040;
TROUBLE WITH TREATIES (S) Lanthorne pb 1975;
THE DIPLOIDS (S8) Avon G1143, 1962; Manor MB 95-228;
COSMIC CHECKMATE (N) (see C. DeVet Co-author)

MACLEOD, ANGUS

THE EIGHTH SEAL (N) Roy 1962;

McMAHON, THOMAS

THE HUBSCHMAN EFFECT (N) S&S 1973; Pocket 78403;

McMICHAEL, R. DAVID

THE JOURNEL OF DAVID Q. LITTLE (N) Arlington 1967;

MACTYRE, PAUL =R. J. ADAM ?

DOOMSDAY 1999 (N) Ace F-201, 1963;

MADDOCK, LARRY = JACK O. JARDINE

WITH J. A. JARDINE = HOWARD L. CORY

AGENT OF T.E.R.R.A.

THE FLYING SAUCER GAMBIT (N) Ace G-605, 1966; 01040;
THE GOLDEN GODDESS GAMBIT (N) Ace G-620, 1967; 01041;
THE EMERALD ELEPHANT GAMBIT (N) Ace G-644, 1967; 01042;
THE TIME TRAP GAMBIT (N) Ace 01043, 1969;

AS CORY

THE MIND MONSTER (N) Ace G+602, 1966;
THE SWORD OF LANKOR (N) Ace F-373, 1966;

MADDUX, RACHEL

THE GREEN KINGDOM (N) S&S 1957; Avon 33803;

MAINE, CHARLES ERIC = DAVID MCILWAIN

ALPH (N) SFBC; 1972; BB 2904;
B.E.A.S.T. (N) BB U6092, 1967;
FIRE PAST THE FUTURE (N) BB360K, 1959;
HE OWNED THE WORLD (N) Avalon 1960; Avon T524;
HIGH VACUUM (N) BBHC 1957; BB 218;
THE ISOTOPE MAN (N) Lipp 1957; SFBC;
THE MAN WHO COULDN'T SLEEP (N) Lipp 1958; SFBC;
THE MIND OF MR. SOAMES (N) Pyramid T2161, 1970;
SPACEWAYS SATELITE (N) Avalon 1958;
THE TIDE WENT OUT (N) BB 290K, 1959;
TIMELINER (N) Rinehart 1955; SFBC; Bant A1470;
SURVIVAL MARGIN (N) GM R1918, 1968;
WORLD WITHOUT MEN (N) Ace D-274, 1958;

MALCOLM, DONALD

THE IRON RAIN (N) Laser 29, 1976;
THE UNKNOWN SHORE (N) Laser 19, 1976;

MALCOLM-SMITH, GEORGE

THE GRASS IS ALWAYS GREENER (N) Dday 1947 Bant 410;

MALEC, ALEXANDER

EXTRAPOLASIS (C12) Dday 1967; Curt 7007;

MALZBERG, BARRY N. Also K. M. O'DONNEL

THE BEST OF BARRY N MALZBERG (C38) Poc 80256, 1976;

BEYOND APOLLO (N) Random 1972; Poc 77687;
CONVERSATIONS (JN) Bobbs-M 1975;
THE DAY OF THE BURNING (N) Ace 13902, 1974;
THE DESTRUCTION OF THE TEMPLE (N) Poc 77696, 1974;
THE FALLING ASTRONAUTS (N) Ace 22690, 1971;
GALAXIES (N) Prmd V3734, 1975;
THE GAMESMAN (N) Poc 80174, 1975;
GUERNICA NIGHT (N) Bobbs-M 1974;
DOWN HERE IN THE DREAM QUARTER (C24) Dday 1976;
IN THE ENCLOSURE (N) Avon 15073, 1973;
HEROVITS WORLD (N) Random 1973; Poc 77753;
THE LAST TRANSACTION (N) Pinn 40-174, 1977;
THE MEN INSIDE (N) Lanc 75486, 1973; Magnum 75486;
OVERLAY (N) Lanc 75345, 1972;
PHASE IV (N) Poc 77710, 1973;
OUT FROM GANYMEDE (C22) Warn 76-538, 1974;
ON A PLANET ALIEN (N) Poc 77766, 1974;
REVELATIONS (N) Warn 64-947, 1972; Avon E 31716;
SCOP (N) Prmd V3895, 1976;
THE SODOM AND GOMORRAH BUSINESS (N) Poc 77789, 1974;
TACTICS OF CONQUEST (N) Prmd N3330, 1974;
UNDERLAY (N) AVON 17939, 1974, (Marg.)
THE MANY WORLDS OF BARRY MALZBERG (C11) Pop 298, 1975;

AS O'DONNELL

GATHER IN THE HALL OF THE PLANETS (N) Ace +27415, 1971;
FINAL WAR AND OTHER FANTASIES (C11) Ace +23775, 1969;
DWELLERS OF THE DEEP (N) Ace +27400, 1970;
IN THE POCKET and other S. F. Stories (C15) Ace +27415, 1971;
THE EMPTY PEOPLE (N) Lanc 74-546, 1969;
UNIVERSE DAY (N) Avon V2394, 1971;

MANNES, MARYA

THEY (N) Dday 1968; Curt 7058;

MANNION, MICHAEL

DEATHCLOUD (N) Leisure LB 323 DK, 1976;

MANNING, LAURENCE

THE MAN WHO AWOKE (N) BB 24367, 1975;

MANO, D. KEITH

THE BRIDGE (N) Dday 1973, Sig Y6144;
HORN (N) Houghton-M 1969; Avon N272;

MANTLEY, JOHN

THE 27TH DAY (N) Dutton 1957; SFBC; Crst 209;

MARCUS, ROBERT P. JR.

SHADOW ON THE STARS (N) Laser 57, 1977;

MARDEN, WILLIAM

THE EXILE OF ELLENDON (N) Dday 1974;

MARGROFF, ROBERT E.

THE E.S.P. WORM (N) (with P. Anthony) PBL 63-357, 1970;
THE RING (N) (see P. Anthony - coauthor)

MARSHALL, EDSON (Partial Listing)

DIAN OF THE LOST LAND (N) KINSEY 1935; Burt 1936; Chilton 1966;
= THE LOST LAND (N) Curt 7227, 1972;
EARTH GIANT (N) Dday 1960; Pop W1110;

MARSTEN, RICHARD - See EVAN HUNTER

MARTEL, SUZANNE

THE CITY UNDERGROUND (N) Viking 1964;

MARTIN, GEORGE, R.R.

DYING OF THE LIGHT (N) S&S, 1977;
A SONG FOR LYA & OTHER STORIES (C10) Avon 27581, 1976;
SONGS OF STARS AND SHADOWS (C9) Poc 81277, 1977;

MARTINSON, HARRY

ANIARA (PN) Knopf 1963; Avon E 30403;

MASON, DAVID

KAVIN HOSTEN
KAVIN'S WORLD (N) Lanc 74-564, 1969; 75372;
THE RETURN OF KAVIN (N) Lanc 75-361; 1972;
THE DEEP GODS (N) Lanc 78762, 1973;
THE SHORES OF TOMORROW (N) Lanc 75-217, 1971;
THE SORCERER'S SKULL (N) Lanc 74-628, 1970;

MASON, DOUGLAS R. also JOHN RANKINE

DILATION EFFECT (N) BB2180, 1971;
FROM CARTHAGE THEN I CAME (N) Dday 1966;
= EIGHT AGAINST UTOPIA (N) PBL 52-599, 1967; 63-496;
THE END BRINGERS (N) BB 3366, 1973;
HORIZON ALPHA (N) BB 2179, 1971;
MATRIX (N) BB 1816, 1970;
THE PHAETON CONDITION (N) Putnam 1973; Berk N2499;
THE RESURRECTION OF ROGER DIMENT (N) BB 2573, 1972;
RING OF VIOLENCE (N) Avon S399, 1969;
SATELITE 54-ZERO (N) BB 2108, 1971;

AS JOHN RANKINE
THE BROMIUS PHENOMENON (N) Ace 08145, 1973;
MOONS OF TRIOPUS (N) PBL 63-228, 1969;
OPERATION UMANAQ (N) Ace 63590, 1973;
SEE ALSO SPACE 1999 SERIES

MASON, GREGORY = DORIS MEEK & ADRIENNE JONES

THE GOLDEN ARCHER (N) Twayne 1956;

MATHESON, RICHARD

BID TIME RETURN (N) Viking 1975; BB 24810;
BORN OF MAN AND WOMAN (C17) Chamberlain 1954;
= THIRD FROM THE SUN (C13) Bant 1294, 1955; J2467; H5548;
HELLHOUSE (N) Viking 1971; Bant N7277;
I AM LEGEND (N) GM 417, 1954; 643; Bant J 2744; Berk S2041; Walker 1970;
SHOCK (C13) Dell B195, 1961;
SHOCK II (C13) Dell 7829, 1964;
SHOCK III (C13) Dell 7830, 1966;
SHOCK WAVES (C14) Dell 7831, 1970;
THE SHORES OF SPACE (C13) Bant A1571, 1957;
THE SHRINKING MAN (N) GM s577, 1956; d1203; Bant H3970;
A STIR OF ECHOES (N) Lipp 1958; Crst 308, Avon S392;

MAUROIS, ANDRE

THE WEIGHER OF SOULS & THE EARTH DWELLERS (2N) Macmil 1963;

MAXWELL, ANN

CHANGE (N) Popular 316, 1975;
THE SINGER ENIGMA (N) Popular 388, 1976;

MAXWELL, JOHN C.

THE WORLD MAKERS (N) Arcadia 1969;

MEAD, HAROLD

THE BRIGHT PHOENIX (N) BBHC 1956; BB 147;

MEAD, SHEPHERD

THE BIG BALL OF WAX (N) S&S 1954; BB 174; Avon G1129; Ace 05785;
THE CAREFULLY CONSIDERED RAPE OF THE WORLD (N) S&S 1966; Ace 09150;

MEADE, RICHARD

EXILE'S QUEST (N) Sig T4348, 1970;
THE SWORD OF MORNING STAR (N) Sig P3774, 1969;

MEEK, S.P. = STERNER ST. PAUL MEEK

SERIES
DRUMS OF TAPAJOS (N) Avalon 1961;
TROYANA (N) Avalon 1961;

MENDELSOHN, FELIX JR.

SUPERBABY (N) Nash 1969; PBL 64-444;

MERAK, A.J.

THE DARK MILLENNIUM (N) Arcadia 1966; Belm B60-1080;
BARRIER UNKNOWN (N) Arcadia 1964;
HYDROSPHERE (N) Arcadia 1967;
NO DAWN AND NO HORIZON (N) Arcadia 1968;
= THE FROZEN PLANET (N) Belm B60-1971, 1970;

MEREDITH, GEORGE

THE SHAVING OF SHAGPAT (N) (Brit 1856) BBAF 1958, 1970;

MEREDITH, RICHARD C.

ERIC MATHERS SERIES
AT THE NARROW PASSAGE (N) Putnam 1973; Berk N2730;
NO BROTHER NO FRIEND (N) Dday 1976;
VESTIGES OF TIME (N) DDAY, 1978;

RUN COME SEE JERUSALEM (N) BB 25066, 1976;
THE SKY IS FILLED WITH SHIPS (N) BB 1600, 1969;
WE ALL DIED AT BREAKAWAY STATION (N) BB 1764, 1969;

MERLE, ROBERT

DAY OF THE DOLPHIN (N) S&S 1969, BC: Crest M1438;
MALEVIL (N) S&S 1974; Warn 79-685; 81-658;
THE VIRILITY FACTOR (N) McGraw-Hill 1977;

MERRIL, JUDITH With KORNBLUTH = CYRIL JUDD

THE BEST OF JUDITH MERRIL (C11) Warn 86-058, 1976;
DAUGHTERS OF EARTH (C3) Dday 1969; Dell 1705;
OUT OF BOUNDS (C7) Prmd G499, 1960; F-830;
SHADOW ON THE HEARTH (N) Dday 1950;
THE TOMORROW PEOPLE (N) Prmd G502, 1960; F806; X1802;

AS CYRIL JUDD
GUNNER CADE (N) S&S 1952; Ace D+227, Dell 3329;
OUTPOST MARS (N) Abelard 1952; Dell 760;
= SIN IN SPACE (N) Galx 312, 1961;

MERRITT, ABRAHAM (partial listing)

THE BLACK WHEEL (N) (completed by H. Bok) New Collectors 1947; Arno 1976;
BURN WITCH, BURN (N) Liveright 1933; Avon MMM5; 43; 392;
CREEP SHADOW (N) Dday 1934 Sun Dial 1938;
=CREEP CHADOW, CREEP (N) Avon MMM 11; MMM 47; 117;
DWELLERS IN THE MIRAGE (N) Liveright 1932; Avon MMM 24; 413; Grandon 1950; Avon S271; 14340; PBL 52-140; 52-516; Avon 30494; Liveright 1953(with Face in the Abyss)
FACE IN THE ABYSS (N) Liveright 1931; Avon MMM 29; 386; T161; 37010;
THE FOX WOMAN (N+The Blue Pagoda by H. Bok) New Collectors 1946;
THE FOX WOMAN (C9) Avon 214, 1949; 33845;

THE FOX WOMAN, THE BLUE PAGODA & THE BLACK WHEEL (3N) Arno 1976
THE METAL MONSTER (N) Avon MMM 41; 315; T172; S231; V2422; 31294;
THE MOON POOL (N) Putnam 1919; Liveright 1932; Avon MMM 18; Avon 370; T135; Coll 2287;
SEVEN FOOTPRINTS TO SATAN (N) Boni & Liveright 1928; Grosset 1929; Avon MMM1; 26: 235; T115; T208; S280; V2417; 28209 Liveright 1953(with Burn Witch Burn)
THE SHIP OF ISHTAR (N) Putnam 1926; Avon MMM 34; 324; T152; S229; 14092; 28936;

MERWIN, SAM

THE HOUSE OF MANY WORLDS (N) Dday 1951; Galaxy 12; Curtis 7049;
THREE FACES OF TIME (N) Ace D+121, 1955;

CHAUVINISTO (N) Major 3085, 1976;
KILLER TO COME (N) Abelard 1953; Galaxy 22;
THE TIME SHIFTERS (N) Lancer 74776, 1971;
THE WHITE WIDOWS (N) Dday 1953; (=); Curtis 6072;
= THE SEX WAR (N) Galaxy 284, 1960;

MESSMAN, JON

THE DEADLY DEEP (N) Sig W6992, 1976;

MEYERS, ROY

JOHN AVERILL
DOLPHIN BOY (N) U6100, 1967;
DAUGHTERS OF THE DOLPHINS (N) 72001, 1968;
DESTINY AND THE DOLPHINS (N) BB 1627, 1969;

MILLARD, JOSEPH

THE GODS HATE KANSAS (N) Monarch 414, 1964;

MILLER, JIMMY

THE BIG WIN (N) Knopf 1969; Bant N5651;

MILLER, P. SCHUYLER

THE TITAN (C9) Fantasy 1953;

MILLER R. DEWITT & ANNA HUNGER

THE MAN WHO LIVED FOREVER (N) Ace D+162, 1956;

MILLER, WALTER M. JR.

A CANTICLE FOR LIEBOWITZ (N) Lipp 1960; Bant F2212; S2973; N5423; Q6737; Q6883; Gregg 1975; Bant 2973; SFBC;
CONDITIONALLY HUMAN (C3) BB F626, 1962;
THE VIEW FROM THE STARS (C9) BB U2212, 1964;

MILLERS, RHEINHOLD R.

TIME EXILE (N) Echo 1972;

MILLS, ROBERT E

STAR QUEST (N) B-T 51259, 1978;

MINOT, STEPHEN

CHILL OF DUCK (N) Dday 64;

MIRRLEES, HOPE

LUD-IN—THE—MIST (N) Knopf 1927; BBAF 1880; 1970; BBDR 25848;

MITCHELL, EDWARD PAGE

THE CRYSTAL MAN (C30) Dday 1973;

MITCHELL, J. LESLIE

THREE GO BACK (N) Bobbs-M 1932; Galx 15, 1953;

MITCHISON, NAOMI

MEMOIRS OF A SPACEWOMAN (N) Berk S2345, 1973;
SOLUTION THREE (N) Warn 76-939, 1975;

MOFFITT, DONALD

THE JUPITER THEFT (N) BBDR 25505, 1977;

MOFFATT, JAMES

THE CAMBRI PLOT (N) B-T 50543, 1973;

MONSARRAT, NICHOLAS

THE TIME BEFORE THIS (N) Sloan 1962; Poc 50499;

MONTELEONE, THOMAS F.

SEEDS OF CHANGE (N) Laser 0. 1975;
THE TIME CONNECTION (N) Pop 417, 1976;
THE TIME SWEEP CITY (N) Pop 4081, 1977;

MOORCOCK, MICHAEL -Also EDWARD P. BRADBURY

THE CHAMPION ETERNAL CYCLE

ELRIC OF MELNIBONE - Original editions
THE DREAMING CITY (N) Lancer 75376, 1972;
THE STEALER OF SOULS (S5) Lancer 73-545, 1967; 78-751;
THE SLEEPING SORCERESS (N) Lancer 75375, 1972;
THE SINGING CITADEL (S2+C2) Berk S1870, 1970;
STROMBRINGER (S3) Lancer 73-579, 1967;

ELRIC OF MELNIBONE (Complete revised series)

ELRIC OF MELNIBONE (N) DAW 214, 1976; Blue Star 1977; Daw UW 1356;
THE SAILOR ON THE SEAS OF FATE (S3) Daw 220, 1976;
THE WEIRD OF THE WHITE WOLF (S3) DAW 233, 1977;
THE VANISHING TOWER (S3) DAW 245, 1977;
THE BANE OF THE BLACK SWORD (S4) Daw 254, 1977;
STORMBRINGER (S4) Daw 264, 1977;

DORIAN HAWKMOON

THE JEWEL IN THE SKULL (N) Lanc 73-688, 1967; 78711; Lode B5015; 75376 DAW 225;
SORCERER'S AMULET (N) Lanc 73-707, 1968;
=THE MAD GOD'S AMULET (N) DAW 238, 1977 (Original British Title)

SWORD OF THE DAWN (N) Lancer 73-761, 1968; DAW 249;
THE SECRET OF THE RUNESTAFF (N) Lancer 73-824, 1969;
= THE RUNESTAFF (N) DAW 257, 1977;;
COUNT BRASS (N) Dell 1541, 1976;
THE CHAMPION OF GARATHORM (N) Dell 1173, 1976;
THE QUEST FOR TANELORN (N) Dell 7193, 1976;

CORUM

THE KNIGHT OF THE SWORDS (N) Berk S1971, 1971;
THE QUEEN OF SWORDS (N) Berk S1999, 1971;
THE KING OF SWORDS (N) Berk S2070, 1971;
All Three = THE SWORDS TRILOGY (3N) Berk 3468, 1977;
THE BULL AND THE SPEAR (N) Berk 2508, 1974;
THE OAK AND THE RAM (N) Berk 2534, 1974;
THE SWORD AND THE STALLION (N) Berk 2548, 1974;

JOHN DAKER

THE ETERNAL CHAMPION (N) Dell 2383, 1970; H&R 1978;
THE SILVER WARRIORS (N) Dell 7994, 1973; 17994;

MICHAEL KANE

WARRIORS OF MARS (N) Lanc 72-118, 1968; (as Bradbury)
= THE CITY OF THE BEAST (N) Lanc 74-668, 1970;
BLADES OF MARS (N) Lanc 72-122, 1968; (as Bradbury)
= THE LORD OF THE SPIDERS (N) Lanc 74-736, 1970;
BARBARIANS OF MARS (N) Lanc 72-127, 1968; (as Bradbury);
= THE MASTERS OF THE PIT (N) Lanc 75-199, 1971;

DANCERS AT THE END OF TIME

AN ALIEN HEAT (N) H&R 1972; SFBC; Avon 34611;
THE HOLLOW LANDS (N) H&R 1974; SFBC; Avon 35386;
THE END OF ALL SONGS (N) H&R 1976; SFBC; Avon 38471;
LEGENDS FROM THE END OF TIME (S3) H&R 1976; DAW 229;
A MESSIAH AT THE END OF TIME (N) Daw 277, 1978;

JERRY CORNELIUS

THE FINAL PROGRAMME (N) Avon S351; 1968; Gregg 1976;
A CURE FOR CANCER (N) H-R-W 1971;
THE ENGLISH ASSASSIN (N) H&R 1974;
THE CONDITION OF MUZAK (N) (Brit) Gregg 1978;
All 4 = THE CORNELIUS CHRONICLES (4N) Avon 31468, 1977;

KARL GLOGAUER

BEHOLD THE MAN (N) Avon V2333, 1970; Avon E28571;
BREAKFAST IN THE RUINS (N) Random 1973;

SERIES

THE WARLORD OF THE AIR (N) Ace 87060, 1971; Daw 291;
THE LAND LEVIATHAN (N) Dday 1974; DAW 178;

THE BLACK CORRIDOR (N) Ace 06530, 1969; SFBC;
THE FIRE CLOWN (N) PBL 52-475, 1967;
= THE WINDS OF LIMBO (N) PBL 63-149, 1969;

DYING FOR TOMORROW (C5) Daw 282, 1978;
THE ICE SCHOONER (N) Berk X1749, 1969; rev. H&R 1977;
THE SUNDERED WORLDS (N) PBL 52-368, 1966;
THE TIME DWELLER (C9) Berk S 1955, 1971;
THE TWILIGHT MAN (N) Berk S1820, 1970;
THE TIME OF THE HAWKLORDS (W) (with M. Butterworth) Warn 78986, 1976;
THE WRECKS OF TIME (N) Ace H+36, 1966;
THE CHINESE AGENT (N) Macmil 1970;Ace 10435;(Not S.F.)

MOORE, C(atherine) L(ucille) MARRIED TO HENRY KUTTNER

Collaborated with Kuttner on many titles

NORTHWEST SMITH AND JIREL OF JOIRY (separate stories)

SHAMBLEAU (S3+S4) Gnome 1953; (s3) Galaxy 31, 1958;
NORTHWEST OF EARTH (S2+S5) Gnome 1954;
S2+S3 = JIREL OF JOIRY (S5) PBL 63-149, 1969;
= BLACK GOD'S SHADOW (S5) Grant 1977;

THE BEST OF C. L. MOORE (C10) SFBC; 1975; BB 24752; Taplinger 1977;
DOOMSDAY MORNING (N) Dday 1957; SFBC; Avon T297; S378;
EARTH'S LAST CITADEL (N) (See H. Kuttner co-author)
JUDGEMENT NIGHT (N + C4) Gnome 1952; (N) PBL 52-863;

MOORE, BRIAN

CATHOLICS (N) Holt 1973; Poc 78356;
THE GREAT VICTORIAN COLLECTION (N) F-S-G 1975; BB 25000;

MOORE, HARRIS

SLATER'S PLANET (N) Pinn P026, 1971;

MOORE, WARD

BRING THE JUBILEE (N) F-S-G 1953; BB 38; Avon V2440;
CADUCEUS WILD (N) (with R. Bradford) Pinn 40-246, 1978;
GREENER THAN YOU THINK (N) Sloane 1947; BB 527;
JOYLEG (N) (See A. Davidson co-author);

MORGAN, DAN

THE 6TH PERCEPTION SERIES

THE NEW MINDS (N) Avon V2271, 1967;
THE SEVERAL MINDS (N) Avon V2302, 1969;
MIND TRAP (N) Avon V2323, 1970;

THE HIGH DESTINY (N) Berk 2434, 1973;
INSIDE (N) Berk N2734, 1974;

SERIES WITH JOHN KIPPAX = John Hynam

A THUNDER OF STARS (N) BB 1922, 1970;
SEED OF STARS (N) BB 2503, 1972;
THE NEUTRAL STARS (N) BB 3086, 1973;

MORLEY, FELIX

GUMPTION ISLAND (N) Caxton 1956;

MORRESSY, JOHN

A LAW FOR THE STARS (N) Laser 21, 1976;
FROST WORLD & DREAM FIRE (N) Dday 1977, SFBC;
NAIL DOWN THE STARS (N) Walker 1973;
= STARDRIFT (N) Pop 256, 1975;
STARBRAT (N) Walker 1972; Curt 7275;
UNDER A CALCULATING STAR (N) Dday 1975; Pop 04240;
THE WINDOWS OF FOREVER (JN) Walker 1975;
THE EXTRATERRITORIAL (N) Laser 52, 1977;
THE HUMANS OF ZIAX II (JN) Walker 1975;

MORRIS, JANET E.

ESTRI SERIES
HIGH COUCH OF SILISTRA (N) Bantam 10522, 1977;
THE GOLDEN SWORD (N) Bant 11276, 1977;
WIND FROM THE ABYSS (N) Bant 11250, 1978;

MORRIS, WILLIAM (Partial Listing)

CHILD CHRISTOPHER AND GOLDILIND THE FAIR (2N) New Castle F111, 1977;
THE GLITTERING PLAIN (N) Newcastle F-100, 1973;
GOLDEN WINGS & OTHER STORIES (C) Newcastle, F107, 1976;
THE HOUSE OF THE WOLFINGS (N) Newcastle 1978;
THE SUNDERING FLOOD (N) BBAF 3261, 1973;
THE WATER OF THE WONDROUS ISLES (N) BBAF 2421; 1971;
THE WELL AT WORLDS END I (N) BBAF 1982, 1970; 2995; 23515;
THE WELL AT WORLDS END II (N) BBAF 2015, 1970; 2996; 23516;
Both = WELL AT WORLD'S END (2N) BB 24482, 1975;
THE WOOD BEYOND THE WORLD (N) BBAF 1652, 1969; Dover 22791; BB23730;

MORRISON, WILLIAM = JOSEPH SAMACHSON

MEL OLIVER AND SPACE ROVER ON MARS(JN) Gnome 1954:
THE TENTH PLANET (as Sterling) (N) Pop 2445, 1969; Captain Future

MOTTLEY, CHARLES C.

THE MUSTARD SEED (N) (with C. M. Mottley) Pop 8599, 1977;

MOUDY, WALTER

NO MAN ON EARTH (N) Berk F987, 1964;

MULLEN, STANLEY

KINSMEN OF THE DRAGON (N) Shasta 1951;
MOON FOAM & SORCERIES (C13+P12) Gorgon 1948;
THE SPHINX CHILD (S) New Collectors P6 1948;

MUNDY, TALBOT (Partial Listing)

TROS OF SAMOTHRACE (Marginal)
TROS (N) Avon S 303, 1967;
= LUD OF LUNDEN (N) Zebra 207, 1976;
HELMA (N) Avon S 309; 1967;
=AVENGING LIAFAIL (N) Zebra 212, 1976;

LIAFALL (N) Avon S 316; 1967;
=THE PRAETOR'S DUNGEON (N) Zebra 218; 1977;
HELENE (N) Avon S 318; 1967;
= THE PURPLE PIRATE (N) Zebra 233 1977;
ALL FOUR = TROS OF SAMOTHRACE (N) Appleton 1934; Gnome 1959;
QUEEN CLEOPATRA (N) Bobbs-M 1929; Ace K149; Avon N247; Zebra 342;
THE PURPLE PIRATE (N) Appleton 1935; Gnome 1959; Avon N251;

OM: THE SECRET OF THE AHBOR VALLEY, (N) Bobbs-M 1924; Avon V2212; Xanadu X2;
THE DEVILS GUARD (N) Bobbs-M 1926; Oriental Club 1945, Avon V2220;
THE NINE UNKNOWN (N) Bobbs-M 1924; Avon V2242;
FULL MOON (N) Appleton 1935;
JIMGRIM (N) Century 1931; Avon V2220;
= JIMGRIM SAHIB (N) Royal 12, 1953;

MUNN, H. WARNER

GWALCHMAI SERIES
KING OF THE WORLD'S EDGE (N) Ace M-152, 1966;
THE SHIP FROM ATLANTIS (N) Ace G+618, 1967;
BOTH = MERLIN'S GODSON (2N) BB 25298, 1976;
MERLIN'S RING (N) BB 24010, 1974;

THE BANNER OF JOAN (P) DMG 1975;
THE WEREWOLF OF PONKERT (N) Grandon 1958; Centaur P6 1976;

MURPHY, SHIRLEY ROSSEAU

THE RING OF FIRE (N) Atheneum 1977;

MYERS, HENRY

O KING, LIVE FOREVER (N) Crown 1953;

MYERS, HOWARD L.

CLOUD CHAMBER (N) Popular 3215, 1977;

MYERS, JOHN MYERS

SILVERLOCK (N) Dutton 1949; Ace A-8;

N

NACE, PIERCE

EAT THEM ALIVE (N) Manor 17157, 1977;

NATION, TERRY

SURVIVORS (N) Coward-McCann 1976;

NEARING, HOMER JR.

THE SINISTER RESEARCHES OF C. P. RANSOM (S9) Dday 1954; SFBC; Curt 7051;

NEEPER, CARY = Carolyn Neeper

A PLACE BEYOND MAN (N) Scribners 1975; Dell 16931;

NELSON, R. FARADAY

BEGGERS SERIES

THEN BEGGERS COULD RIDE (N) Laser 32, 1976;
THE REVOLT OF THE UNEMPLOYABLES (N) Anthewon, pb 1977 ?

BLAKES PROGRESS (N) Laser 13, 1975;
THE GANEMEDE TAKEOVER (N) (see P. Dick - coauthor)
THE ECOLOG (N) Laser 53, 1977;

NESVADBA, JOSEF

THE LOST FACE (C8) Taplinger 1971;

NEVILLE, KRIS

BETTYANN (N) Towr T-075-7, 1970;
INVADERS ON THE MOON (N) Belm B75-1085, 1970;
MISSION: MANSTOP (C7) Leis LB 225, 1971;
THE MUTANTS (N) Belm B50-730, 1966;
PERIL OF THE STARMEN (N) Belm B50+759, 1967;
SPACIAL DELIVERY (N) Belm B50+788, 1967;
THE UNEARTH PEOPLE (N) Belm B92-611, 1964, 50843;

NEWBOLT, HENRY

ALADORE (N) Newcastle pb F-104, 1975;

NEWBY, P. H.

THE SPIRIT OF JEM (N) Delacorte 1967;

NEWTON, JULIUS

THE FORGOTTEN RACE (N) Arcadia 1967;

NIALL, IAN =JOHN McNEILLIE

THE BOY WHO SAW TOMORROW (N) Appleton 1952;

NIVEN, LARRY =LAURENCE VAN COTT NIVEN

KNOWN SPACE SERIES

WORLD OF PTAVVS (N) BB U2328, 1966; 233; 23440; 24591;
A GIFT FROM EARTH (N) BB 72113, 1968; Walker 1970; BB 2296; 23442; 24509;
NEUTRON STAR (S8) BB U6120, 1968; 2297; 23441; 24047; 24794;
RINGWORLD (N) BB 2046, 1970; 2759; 22046; 22759; 24795; 25776; H-R-W 1977;
PROTECTOR (N) BB 23486, 1973; 24778; THE RINGWORLD ENGINEERS 80
TALES OF KNOWN SPACE (S13) BB 24563, 1975; 25836;
THE LONG ARM OF GIL HAMILTON (S3) BB 24868, 1976; 25808;

ALL THE MYRIAD WAYS (C14) BB 2280, 1971; 24084;
THE FLIGHT OF THE HORSE (S5+C3) BB 23487, 1973; 24692; 25577;
THE FLYING SORCERERS (N) (with D. Gerrold) BB 2331, 1971;

A HOLE IN SPACE (S4+C6) BB 24011, 1974; 25287;
INFERNO (N) (with Pournelle) Poc 80490, 1976;
LUCIFER'S HAMMER (N) (with J. Pournelle) Playboy, 1977; Crest 23599;(fc 7/78)
THE MOTE IN GODS EYE (N) (with Pournelle) S&S 1974; SFBC; Poc 80107;
THE SHAPE OF SPACE (C7+S3-Known Space) BB 1712, 1969;
A WORLD OUT OF TIME (N) H-R-W 1976; SFBC; BBDR 25750;

NOBLE, MARK (See B. STRICKGOLD)

NOEL, STERLING

WE WHO SURVIVED (N) Avon T360, 1959;

NOLAN, WILLIAM F.

SERIES

LOGAN'S RUN (N) (with G. C. Johnson) Dial 1967; Dell 4933; Bant X2517;
LOGAN'S WORLD (N) Bantam 11418, 1977;

ALIEN HORIZONS (C19) Poc 77928, 1974;
IMPACT 20 (C20) PBL 52-250, 1963; 52-971;
SPACE FOR HIRE (N) Lanc 74-778, 1971;

NORDEN, ERIC

THE ULTIMATE SOLUTION (N) Warn 75-154; 1973;

NORMAN, JOHN =JOHN F. LANGE JR.

TARL CABOT

TARNSMAN OF GOR (N) BB U6071, 1966; 1830; 2485; 22485; 24775; 25179;
OUTLAW OF GOR (N) U6072, 1967; 1831; 2486; 22486; 24782; 25180;
PRIEST-KINGS OF GOR (N) BB 72015, 1968; 1832; 2487; 22487; 24783; 25181;
NOMADS OF GOR (N) BB 1765, 1969; 2488; 22488; 24784; 25182;
ASSASSIN OF GOR (N) BB 2094, 1970; 2489; 22489; 25183;
RAIDERS OF GOR (N) BB 2447, 1971; 22447; 25184;
HUNTERS OF GOR (N) DAW 96, 1974; UE1294;
MARAUDERS OF GOR (N) DAW 141, 1975; UE1295; UM1369;
TRIBESMEN OF GOR (N) DAW 185, 1976; UE1296;
BEASTS OF GOR (N) Daw 280, 1978;

SLAVERY IS FUN SERIES

CAPTIVE OF GOR (N) BB 2994, 1972; 22994, 24384; 25185; BBDR 27114;
SLAVE GIRL OF GOR (N) Daw 232, 1977;
TIME SLAVE (N) Daw 169, 1975; UJ 1322

NORRIS, FRANK

NUTRO 29 (N) Rinehart 1950;

NORRIS, KATHLEEN

THROUGH A GLASS DARKLY (N) Dday 1957;

NORTH, ERIC =BERNARD CHARLES CRONIN

THE ANT MEN (JN) Winston 1955; M-B 60-277; 60-434; 75443;

NORTON, ANDRE =ALICE MARY NORTON

ALSO ANDREW NORTH

WITCH WORLD SERIES

WITCH WORLD (N) Ace F-197, 1963; G-655; 89700; Gregg 1977;
WEB OF THE WITCH WORLD (N) Ace F-263, 1964; 87870; Gregg 1977;
THREE AGAINST THE WITCH WORLD (N) Ace F-332, 1965; 80800; Gregg 1977;
YEAR OF THE UNICORN (N) Ace F-357, 1965; 94250; Gregg 1977;
WARLOCK OF THE WITCH WORLD (N) Ace G-630, 1967; 87319; Gregg 1977;
SORCERESS OF THE WITCH WORLD (N) Ace H-84, 1968; 77550; Gregg 1977;
SPELL OF THE WITCH WORLD (S3) DAW 1, 1972; UY1179; Gregg 1977;
TREY OF SWORDS (S3) G&D 1977; Ace 82355;

ON WITCHWORLD - NOT PART OF SERIES

THE CRYSTAL GRYPHON (JN) Athenum 1972; DAW 75, 1973; UY1187;
THE JARGOON PARD (JN) Atheneum 1974; Crest P2657; 2911; 22911;

TIME TRAVEL SERIES

THE TIME TRADERS (N) World 1958; Ace D-461; F-236; F-386; 81251;
GALACTIC DERELICT (N) World 1959; Ace D-498; F-310; 27225;
THE DEFIANT AGENTS (N) World 1962; Ace F-183; M-150; 14232;
KEY OUT OF TIME (N) World 1963; Ace F-287; M-156; 43672;;

CENTRAL CONTROL

STAR RANGERS (N) Harcourt 1953;
= THE LAST PLANET (N) Ace D+96, 1955; D-96; D-542; M-151; 47161;
STAR GUARD (N) Harcourt-B 1955; Ace D+199; D-527; G-599; 78130;

PAX

THE STARS ARE OURS (N) World 1954; Ace D+121; D-121; F-207; F-366; M-147; 78430;
STAR BORN (N) World 1957; Ace D+299; F-192; M-148; 78010;

JANUS

JUDGEMENT ON JANUS (N) H-B-W 1963; Ace F-308, 1964; 41550;
VICTORY ON JANUS (N) H-B-J 1966; Ace G-703, 1968; 86321;

SOLAR QUEEN (First Three as Andrew North)

SARGASSO OF SPACE (N) Gnome 1955; Ace D+249; F-279; 74981; Gregg 1978;
PLAGUE SHIP (N) Gnome 1956; Ace D+345, F-291; 68832; Gregg 1978;
VOODOO PLANET (N) Ace D+345, 1959; G+723; 78191; Gregg 1978;
POSTMARKED THE STARS (N) H-B-J 1969; Ace 67555;

BLAKE WALKER

THE CROSSROADS OF TIME (N) Ace D+164, 1956; D-546; F-391; 12311; Gregg 1978;
QUEST CROSSTIME (N) Viking 1965; Ace G-595; 69681;

JERN MURDOCK

THE ZERO STONE (N) Viking 1968; Ace 95960;
UNCHARTED STARS (N) Viking 1969; Ace 84000;

FREE TRADERS
MOON OF THREE RINGS (N) Viking 1966; Ace H-33; 54101;
EXILES OF THE STARS (N) Viking 1971; Ace 22365;

HOSTEEN STORM
THE BEAST MASTER (N) Harbourt-B 1959; Ace D+509; F-315; G-690; 05160;
LORD OF THUNDER (N) H-B-W 1962; Ace F-243; G-691; 49235;

PLANET WARLOCK
STORM OVER WARLOCK (N) World 1960; Ace F-109; F-329; 78740;
ORDEAL IN OTHEWHERE (N) H-B-W 1964; Ace F-325; 63821;

STAR KAAT SERIES
STAR KA'AT (JN) Walker 1976 (with D. Madler) Poc 29810;
STAR KA'AT WORLD (JN) (with D. Madler) Walker, 1978;

ANDROID AT ARMS (N) H-B-J 1971; Ace 02275;
BREED TO COME (N) Viking 1972; Ace 07895;
CATSEYE (N) H—B—W 1961; Ace F-167; G-654; 09265;
DARK PIPER (N) H-B-W 1968; Ace 13795;
DRAGON MAGIC (N) Crowell 1972; Ace 16647;
THE DAY OF THE NESS (JN) (with M. Gilbert) Walker 1975; Dell Yearling;
DREAD COMPANION (N) H-B-J 1970; Ace 16669;
EYE OF THE MONSTER (N) Ace F+147, 1962;
FORERUNNER FORAY (N) Viking 1973; SFBC;
FUR MAGIC (JN) World 1968;
GARAN THE ETERNAL (C5) FPCI 1972; DAW 45, UY 1186;
HIGH SORCERY (C5) 33700, 1970;
HERE ABIDE MONSTERS (N) Atheneum 1973; DAW 121; UW1334;
ICE CROWN (N) Viking 1970; Ace 35840;
IRON CAGE (N) Viking 1974; SFBC; Ace 37290;
KNAVE OF DREAMS (N) Viking 1975; Ace 45000;
LAVENDER GREEN MAGIC (JN) Crowell 1974; Ace 47440;
MERLINS MIRROR (N) DAW 152, 1975; UW1340;
THE MANY WORLDS OF ANDRE NORTON (C7+) Chilton 1974;
= THE BOOK OF ANDRE NORTON (C7) DAW 165, 1975; UW1341;
NO NIGHT WITHOUT STARS (N) Atheneum 1975; Crest 23264;
NIGHT OF MASKS (N) H-B-W 1964; Ace F-365; 57751;
OCTAGON MAGIC (N) World 1967;
OPERATION TIME SEARCH (N) H-B-W 1967; Ace 63410;
OUTSIDE (JN) Walker 1975; Avon 26221;
PERILOUS DREAMS (C4) DAW 196, 1976;
QUAG KEEP (JN) Atheneum 1978;
RED HART MAGIC (JN) Crowell 1976;
SEA SIEGE (N) Harcourt 1957; Ace F+147, 75695;
SECRET OF THE LOST RACE (N) Ace D+381, 1959; 75831; Gregg 1978;
STAR GATE (N) Harcourt-B 1958; Ace F-231; M-157; 78071;
STAR HUNTER (N) Ace D+509, 1961; G-723; +78191; Gregg 1978;
STARMAN'S SON (N) Harcourt 1952;
= DAYBREAK 2250 A.D. (N) Ace D+69; D-534; F-323; 13990;

THE SIOUX SPACEMAN (N) Ace D+437, 1960; F-408; 76801; Gregg 1978;
STEEL MAGIC (N) World 1965;
THE X FACTOR (N) H-B-J 1965; Ace G-646; 92551;
WRAITHS OF TIME (N) Atheneum 1976; Crest 03532;

HISTORICAL NOVELS (Partial Listing)
HUON OF THE HORN (N) Harcourt-B 1951; Ace F-226; 354225;
SHADOW HAWK (N) Harcourt 1960; Ace G-538; 75991;

NORVIL, MANNING

ODAN THE HALF GOD SERIES
DREAM CHARIOTS (N) Daw 260, 1977;
WHETTED BRONZE (N) Daw 281, 1978;

NOURSE, ALAN E.

THE BLADE RUNNER (JN) McKay 1974; BB24654;
THE COUNTERFEIT MAN (C11) McKay 1963; SBS T941;
THE INVADERS ARE COMING (N) (with J.A. Meyer) Ace D-366, 1959;
A MAN OBSESSED (N) Ace D+96, 1955;
=+ THE MERCY MAN (N) McKay 1968; SFBC; Ace 52560;
PSI HIGH AND OTHER STORIES (C3) McKay 1967; Ace G-730;
RAIDERS FROM THE RINGS (N) McKay 1962; Prmd F933;
ROCKET TO LIMBO (N) McKay 1957; Ace D+385;
SCAVENGERS IN SPACE (N) McKay 1959; Ace D-541;
STAR SURGEON (N) McKay 1959; SBS T625;
TIGER BY THE TAIL (C9) McKay 1961; SFBC; M-B 50-199; 60-309;
TROUBLE ON TITAN (JN) Winston 1955; Lanc L72-159;
THE UNIVERSE BETWEEN (N) McKay 1965; PBL 52-462;
RX FOR TOMORROW (JC 11) McKay 1971;

NOWLAN, PHILIP FRANCES

ARMAGEDDON 2419 A.D. (N) Avalon 1962; Ace F-188; 02935; 02939;

NUETZEL, CHARLES - Also ALBERT AUGUSTUS, JR.

TORLO HANNIS
WARRIOR OF NOOMAS (N) Pow PP149, 1969;
RAIDERS OF NOOMAS (N) Pow PP157, 1969;

IMAGES OF TOMORROW (C13) Pow Pp135, 1969;
SWORDMEN OF VISTAR (N) Pow PP121, 1969;
LAST CALL FOR THE STARS (N) Lenox Hill 1970;
THE SLAVES OF LOMOORO (N) (as Augustus) Pow PP189, 1969;

NUNES, CLAUDE

INHERIT THE EARTH (N) Ace G+580, 1966;
RECOIL (N) (with R. Nunes) Ace +71082; 1971;

O

OAKES, PHILIP

EXPERIMENT AT PROTO (N) Coward-McCann 1973; Avon 22582;

O'DONNELL, K.M. =MALZBERG, BARRY

OFFUTT, ANDREW J.

CORMAC MAC ART

SWORD OF THE GAEL (N) Zebra 138, 1975;
THE UNDYING WIZARD (N) Zebra 197, 1976;
THE SIGN OF THE MOONBOW (N) Zebra 254, 1977;
THE MISTS OF DOOM (N) Zebra 302, 1977;

ARDOR ON AROS (N) Dell 0931, 1973; 10931;
THE BLACK SORCERER OF THE BLACK CASTLE (S) Hall 1976 PB 12pp; (Satire)
THE CASTLE KEEPS (N) Berk S2187, 1972;
CHIEFTON OF ANDOR (N) Dell 4551, 1976;
DEMON IN THE MIRROR (N) (with R. Lyon) Poc 81720, 1978;
EVIL IS LIVE SPELLED BACKWARDS (N) PBL 64-490, 1970;
THE GALACTIC REJECTS (JN) Lothrop-Lee 1973; Dell 3361;
GENETIC BOMB (N) (with D.B. Berry) Warn 76-868, 1975;
MESSENGER OF ZHUVASTOU (N) Berk S 2317, 1973;
MY LORD BARBARIAN (N) BBDR 25713, 1977;

OLEMY, P. T.

THE CLONES (N) Flagship 92-840, 1968;

OLIVER, CHAD = SYMMES CHADWICK OLIVER

ANOTHER KIND (C7) BBHC 1954; BB113;
THE EDGE OF FOREVER (C6) Sherbourne 1971;
GIANTS IN THE DUST (N) Prmd V3670, 1976;
MISTS OF DAWN (JN) Winston 1952;
SHADOWS IN THE SUN (N) BBHC 1954; BB 91; U2857;
THE SHORE OF ANOTHER SEA (N) Sig T4526, 1971;
UNEARTHLY NEIGHBORS (N) BB 365k, 1960;
THE WINDS OF TIME (N) Dday 1957; SFBC; Poc 1222; Avon E 23887;

OLSEN BOB = ALFRED JOHN OLSEN, JR.

RHYTHM RIDES THE ROCKET (S) Columbia 6, about 1940;

O'NEIL, DENNIS

THE BITE OF MONSTERS (N) Belm B75-2134, 1971;

ORKAW, BEN

WHEN TIME STOOD STILL (N) Signet D2150, 1962;

O'ROUKE, FRANK

INSTANT GOLD (N) Morrow 1964; SFBC;

ORWELL, GEORGE = ERIC ARTHUR BLAIR

ANIMAL FARM (N) Harcourt 1946; BC; Signet 1289; S 1615; CD3; CP121; CT304; CQ706;+
1984 (N) Harcourt 1949; BC; Signet 798; S1640; CP100; CT311; CO522; CY688;+

OSBORNE, DAVE = R. SILVERBERG

OTTUM, BOB

ALL RIGHT, EVERYBODY OFF THE PLANET (N) Random 1972; Bant N7598;

OWEN, DEAN =DUDLEY DEAN MCGAUGHY

THE END OF THE WORLD (N) Ace D-548, 1962;
KONGA (N) Mon MM604, 1960;
REPTILICUS (N) Mon MM605, 1961;
THE BRIDES OF DRACULA (N) Mon MM602; 1960;

OWEN, FRANK (Partial Listing) = ROSWELL WILLIAMS

THE PORCELAIN MAGICIAN (C14) Gnome 1948;

P

PAGE, NORVELL W.

FLAME WINDS (N) Berk X1741, 1969;
SONS OF THE BEAR-GOD (N) Berk X1769, 1969;

PAGE, THOMAS = ROBERT PAGE JONES & DANIEL THOMAS STREIB

THE HEPHAESTUS PLAGUE (N) Putnam 1973; Bantam X8550;

PANGBORN, EDGAR

THE COMPANY OF GLORY (N) Pyramid V3568, 1975;
DAVY (N) St. Martins 1964; BB U6018; 3263; 24968; Garland 1975;
GOOD NEIGHBORS AND OTHER STRANGERS (C10) Macmil 1972; Collier 2360;
THE JUDGEMENT OF EVE (N) S&S 1966; Dell 4292; Avon E30387;
A MIRROR FOR OBSERVERS (N) Dday 1954; SFBC; Dell D246; Avon E24703;
WEST OF THE SUN (N) Dday 1953; SFBC; Dell 9422;

PANSHIN, ALEXEI

ANTHONY VILLIERS
STARWELL (N) Ace G-756, 1968;
THE THURB REVOLUTION (N) Ace G-762, 1968;
MASQUE WORLD (N) Ace 02320, 1969;

FAREWELL TO YESTERDAY'S TOMORROW (C12) Berk/Put 1975; (C11) Berk Z3211;
RITE OF PASSAGE (N) Ace A-16, 1968; 72781; Gregg 1976; Ace 72785;

PARNOV, EREMEI (See EMTSEV, M.)

PARRY, MICHEL

BOAZ SERIES (see G. Rusoff)

CHARIOTS OF FIRE (N) Popular 3175, 1977;
THRONE OF FIRE (N) Pop 3232, 1977;

PAULSEN, GARY

THE IMPLOSION EFFECT (N) Major 3048, 1976;

PEAKE, MERVYN LAURENCE

GORMENGHAST TRILOGY

TITUS GROAN (N) Reynal & Hitchcock 1946; W-T 1967; BB 73007; 23518; 24321; 27096;
GORMENGHAST (N) W-T 1967; BB 73008; 23519; 24322; 25790;
TITUS ALONE (N) W-T 1967; BB 73009; 23520; 24323; 25791;

PEARSON, EDWARD

CHAMIEL (N) Poc 77790, 1974;

PECK, RICHARD E.

FINAL SOLUTION (N) Dday 1973;

PEDLER, KIT & GERRY DAVIS

MUTANT 59; THE PLASTIC EATERS (N) Viking 1972; SFBC; Bant T7499;
THE DYNOSTAR MENACE (N) Scribners 1976;
BRAINRACK (N) Pocket 78943, 1975;

PENDELTON, DON Also DAN BRITAIN

CATACLYSM, THE DAY THE WORLD ENDED (N) Pinn 003, 1969; 356;
THE GOD MAKERS (N) Pinn 010 (as Britain) 1969; Pinn 323 (as Pendelton)
1989: POPULATION DOOMSDAY (N) Pinn 007, 1970; 329;
THE GUNS OF TERRA 10 (N) Pinn 006, 1969; 377;
REVOLT! (N) Beeline 3130N, 1968;
=+ CIVIL WAR II (N) Pinn 055 (as Britain) 1971; Pinn 758 (as Pendelton)

PERCY, WALKER

LOVE IN THE RUINS (N) F-S&G 1971; Dell 5053;

PETAJA, EMIL

KALEVALLA SERIES

SAGA OF LOST EARTHS (N) Ace F-392, 1966;
THE STAR MILL (N) Ace F-414, 1966;
THE STOLEN SUN (N) Ace G+618, 1967;
TRAMONTANE (N) Ace H+36, 1967;

GREEN PLANET

LORD OF THE GREEN PLANET (N) Ace H+22, 1967;
DOOM OF THE GREEN PLANET (N) Ace H+70, 1968; +78370;

ALPHA YES, TERRA NO (N) Ace M+121, 1965;
AS DREAM AND SHADOW (P45) SISU; 1972;
THE CAVES OF MARS (N) Ace M+133, 1965;
THE PATH BEYOND THE STARS (N) Dell 6864, 1969;
THE NETS OF SPACE (N) Berk X1692, 1969;
THE PRISM (N) Ace H+51, 1968; +12375;
SEED OF THE DREAMERS (N) Ace +06707, 1970;
STARDRIFT (C14) FPCI 1971;
THE TIME TWISTER (N) Dell 8911, 1968;

PETERS L. T. = ALBERT & JO ANN KLAINER

THE 11TH PLAGUE (N) S&S 1973; Pinn 531;

PETERSON, JOHN VICTOR

ROCK THE BIG ROCK (N) Curtis 7082, 1970;

PFEIL, DONALD J.

LOOK BACK TO EARTH (N) Manor 15299, 1977;
THROUGH THE REALITY WARP (N) BB 25377, 1976;
VOYAGE TO A FORGOTTEN SUN (N) BB 24338, 1975;
See Also RETURN TO PLANET OF THE APES SERIES

PHELPS, GILBERT

THE WINTER PEOPLE (N) S&S 1964;

PHILLIFENT, JOHN T. Also JOHN RACKHAM

GENIUS UNLIMITED (N) Daw 16, 1972;
HIERARCHIES (N) Ace +53415, 1973;
LIFE WITH LANCELOT (N) Ace +48245, 1973;
KING OF ARGENT (N) Daw 46, 1973;

AS JOHN RACKHAM

ALIEN SEA (N) Ace H+40, 1968; +11500;
THE ANYTHING TREE (N) Ace +89250, 1970;
BEANSTALK (N) Daw 78, 1973;
THE BEASTS OF KOHL (N) Ace G+592, 1966;
BEYOND CAPELLA (N) Ace +05595, 1971;
DANGER FROM VEGA (N) Ace G+576, 1966;
DARK PLANET (N) Ace +13805, 1971;
THE DOUBLE INVADERS (N) Ace G+623, 1967;
EARTHSTRINGS (N) Ace +10293, 1972;
FLOWER OF DORADIL (N) Ace +24100, 1970;
IPOMOEA (N) Ace +37250, 1969;
THE PROXIMA PROJECT (N) Ace H+91, 1968; +68600;
TIME TO LIVE (N) Ace G+606, 1966;

TREASURE OF TAU CETI (N) Ace +23775, 1969;
WE, THE VENUSIANS (N) Ace M+127, 1965;

PHILLIPS, ALEXANDER M.

THE MISLAID CHARM (N) Prime 1947;

PHILLIPS, MARK See LAWRENCE JANIFER & RANDALL GARRETT

PHILLIPS, ROG = ROGER PHILLIPS GRAHAM

THE INVOLUNTARY IMMORTALS (N) Avalon 1959;
TIME TRAP (N) Cent 116, 1949;
WORLDS WITHIN (N) Cent 124, 1950;
WORLD OF IF (N) Cent B13, 1951;

PIERCY, MARGE

WOMAN ON THE EDGE OF TIME (N) Knopf 1976; Crest 3208;
DANCE THE EAGLE TO SLEEP (N) Dday 1970; GM M1616;

PINCER, CHAPMAN

NOT WITH A BANG (N) NAL 1965; SFBC; Sig P 2888;

PIPER, H. BEAM

LITTLE FUZZY (N) Avon F118, 1962; Ace 48490;
THE OTHER HUMAN RACE (N) Avon G1220, 1964;
= FUZZY SAPIENS (N) Ace 26190, 1976; 26192;
BOTH = THE FUZZY PAPERS (2N) SFBC; 1977;

CRISIS IN 2140 (N) (with J. J. McGuire) Ace D+227, 1957;
FOUR DAY PLANET (JN) PUTNAM 1961;
JUNKYARD PLANET (N) Putnam 1963;
= THE COSMIC COMPUTER (N) Ace F-274, 1964; 11756;
LORD KALVAN OF OTHERWHEN (N) Ace F-342, 1965; Garland 1975; Ace 49051;
A PLANET FOR TEXANS (N) (with J.J. McGuire) Ace D+299, 1958;
SPACE VIKING (N) Ace F-255, 1963; Garland 1975; 77780;

PISERCHIA, DORIS

A BILLION DAYS OF EARTH (N) Bant 8805, 1976;
EARTHCHILD (N) Daw 241, 1277;
MISTER JUSTICE (N) Ace +53415, 1973;
STAR RIDER (N) Bant Q8408, 1974;

PLATT, CHARLES

GARBAGE WORLD (N) Berk X1470, 1967; Bel-T BT 50509; 51-164;
PLANET OF THE VOLES (N) Putnam 1971; Berk S2248;
TWILIGHT OF THE CITY (N) Macmil 1977;

POHL, FREDERICK WITH L. DEL REY = EDSON McCANN

THE ABOMINABLE EARTHMAN (C7) BB685, 1963; 1748;
THE AGE OF THE PUSSYFOOT (N) Trident 1969; BB 1732; BBDR 27129;

BEYOND THE BLUE EVENT HORIZON 1980 BAL

ALTERNATING CURRENTS (C10) BBHC 1956; BB 130; 1663;
THE BEST OF FREDERICK POHL (C19) SFBC 1975; BB24507; Taplinger 1977;
THE CASE AGAINST TOMORROW (C6) BB 206, 1957; U2175; 1945;
DAY MILLION (C9) BB 1939, 1970; THE COOL WAR (N) 1982 DEL RAY
DIGITS AND DASTARDS (C8) BB U2178, 1966; 1947;
DRUNKARDS WALK (N) BB 439K, 1960; Gnome 1961; BB 1743; 23439;
THE EARLY POHL (C8) Dday 1976; SFBC;
GATEWAY (N) St. Martins 1977; SFBC; BBDR 25378;
THE GOLD AT THE STARBOW'S END (C5) BB 2775, 1972; 22775;
IN THE PROBLEM PIT (C11) Bant T8857, 1976;
THE MAN WHO ATE THE WORLD (C5) BB 397K, 1960; 597; 1946;
A PLAGUE OF PYTHONS (N) BB U2174, 1965; 1745; 23438;
MAN PLUS (N) Random 1976; SFBC; Bant 10779;
SLAVE SHIP (N) BBHC 1957; BB 192; U2177; 1744; 24586;
TOMORROW TIMES SEVEN (C7) BB 325K, 1959; 1746;
TURN LEFT AT THURSDAY (C7) BB 476K, 1961; 1747;

WITH JACK WILLIAMSON

STARCHILD

THE REEFS OF SPACE (N) BB U2172, 1964; 23448;
STAR CHILD (N) BB U2176, 1965; 23449;
ROGUE STAR (N) 1797, 1969; 23450;
ALL 3 = THE STARCHILD TRILOGY (3N) SFBC 1977; Poc 81105;

JIM EDEN

UNDERSEA QUEST (JN) Gnome 1954; BB 2207; BBDR 25617;
UNDERSEA FLEET (JN) Gnome 1956; BB 2208; BBDR 25618;
UNDERSEA CITY (JN) Gnome 1958; BB 2209; BBDR 25619;

FARTHEST STAR (N) BB 24330, 1975;

WITH CYRIL KORNBLUTH

CRITICAL MASS (C10) Bant 10948, 1977;
GLADIATOR AT LAW (N) BBHC; 1955 BB 107; F570; U2343; 1659; 2764; Bant 6422;
SEARCH THE SKY (N) BBHC 1954; BB 61; F738; 1660; Pant 2983;
THE SPACE MERCHANTS (N) BBHC 1953; BB 21; 381K; U2173; 1658; Walker 1969; BB 2600; 24290; 25596;
WOLFBANE (N) BB 335K, 1959; 1661; Bant T2062; Garland 1976;
THE WONDER EFFECT (C9) BB F638, 1962; 1662;
PRESIDENTIAL YEAR (N) (not Science Fiction) BB 144, 1956;
A TOWN IS DROWNING (N) (not Science Fiction) BB 123, 1955;

WITH LESTER DEL REY (as EDSON McCANN)

PREFERRED RISK (N) S&S 1955; Dell R114;

POURNELLE, JERRY

JOHN CHRISTIAN FALKENBERG

WEST OF HONOR (N) Laser 50, 1976;
THE MERCENARY (N) Pocket 80903, 1977

HIGH JUSTICE (C7) Pocket 81104, 1977;
BIRTH OF FIRE (N) Laser 23, 1976;
A SPACESHIP FOR THE KING (N) Daw 42, 1973;

JANISSARIES: CLAN AND CROWN; ACE 83

LUCIFERS HAMMER (See Larry Niven co-author)
A MOTE IN GOD'S EYE (N) (See Larry Niven Co-author)
INFERNO (N) (See Larry Niven co-author)
EXILES TO GLORY (N) Ace 22215, 1978;(fc 7/78)
See Also PLANET OF THE APES SERIES

POWE, BRUCE

THE LAST DAYS OF THE AMERICAN EMPIRE (N) St. Martins 1974;

POWERS, J. L.

BLACK ABYSS (N) Arcadia 1966;

POWERS, TIMOTHY

THE SKIES DISCROWNED (N) Laser 28, 1976;
EPITAPH IN RUST (N) Laser 47, 1976;

POYER, JOE

NORTH CAPE (N) Dday 1969;
OPERATION MALACCA (N) Dday 1968; Curt 7032 Prmd, A3935;

PRAGNELL, FESTUS

THE GREEN MAN OF GRAYPEC (N) Greenberg 1950;
THE MACHINE GOD LAUGHS (N+A2) FPCI 1949;

PRATCHETT, TERRY

THE DARK SIDE OF THE SUN (N) St. Martins 1976;

PRATT, FLETCHER Also George U Fletcher

ALIEN PLANET (N) Avalon 1962; Ace F-257; 01570;
THE BLUE STAR (N) (In 'Witches Three Twayne 1952) BB 1602; 24537;
DOUBLE IN SPACE (2N) Dday 1951; Curtin 7043;
DOUBLE JEOPARDY (2N) Dday 1952; SFBC; Galaxy 30; Curtis 7044;
INVADERS FROM RIGEL (N) Avalon 1960; Airmont SF 4;
LAND OF UNREASON (N) (With De Camp) Holt 1942; BB 1814;
THE UNDYING FIRE (N) BBHC 1953; BB25;
THE WELL OF THE UNICORN (N) Sloane 1948; (as Fletcher)
Lancer 74-911; BB 25012; Garland 1976;

PREUSS PAUL THE GATES OF HEAVEN 1980 BANT

PRICE, E. HOFFMAN

FAR LANDS, OTHER DAYS (C31) Carcossa 1975; OPERATION LONGLIFE 82
STRANGE GATEWAYS (C12) Arkham 1967;

PRIEST, CHRISTOPHER

DARKENING ISLAND (N) H&R 1972; Manor 12230;
INDOCTRINAIRE (N) H&R 1970; Pocket 77367;
THE INVERTED WORLD (N) H&R 1974; SFBC; Popular 309;
THE PERFECT LOVER (N) Scrib 1977;
THE SPACE MACHINE (N) H&R 1976; Pop 04142;

PRIESTLY, JOHN B. (partial listing)

THE DOOMSDAY MEN (N) Harper 1938; Pop SP195;
SATURN OVER THE WATER (N) Dday 1961; Poc GC-165;
THE 31ST OF JUNE (N) Dday 1962;

PURDOM, TOM

THE BARONS OF BEHAVIOR (N) Ace 04760, 1972;
FIVE AGAINST ARLANE (N) Ace H+22, 1967;
I WANT THE STARS (N) Ace F+289, 1964;
REDUCTION IN ARMS (N) Berkley S2088, 1971;
THE TREE LORDS OF IMETEN (N) Ace M+139, 1966;

PUTNEY, SUSAN K.

AGAINST ARCTURUS (N) Ace + 00990, 1972;

PYCHON, THOMAS

GRAVITY'S RAINBOW (N) Viking 1973; Bant; T8099; 10271;
THE CRYING OF LOT 49 (N) Chilton 1973; Bant N5764;

Q

QUINN, SEABURY

JULES DeGRANDIN (Borderline)
THE PHANTOM FIGHTER (S10) Mycroft and Moran 1966;
THE ADVENTURES OF JULES DE GRANGIN (S7)Pop 394, 1976;
THE CASEBOOK OF JULES DE GRANDIN (S7) Pop, 404, 1976;
THE SKELETON CLOSET OF JULES de GRANDIN (S6) Pop 8527, 1976;
THE DEVILS BRIDE (N) Pop 424, 1976;
THE HELLFIRE FILES OF JULES de GRANDIN (S6) Pop 428, 1976;
THE HORROR CHAMBERS OF JULES de GRANDIN (S6) Pop 3183, 1977;

ALIEN FLESH (N) Train 1977;
IS THE DEVIL A GENTLEMEN (C) Mirage 1970;
ROADS (N) Arkham 1948;

R

RACKHAM, JOHN See PHILLIFENT, JOHN

RAE, H.C.

THE TRAVELING SOUL (N) Avon 36517, 1978;

RAND, PETER

THE TIME OF THE EMERGENCY (N) Dday 1977;

RANDALL, FLORENCE ENGLE

HALDANE STATION (N) Harcourt 1973; Crest; P2217;
A WATCHER IN THE WOODS (JN) Atheneum 1976;

RANDALL, MARTA

A CITY IN THE NORTH (N) Warn 88117, 1976;
ISLANDS (N) Pyramid V3664, 1976;
JOURNEY (N) Pocket 81207, 1978

RANDALL, ROBERT =R. GARRETT & R. SILVERBERG

RANKINE, JOHN SeeMASON, DOUGLAS R.

RAPHAEL, RICK

CODE THREE (N) S&S 1965; Berk X1394;

RAYER, F. G.

JOURNEY TO THE STARS (N) Arcadia 1964;
THE IRON AND THE ANGER (N) Arcadia 1967;

READE, QUINN

QUEST OF THE DARK LADY (N) Belm B60-1067, 1960; B-T 51101;

REED, KIT

MISTER DA V. (C13) Berk 2380, 1973;
ARMED CAMPS (N) Dutton 1970; Berk S2086;

REED, DAVID V. =DAVID VERN

MURDER IN SPACE (N) Galaxy 23, 1954;

REIDA, ALVAH

FAULT LINES (N) World 1972; Berk 2437;

REIN, HAROLD

FEW WERE LEFT (N) Day 1955;

RENARD, JOSEPH

THE MONODYNE CATASTROPHE (N) Major 122, 1977;

REPP, ED EARL

THE RADIUM POOL (C3) FPCI 1949; HC & PB;
THE STELLAR MISSILES (C3) FPCI 1950; HC & PB;

RESNICK, MICHAEL

ADAM THANE

THE GODDESS OF GANYMEDE (N) DMG 1965; PBL 52-687;
PURSUIT ON GANYMEDE (N) PBL 53-760, 1968;

FORGOTTEN SEA OF MARS (N) Casedessus 1965;
REDBEARD (N) Lancer 74-579, 1969; Magnum 74-579;

REYNOLDS, MACK = DALLAS McCORD REYNOLDS

HOMER CRAWFORD

BLACKMAN'S BURDEN (N) Ace +06612, 1972;
BORDER, BREED NOR BIRTH (N) Ace +06612, 1972;
THE BEST YE BREED (N) Ace 05481, 1978;

UNITED PLANETS ORGANIZATION (first 4 - Ronny Bronston)

PLANETARY AGENT X (N) Ace M+131, 1965; +66995;
DAWNMAN PLANET (N) Ace G+580, 1966; +14250;
CODE DUELLO (N) Ace H+103, 1968; +11650;
AMAZON PLANET (N) Ace 01950, 1975;
SECTION G. UNITED PLANET (N) Ace 75860, 1976;

JOE MAUSER

THE EARTH WAR (N) Prmd F886, 1963;
TIME GLADIATOR (N) Lan 74-537, 1969;
MERCENARY FROM TOMORROW (N) Ace H+65, 1968; +52500; +24035;

JULIAN WEST

LOOKING BACKWARD FROM THE YEAR 2000 (N) Ace 48970, 1973;
EQUALITY IN THE YEAR 2000 (N) Ace 21430, 1977;

BAT HARDIN

THE TOWERS OF UTOPIA (N) Bant T6884, 1975;
ROLLTOWN (N) Ace 73450, 1976;
COMMUNE 2000 AD (N) Bant N8402, 1974;

ABILITY QUOTIENT (N) Ace 00265, 1975;
AFTER UTOPIA (N) Ace 00958, 1977;
AFTER SOME TOMORROW (N) Belmont B50-795, 1967;
THE BEST OF MACK REYNOLDS (C22) Poc 80403, 1976;
THE CASE OF THE LITTLE GREEN MEN (N) Phoenix 1951;
COMPUTER WAR (N) H+34, 1967; +11650;
COMPUTER WORLD (N) Curtis 7098, 1970;
THE COSMIC EYE (N) Belmont B60-1040, 1969; BT 50802;
DAY AFTER TOMORROW (N) Ace 13960, 1976;
DEPRESSION OR BUST (N) Ace +14250, 1974;
THE FIVE WAY SECRET AGENT (N) Ace +24035, 1976;
GALACTIC MEDAL OF HONOR (N) Ace 27240, 1976;
MISSION TO HORATIUS (JN) Whitman 1968; (Star Trek)
OF GODLIKE POWER (N) Belmont B50-680, 1966;
= EARTH UNAWARE (N) Belmont B50-826, 1968;
ONCE DEPARTED (N) Curtis 6122, 1970;
PERCHANCE TO DREAM (N) Ace 65948, 1977;

POLICE PATROL 2000 A.D. (N) Ace 67460, 1977;
THE RIVAL RIGELIANS (N) Ace G+632, 1967; +66995;
SATELLITE CITY (N) Ace 75045, 1975;
SPACE VISITOR (N) Ace 77782, 1977;
THE SPACE BARBARIANS (N) Ace +77710, 1969;
TOMORROW MIGHT BE DIFFERENT (N) Ace 81670, 1975;

REYNOLDS, PHILLIP

WHEN AND IF (N) Sloane 1952;

RHEINGOLD, HOWARD

SERIES
THE SAVAGE REPORT: 1994 (N) Freeway FP 2033, 1974;
WAR OF THE GURUS (N) Freeway FP 2045, 1974;

RICCI, BARBARA GUIGNON

THE YEAR OF THE RATS (N) Walker 1973;

RICHARDS, HENRY See RICHARD SAXON

RICHMOND, WALT & LEIGH

CHALLENGE THE HELLMAKER (N) Ace 10150, 1976;
GALLAGHER'S GLACIER (N) Ace +27235, 1970;
THE LOST MILLENNIUM (N) Ace H+29, 1967;
PHOENIX SHIP (N) Ace +66160, 1969;
POSITIVE CHARGE (C8) Ace +27235, 1970;
THE PROBABILITY CORNER (N) Ace 37088, 1977;
SHOCK WAVE (N) ACE G+2614, 1967;

RIENOW, LEONA TRAIN & ROBERT REINOW

THE YEAR OF THE LAST EAGLE (N) BB 2065, 1970;

RIVERE, ALEC

LOST CITY OF THE DAMNED (N) Pike 101, 1961;

ROBERTS, JANE

THE REBELLERS (N) F+215, 1963;

ROBERTS, TERRENCE

REPORT ON THE STATUS QUO (N) Merlin 1955;

ROBERTS, JOHN MADDOX

THE STRAYED SHEEP OF CHARUM (N) Dday 1977;

ROBERTS, KEITH

THE CHALK GIANTS (N) Berk/Put 1975; Berk Z3115;
THE FURIES (N) Berk F1177, 1966;
THE INNER WHEEL (N) Dday 1970; Play 16143;
PAVANE (N) Dday 1968; Ace 65430; Berk D3142;

ANITA (S15) Ace 02295, 1970; (Marginal Supernatural);
THE PASSING OF DRAGONS (C12) Berk 3477, 1977;

ROBINETT, STEPHEN

THE MAN RESPONSIBLE (N) Ace 51899, 1977;
STARGATE (N) St. Martins 1976; Sig W7757;

ROBINSON, ELEANOR

CHRYSALIS OF DEATH (N) Poc 80516, 1976;

ROBINSON, FRANK M.

THE POWER (N) Lipp 1956; SFBC; Bant A1593; Pop 8059; Berk 03600;
See Also T. SCORTIA - co-author

ROBINSON, FRANK S.

CHILDREN OF THE DRAGON (N) Avon 35774, 1978;

ROBINSON, SPIDER

TELEMPATH (N) Berk/Put 1976; Berk 3548;
CALLAHANS CROSSTIME SALOON (S9) Ace 09034, 1977;

ROCKLYNNE, ROSS =R. L. ROCKLIN

THE MEN AND THE MIRROR (C6) Ace 52460, 1973;
THE SUN DESTROYERS (N) Ace +93900, 1973;

ROGERS, MICHALE

MINDFOGGER (N) Knopf 1973; Dell 4895,

ROHMER, SAX = ARTHUR S. WARD (partial listing)

FU MANCHU VS. NAYLAND SMITH
THE INSIDIOUS DR. FU-MANCHU (N) Mcbride 1913; Prmd G579; F-908; R1301;
THE RETURN OF DR. FU—MANCHU (N) McBride 1916; Prmd G641; R1302;
THE HAND OF FU-MANCHU (N) McBride 1917; Prmd F-688; R1306; X2342;
THE MASK OF FU-MANCHU (N) Dday 1932; Prmd F-740; R1303;
THE BRIDE OF FU-MANCHU (N) Dday 1933; Prmd F-761; X2113; V3940;
THE DRUMS OF FU-MANCHU (N) Dday 1939; Prmd F-804; X2531;
SHADOW OF FU-MANCHU (N) Dday 1948; Prmd F-837;
THE ISLAND OF FU-MANCHU (N) Dday 1941; Prmd F-858; V4055;
PRESIDENT FU-MANCHU (N) Dday 1936; Prmd F-946;
THE TRAIL OF FU-MANCHU (N) Dday 1934; Prmd R-1003; R1308;
DAUGHTER OF FU-MANCHU (N) Dday 1931; Avon 189; Prmd R 1032; V4024;
RE-ENTER FU-MANCHU (N) GM s684, 1957; K1458; Prmd X1774; V3944;
EMPEROR FU-MANCHU (N) GM s929; 1959; Prmd R 1310;
THE WRATH OF FU-MANCHU (S4+) (C8) Daw 186, 1976;

SUMURU
NUDE IN MINK (N) GM105, 1950; 321;
SUMURU (N) GM 199, 1951; S757;

FIRE GODDESS (N) GM283, 1953;
RETURN OF SUMURU GM 408, 1954; 868;
SINISTER MADONNA (N) GM 555, 1955;

THE DAY THE WORLD ENDED (N) Dday 1930; Ace F-283;

ROMANO, DEANE

FLIGHT FROM TIME ONE (N) Walker 1972;

RONALD, BRUCE W.

OUR MAN IN SPACE (N) Ace M+117, 1965;

ROSHWALD, MORDECAI

LEVEL 7 (N) McGraw-H 1959; SFBC; Sig D1956; D2650; T3904; Q5956;
A SMALL ARMAGEDDON (N) (Brit 1962) Sig W7194, 1976; W7235;

ROSNY, J. H. = J. H. H. BOEX

THE GIANT CAT (N) McBride 1924;
= QUEST OF THE DAWN MAN (N) Ace F-269, 1964;
IRONCASTLE See P.J. Farmer, co-author

ROSSITER, OSCAR = VERNON SKEELS

TETRASOMY TWO (N) Dday 1974; Bant T2052;

ROTHBERG, ABRAHAM

THE SWORD OF THE GOLEM (N) McCall 1971; Bant Q6967;
THE BOY AND THE DOLPHIN (JN) Norton 1969;

ROTSLER, WILLIAM Also JOHN RYDER HALL

PATRON OF THE ARTS (N) BB 24062, 1974;
FUTUREWORLD (N) (as Hall) BB 25559, 1976; (Movie Tie In)
SINBAD AND THE EYE OF THE TIGER (N) (as Hall) Poc 80933, 1977; (Movie Tie In)
TO THE LAND OF THE ELECTRIC ANGEL (N) BB 24517, 1976;
ZANDRA (N) Dday 1978;
See Also RETURN TO PLANET OF THE APES SERIES

ROUECHE, BERTON

FERAL (N) H&R 1974; Poc 80152;

RUBEN, WILLIAMS S. Also FRED SHANNON

WEIGHTLESS IN GAZA (N) (as Shannon) Tower T 060, 1970;
=+ DIONYSUS: THE ULTIMATE EXPERIMENT (N) Manor 15232, 1977;

RUNYON, CHARLES W.

AMES HOLBROOK, DIETY (N) Curt 7202, 1972;
PIGWORLD (N) Dday 1971; Lanc 75-446;
I WEAPON (N) Dday 1974; Pop 4127;
SOULMATE (N) Avon 18028; 1974;

RUSOFF, GARRY (see M. Parry)

SPEAR OF FIRE (N) Pop 04211, 1977;

RUSS, JOANNA

THE FEMALE MAN (N) Bant Q8765, 1975; Gregg 1977; Bant 11175;
PICNIC ON PARADISE (N) Ace H-72, 1968; 66200;
AND CHAOS DIED (N) Ace 02268, 1970; Gregg 1978;
ALYX (N+S4) Gregg, 1976; (N=Picnic on Paradise)
WE WHO ARE ABOUT TO... (N) Dell 19428, 1977;
THE TWO OF THEM (N) Berk/Put 1978; (fc 5/78)

RUSSELL, ERIC FRANK

DEEP SPACE (C9) Fantasy 1954; (C8) Bant 1362;
DREADFUL SANCTUARY (N) Fantasy 1951; Lanc 74-819; 72-149;
THE GREAT EXPLOSION (N) Torquil 1962; SFBC; Prmd F-862; Avon E 23820;
MEN, MARTIANS AND MACHINES (C4) Roy 1956; Berk G148; F1088;
THE MINDWARPERS (N) Lancer 72-942, 1965; 75-414;
SENTINELS FROM SPACE (N) Bourgey & C 1953; (=) Ace D-468; 75894;
= SENTINELS OF SPACE (N) Ace D+44, 1954;
SINISTER BARRIER (N) Fantasy 1948; Galx 1; PBL 52-287; 52-384;
SIX WORLDS YONDER (C6) Ace D+315, 1958; +77785;
SOMEWHERE A VOICE (C7) Ace F-398, 1965;
THE SPACE WILLIES (N) Ace D+315, 1958; +77785;
THREE TO CONQUER (N) Avalon 1956; Ace D+215;
WASP (N) Avalon 1957; Perm M4120; Bant X5913;

RUSSELL, JOHN ROBERT

CABU (N) Pocket 77718, 1974;
SAR (N) Pocket 77726, 1974;
TA (N) Pocket 78890, 1975;

RUSSELL, RAY

WEIRD & HORROR FICTION ONLY;

RYAN, THOMAS J.

THE ADOLESCENCE OF P-1 (N) Macmil, 1977;

S

SABERHAGEN, FRED

BERSERKER TALES
BERSERKER (C10) BB U5063, 1967;
BROTHER ASSASSIN (N) BB 72018, 1969;
BERSERKER'S PLANET (N) DAW 147, 1976;

CHUP SERIES
THE BROKEN LANDS 9N) Ace G-740, 1968;
THE BLACK MOUNTAINS (N) Ace 06615, 1971;

THE BOOK OF SABERHAGEN (C10) DAW 136, 1975;
CHANGLING EARTH (N) DAW 41, 1973;
THE GOLDEN PEOPLE (N) Ace M+103, 1964;
SPECIMENS (N) Pop 335, 1976;
THE WATER OF THOUGHT (N) Ace M+127, 1965;

SABINE, TED

THE SOULSUCKER (N) Pinn 592, 1975;

ST. CLAIR, MARGARET

AGENT OF THE UNKNOWN (N) Ace D+150, 1956;
CHANGE THE SKY & OTHER STORIES (C18) Ace 10258, 1974;
THE DANCERS OF NOYO (N) Ace 13600, 1973;
THE DOLPHINS OF ALTAIR (N) Dell 2079, 1967;
THE GAMES OF NEITH (N) Ace D+453, 1960;
THE GREEN QUEEN (N) Ace D+176, 1956;
MESSAGE FROM THE EOCENE (N) Ace M+105, 1964;
THE SHADOW PEOPLE (N) Dell 7820, 1969;
SIGN OF THE LABYRS (N) Bant J2617, 1963;
THREE WORLDS OF FUTURITY (C5) Ace M+105, 1964;

ST. JOHN, PHILLIP =LESTER DEL DEY

SALLIS, JAMES

A FEW LAST WORDS (C19) Macmil 1971; Coll 6175;

SAMBROT, WILLIAM

ISLAND OF FEAR AND OTHER S. F. STORIES (C14) Perm M4278, 1963;

SANBORN, ROBIN

THE BOOK OF STIER (N) Berk S2019, 1971;

SANDERS, LAWRENCE

THE TOMORROW FILE (N) Put 1976; Berk T3200, 3450;

SARAC, ROGER = ROGER CARAS

THE THROWBACKS (N) Belm B50-642, 1965; 60-1064;

SARGENT, PAMELA

CLONED LIVES (N) G-M Q3529, 1976;
STAR SHADOWS (C10) Ace 78318, 1977;

SAUNDERS, JAKE

THE TEXAS-ISRAELI WAR: 1999 (N) (with H. Waldrop) BB 24182, 1974;

SAXON, PETER = WEIRD & HORROR FICTION ONLY

SAXON, RICHARD also HENRY RICHARDS

THE STARS CAME DOWN (N) Arcadia 1967;
COSMIC CRUSADE (N) Arcadia 1966;
FUTURE FOR SALE (N) Arcadia 1966;
THE HOUR OF THE PHOENIX (N) (as Richards) Arcadia 1965;

SAXTON, JOSEPHINE

GROUP FEAST (N) Dday 1971;
THE HIEROS GAMOS OF SAM AND AN SMITH (N) Dday 1969; Curt 7197;
VECTOR FOR SEVEN (N) Dday 1970;

SAXTON, MARK

THE ISLAR (N) Houghton-M 1969; Sig Q4620; Pop 04171;
Sequel to ISLANDIA by A. T. Wright;

SCHACHNER, NAT(han)

SPACE LAWYER (N) Gnome 1953;

SCHMIDT, STANLEY

NEWTON AND THE QUASI-APPLE (N) Dday 1975; Pop 3223;
THE SINS OF THE FATHERS (N) Berk Z3089, 1976;

SCHMITZ, JAMES H.

TELZEY AMBERDON
THE UNIVERSE AGAINST HER (N) Ace F-314, 1964;
THE LION GAME (N) DAW 38, 1973;
THE TELZEY TOY (S4) DAW 82, 1973;

AGENT OF VEGA (S4) Gnome 1960; Perm M4242; Temp 5403;
THE DEMON BREED (N) Ace H-105, 1968; SFBC;
THE ETERNAL FRONTIERS (N) Putnam 1973; Berk 2458;
A NICE DAY FOR SCREAMING & OTHER TALES OF THE HUB (C6) Chilton 1965;
A PRIDE OF MONSTERS (C5) Macmil 1970; Coll 2486;
A TALE OF TWO CLOCKS (N) Torquil 1962; SFBC; Belm B50-643;
THE WITCHES OF KARRES (N) Chilton 1966; Ace A-13; 89851;

SCHOONER, LAWRENCE

CENTRAL PASSAGE (N) Sloane 1962; BC ; Dell 1155;

SCHRAM, IRENE

ASHES, ASHES, WE ALL FALL DOWN (N) S&S 1973;

SCHWARTZ, ALAN

THE WANDERING TELLURIAN (N) Ace H+20, 1967;

SCORTIA, THOMAS N.

ARTERY OF FIRE (N) Dday 1972; Pop 535;
CAUTION INFLAMMABLE (C20) Dday 1975; Bant 2580;
EARTHWRECK (N) GM M2963, 1974;
THE INFERNO (N) (with Frank M. Robinson) Dday 1975; (Not S.F)
THE NIGHTMARE FACTOR (N) (with F.M. Robinson) Dday 1978;
THE PROMETHEUS CRISIS (N) (with Frank M. Robinson) Dday, 1975; Bant 2270;

SCOTT, ALAN

THE ANTHRAX MUTATION (N) Prmd A3949, 1976;

SCOTT, JODY

PASSING FOR HUMAN (N) Daw 262, 1977;

SEARLS, HANK = HENRY HUNT SEARLS

THE PILGRIM PROJECT (N) McGraw-H, 1964; SFBC; Crst D798;
THE BIG X (N) Harper 1959; Pocket 81164, 1977;

SELLERS, CON

F.S.C. (N) Novel Book 6081, 1963;
= MR. TOMORROW (N) Papillon OSF-502, 1974;

SELLINGS, ARTHUR = ROBERT ARTHUR LEY

also RAY LUTHER

INTERMIND (N) (as Ray Luther) Banner B50-117, 1967;
THE POWER OF X (N) Berk X1801, 1970;
THE QUY EFFECT (N) Berk X1350, 1967;
TELEPATH (N) BB F609, 1962;
THE UNCENSORED MAN (N) Berk X1379, 1967;

SERVISS, GARRETT P. (Partial Listing)

A COLOMBUS OF SPACE (N) Appleton 1911; Hyperion 1975;
EDISON'S CONQUEST OF MARS (N) Carcosa 1947;
= INVASION OF MARS (N) Pow PP173, 1969;
THE MOON METAL (N) Harper 1900; Fax 1972;
THE SECOND DELUGE (N) McBride 1912; Hyperion 1975;

SHAFER, ROBERT

THE CONQUERED PLACE (N) Putnam 1954
= THE NAKED AND THE DAMNED (N) Pop 686, 1955;

SHAFFER, EUGENE CARL

THE LAST BREATH (N) Pap OSF 501, 1974;

SHANNON, FRED See WILLIAM S. RUBEN

SHAPIRO, NEIL

PLANET WITHOUT A NAME (N) Major 3099, 1976;

SHARKEY, JACK

THE SECRET MARTIANS (N) Ace D+471, 1960;
ULTIMATUM IN 2050 A.D. (N) Ace M+117, 1965;

SHAVER, RICHARD

I REMEMBER LEMURIA AND RETURN OF SATHANAS (2N) Venture 1948;

SHAW, BOB

COSMIC KALEIDOSCOPE (C10) Dday 1977;
GROUND ZERO MAN (N) Avon V2414, 1971;
NIGHT WALK (N) Belm B60-110, 1967; Avon S406;
ONE MILLION TOMORROWS (N) Ace 62938, 1970;
OTHER DAYS, OTHER EYES (N) Ace 64240, 1972;
THE PALACE OF ETERNITY (N) Ace 65050, 1969;
SHADOW OF HEAVEN (N) Avon S398, 1969;
TOMORROW LIES IN AMBUSH (C13) Ace 81656, 1973;
THE TWO-TIMERS (N) Ace H-79, 1968; 83550;
A WREATH OF STARS, (N) Dday 1977; Dell 19710;
ORBITSVILLE (N) Ace 63780, 1977;

SHAW, FREDERICK L. JR.

ENVOY TO THE DOG STAR (N) Ace G+614, 1967;

SHEA, MICHAEL

A QUEST FOR SIMBILIS (N) Daw 88, 1974; (set in J. Vance's Dying Earth)

SHEA, ROBERT

WITH R. A. WILSON
ILLUMINATUS I: THE EYE IN THE PYRAMID (N) Dell 4688, 1975;
ILLUMINATUS II: THE GOLDEN APPLE (N) Dell 4691, 1975;
ILLUMINATUS III: LEVIATHAN (N) Dell 4724, 1975;

SHEAR, DAVID

CLONING (N) Walker 1972; Pinn 461;

SHECKLEY, ROBERT

CAN YOU FEEL ANYTHING WHEN I DO THIS (C16) Dday 1971; SFBC; DAW 99;
CITIZEN IN SPACE (C12) BBHC 1955; BB 126; F648; U2862;
DIMENSION OF MIRACLES (N) Dell 1940, 1968;
IMORTALITY DELIVERED (N) Avalon 1958;
=+ IMMORTALITY, INC. (N) Bant A1991, 1959;
JOURNEY BEYOND TOMORROW (N) Sig D2223, 1962; Dell 4268;
MINDSWAP (N) Delacorte 1966; SFBC; Dell; 5643; Ace 53351;
NOTIONS UNLIMITED (C12) Bant A2003, 1960; F3850;
OPTIONS (N) Prmd V3688, 1975;
THE PEOPLE TRAP (C14) Dell 6881, 1968;
PILGRIMAGE TO EARTH (C15) Bant A1672, 1957; F2812;
SHARDS OF SPACE (C11) Bant J2443, 1962; S5927;
THE STATUS CIVILIZATION (N) Sig S1840, 1960; Dell 8249;

STORE OF INFINITY (C8) Bant A2170, 1960; H5229;
THE 10TH VICTIM (N) BB U5050, 1965; Gregg 1978;
UNTOUCHED BY HUMAN HANDS (C13) BBHC, 1954; BB 73; 437K; U2855;

SHEEHAN, PERLEY POORE

THE ABYSS OF WONDERS (N) Polaris 1953;

SHELDON, LEE = WAYNE C. LEE

DOOMED PLANET (N) Avalon 1967;

SHERMAN, HAROLD M.

THE GREEN MAN (N) Century 104, 1946;

SHERRED, T.L.

ALIEN ISLAND (N) BB 1815, 1970;
FIRST PERSON PECULIAR (C4) BB 2469, 1972;

SHERRIFF, R. C.

THE HOPKINS MANUSCRIPT (N) Macmil 1939; Macmil 1963; SFBC;

SHERRELL, CARL

RAUM (N) Avon 33043, 1977;

SHIEL, M. P. (partial listing)

LORD OF THE SEA (N) Stokes 1901; Crown Xanadu
THE PURPLE CLOUD (N) Vang 1930; World 1946; PBL 52-232; 52-944; Warn 75-477; Gregg 1977;
XELUCHIA & OTHERS ( ) Arkham 1975;

SHIRAS, WILMAR H.

CHILDREN OF THE ATOM (S5) Gnome 1953; Avon T221;

SHIRLEY, ROBERT

TEENOCRACY (N) Ace 80200, 1969;

SHUTE, NEVIL = NEVIL SHUTE NORWAY

ON THE BEACH (N) Morrow 1957; Sig D1562; P2279; N5505; Bant S3875; SBS TK1172; BB23732; 24049;
IN THE WET (N) Morrow 1953; Perm M4095; BB 5004; 1834; 2272; 2990; 3159;

SIEGEL, MARTIN

AGENT OF ENTROPY (N) Lanc 74-753, 1969;
THE UNREAL PEOPLE (N) Lanc 78-763, 1973;

SILENT, WILLIAM T. = JOHN JACKSON

LORD OF THE RED SUN (N) Walker 1971;

SILVERBERG, ROBERT also IVAR JORGENSON, DAVID OSBORNE, CALVIN M. KNOX

as ROBERT RANDALL - See R. GARRETT CoAuthor

THE BEST OF ROBERT SILVERBERG (C10) Pocket 80282, 1976;
THE BOOK OF SKULLS (N) Scrib 1972; Sig Q5177;
BORN WITH THE DEAD (C3) Random 1974; Vintage V447;
CAPRICORN GAMES (C8) Random 1976;
COLLISION COURSE (N) Avalon 1959; Ace F+123; 11510;
THE CUBE ROOT OF UNCERTAINTY (C12) Macmil 1970; Coll 2539;
DIMENSION THIRTEEN (C13) BB 1601, 1969;
DOWNWARD TO THE EARTH (N) SFBC; 1970; Sig T4497; W7134;
DYING INSIDE (N) Scrib 1972; BB 23563; 24822;
EARTH'S OTHER SHADOW (C9) Sig Q5538, 1975;
THE FEAST OF ST. DIONYSUS (C5) Scrib 1975;
GODLING, GO HOME, (C11) Belm L92-591, 1964;
HAWKSBILL STATION (N) Dday 1968; SFBC; Avon S411; Berk 03679;
INVADERS FROM EARTH (N) Ace D+286, 1958; Avon S365;
= WE THE MARAUDERS (N) (in 'A PAIR FROM SPACE Belm 92-612, 1965; 50-813;)
THE MAN IN THE MAZE (N) Avon V2262, 1969; E 21915; 38539;(fc 7/78)
THE MASKS OF TIME (N) BB U6121, 1968; 23446;
MASTER OF LIFE AND DEATH (N) Ace D+237, 1957; Avon S329;
MOONFERNS AND STARSONGS (C11) BB 2278, 1971;
NEEDLE IN A TIME STACK (C10) BB U 2330, 1966; 2024;
NEXT STOP THE STARS (C5) Ace F+145, 1962; 57420;
NIGHTWINGS (N) Avon V2303, 1969; Walker 1970; Avon E 28068;
PARSECS AND PARABLES (C10) Dday 1970;
THE PLANET KILLERS (N) Ace D+407, 1959;
THE REALITY TRIP AND OTHER IMPLAUSIBILITIES (C8) BB 2548, 1972;
RECALLED TO LIFE (N) Lanc 74-810, 1962; 72-156; rev. Dday 1972; Ace 71085;
REGAN'S PLANET (N) Prmd F986, 1964;
THE SECOND TRIP (N) SFBC 1972; Sig Q5402;
THE SEED OF EARTH (N) Ace F+145, 1962; 75875;
SHADRACH IN THE FURNACE (N) Bobbs-M 1976; SFBC; Poc 81273;
THE SHORES OF TOMORROW (C8) Nelson 1976;
THE SILENT INVADERS (N) Ace F+195, 1963; 76390;
SON OF MAN (N) BB 2277, 1971; BBDR 25745;
STEPSONS OF TERRA (N) Ace D+311, 1958; 78600;
THE STOCHASTIC MAN (N) H&R 1975; G M 13570;
SUNRISE ON MERCURY & OTHER S. F. STORIES (JC8) Nelson 1975;
THE THIRTEENTH IMMORTAL (N) Ace D+223, 1957;
THORNS (N) BB U6097, 1967; Walker 1969; BB 2026; 23447;
THOSE WHO WATCH (N) Sig P3160, 1967; T4496; W8149;(fc 7/78)
THE TIME HOPPERS (N) Dday 1967; SFBC; Avon S372; BT 50-716; Leis LB512;
A TIME OF CHANGES (N) SFBC 1971; Sig Q4729; W7386;
TO LIVE AGAIN (N) Dday 1969; Dell 8973; Berk 03774;
TO OPEN THE SKY (S5) BB U6093, 1967; 2025; Gregg 1977;
TO WORLDS BEYOND (C9) Chilton 1965;
TOWER OF GLASS (N) Scrib 1970; Bant S6902;
UP THE LINE (N) BB 1680, 1969; 23445; BBDR 27388;
SUNDANCE AND OTHER S. F. STORIES (C9) Nelson 1974;
UNFAMILIAR TERRIRORY (C14) Scrib 1973;
VALLEY BEYOND TIME (C4) Dell 9249, 1973;

WORLDS FAIR 1992 (N) Follett 1970; (rewritten from Regan's Planet);
THE WORLD INSIDE (N) Dday 1971; SFBC; Sig Q5176;

AS CALVIN M. KNOX

LEST WE FORGET THEE EARTH (N) Ace D+291, 1958;
ONE OF OUR ASTEROIDS IS MISSING (N) Ace F+253, 1964;
THE PLOT AGAINST EARTH (N) Ace D+358, 1959;

AS DAVID OSBORNE

ALIENS FROM SPACE (N) Avalon 1958;
INVISIBLE BARRIERS (N) Avalon 1958;

AS IVAR JORGENSON

STARHAVEN (N) Avalon 1958; Ace D+351;

JUVENILES

ACROSS A BILLION YEARS (JN) Dial 1969;
THE CALIBRATED ALLIGATOR (J) Holt 1969;
CONQUERORS FROM THE DARKNESS (JN) H-R-W 1965; Dell 1456;
THE GATE OF WORLDS (JN) H-R-W 1967;
LOST RACE OF MARS (JN) H-R-W 1959; SBS TX 535;
PLANET OF DEATH (JN) H-R-W 1967;
REVOLT ON ALPHA C (JN) Crowell 1955; SBS TX137;
STARMAN'S QUEST (JN) Gnome 1958; Meredith 1969;
THREE SURVIVED (JN) Holt 1969;
TIME OF THE GREAT FREEZE (JN) H-R-W 1964; Dell 8922;

SIMAK, CLIFFORD

ALL FLESH IS GRASS (N) Dday 1965; Berk X1312; 2430;
ALL THE TRAPS OF EARTH (C9) Dday 1962; SFBC; (C6) MB 50-165; 50-388; 95-315;
BEST S. F. STORIES OF CLIFFORD SIMAK (C7) Dday 1971; SFBC; WPBL 65-808;
CEMETERY WORLD (N) Putnam 1973; SFBC; Berk 2626; D3301;
A CHOICE OF GODS (N) Putnam 1972; SFBC; Berk S2412; 3415;
CITY (S8) Gnome 1952; Perm 264; Ace D-283; H-30; 10620;
COSMIC ENGINEERS (N) Gnome 1950; PBL 52-506; 52-498; 63-133; 63432;
THE CREATOR (S) Crawford pb 1946;
DESTINY DOLL (N) Putnam 1971; Berk S2103; Z2996;
EMPIRE (N) Galaxy 7, 1951;
ENCHANTED PILGRIMAGE (N) Berk/Put 1975; SFBC; Berk Z2987;
THE GOBLIN RESERVATION (N) Putnam 1968; Berk S1671; 3399;
MASTODONIA (N) Del Rey 1978; SFBC;
OUR CHILDREN'S CHILDREN (N) Putnam 1974; Berk N2759;
OUT OF THEIR MINDS (N) Putnam 1970; Berk S1879; Z2997;
RING AROUND THE SUN (N) S&S 1953; SFBC; Ace D+61; D-339; Avon S270; V2317;
SHAKESPEARE'S PLANET (N) Berk/Put 1976; SFBC; Berk 3394;
SKIRMISH (C10) Berk/Put 1977;
SO BRIGHT THE VISION (C4) Ace H+95, 1968; +51905; 77220;
STRANGERS IN THE UNIVERSE (C11) S&S 1956; SFBC; (C7) Berk G-71; F835; X1589;
THEY WALKED LIKE MEN (N) Dday 1962; SFBC; M-B 50-184; 50-381; Manor 95-390;
TIME AND AGAIN (N) S&S 1951; (=) Ace F-239; 81000;
= FIRST HE DIED (N) Dell 680; 1953;
TIME IS THE SIMPLEST THING (N) Dday 1961; SFBC; Crst d547; d752; Leis LB 198NK; 480DK;

THE TROUBLE WITH TYCHO (N) Ace D+517, 1961; 82442;
WAY STATION (N) Dday 1963; SFBC; M-B 60-198; 60-397; Man 95-270; 12285;
THE WEREWOLF PRINCIPLE (N) Putnam 1967; SFBC; Berk S1463;
WHY CALL THEM BACK FROM HEAVEN (N) Dday 1967; SFBC; Ace H-42; 88601;
THE WORLDS OF CLIFFORD SIMAK (C12) S&S 1960; SFBC; (C6) Avon G1096;
=& OTHER WORLDS OF SIMAK (C6) Avon G1124;
WORLDS WITHOUT END (C3) Belm 92-584, 1964; 50-791;
A HERITAGE OF STARS (N) Berk/Put 1977; SFBC; Berk 03773;

SINCLAIR, ANDREW

GOG (N) Macmil 1967; Avon N208;
THE PROJECT (N) S&S 1960;

SINGER, JUDITH

THRESHOLD (N) Bant Q8186, 1975;

SIROTA, MIKE

DANNUS SERIES
THE PRISONER OF REGAATHIUM (N) Manor 22122, 1978;

SIODMAK, CURT

DR. PATRICK CORY
DONOVAN'S BRAIN (N) Knopf 1942; Mercury 87; Bant 819; Pop G560; Berk X1716;
HAUSER'S MEMORY (N) Putnam 1968; SFBC; Berk X1649;

CITY IN THE SKY (N) Putnam 1974; Pinn 582;
F.P. 1 DOES NOT REPLY (N) Little-B 1933;
RIDERS TO THE STARS (N) BB 58, 1954; (from screenplay-novel by R. Smith)
SKYPORT (N) Crown 1959; Signet S1939;
THE THIRD EAR (N) Putnam 1971; SFBC; Pinn 345;

SKINKLE, DOROTHY E.

STAR GIANT (N) Tower 43-275, 1969;

SKY, KATHLEEN Married to STEPHEN GOLDIN

BIRTHRIGHT (N) Laser 14, 1975;
ICE PRISON (N) Laser 38, 1976;

SLADEK, JOHN

MECHASM (N) Ace 71435, 1969;
= THE REPRODUCTIVE SYSTEM (N) Avon E 20917, 1974;
THE MULLER-FOKKER EFFECT (N) Morrow 1971; Poc 77622;

SLATER, HENRY J.

SHIP OF DESTINY (N) Crowell 1952;

SLEATOR, WILLIAM

HOUSE OF STAIRS (N) Dutton 1974, Avon 25510;

SLESAR, HENRY

20 MILLION MILES TO EARTH (N) Amazing S.F. Novel, pb 1953;

SLOANE, WILLIAM M. III

THE EDGE OF RUNNING WATER (N) Farrar & R 1939; World 1945; Dodd-M 1954; SFBC;
= THE UNQUIET CORPSE (N) Dell 928; 1956;
TO WALK THE NIGHT (N) Farrar & R 1937; Dodd Mead 1954; Penquin 550; Dell 856; Bant H3426;
BOTH= THE RIM OF MORNING (2N) Dodd-Mead 1964;

SMITH, ARTHUR D. HOWDEN

GREY MAIDEN (N) Longmans Green 1929; Centaur 1974;

SMITH, CLARK ASHTON (Partial Listing)

IMMORTALS OF MERCURY (S) Stellar 16, 1932;
HYPERBORIA (C15) BBAF 2206, 1971;
POSEIDONIS (C22) BBAF 3353, 1973;
XICCARPH (C10) BBAF 2501, 1972;
ZOTHIQUE (C16) BBAF 1938, 1970;

SMITH, CORDWAINER = PAUL LINEBARGER

THE INSTRUMENTALITY
THE UNDERPEOPLE (N) Prmd1910, 1968;
SPACE LORDS (S5) Prmd R1183, 1965; X1911;
THE PLANET BUYER (N) Prmd R1084, 1964; V3969;
NORSTRILIA (2n+) BB 24366, 1975; (Planet Buyer + Underpeople +);

THE BEST OF CORDWAINER SMITH (C12) SFBC 1975; BB24581; BBDR 27202;
QUEST OF THE THREE WORLDS (C4) Ace F-402, 1966;
STARDREAMER (C8) Begl 95127, 1971;
YOU WILL NEVER BE THE SAME (C8) Regency RB 309, 1963; Berk S1894; Garland 1976;

SMITH, DAVID C.

(Characters created by R E Howard)
THE WITCH OF THE INDIES (N) Zebra 267, 1977; (Black Vulmea Series)
FOR THE WITCH OF THE MISTS (N)(with R. Tierney) Zebra 313, 1978; (Bran Mac Morn)
ORON (N) Zebra 358, 1978;(fc 8/78)

SMITH, E. E. 'DOC' = EDWARD ELMER SMITH

LENSMAN SERIES
TRIPLANETARY (N) Fantasy 1948; Prmd R1222; X1455; T2174; N2890;
FIRST LENSMAN (N) Fantasy 1950; Prmd R1114; X1456; T2172; N2925;
GALACTIC PATROL (N) Fantasy 1950; Fantasy GSFL 3; Prmd X1457; T2176; N3084;
GRAY LENSMAN (N) Fantasy 1951; Prmd X1245; T2199; N3120;
SECOND STAGE LENSMEN (N) Fantasy 1953; Prmd R1262; T2159; N3172;
CHILDREN OF THE LENS (N) Fantasy 1954; Prmd R1294; T2195; N3251;
THE VORTEX BLASTER (N) Fantasy-Gnome 1960;
= MASTERS OF THE VORTEX (N) Prmd X1851; T2230; V3000;
SKYLARK SERIES
THE SKYLARK OF SPACE (N) Buffalo 1946; Hadley; FFF; Prmd G332; F764; R1350; T2232; N2969; Garland 1975;

SKYLARK THREE (N) Fantasy 1948; Prmd F924; X1459; T2233; N3160; Garland 1975;
SKYLARK OF VALERON (N) Fantasy 1949; Prmd F948; X1458; T2237; V3022; Garland 1975;
SKYLARK DUQUESNE (N) Prmd X1539, 1966; T2238; N3050; Garland 1975;

THE GALAXY PRIMES (N) Ace F-328, 1965; 27291;
SPACEHOUNDS OF IPC (N) Fantasy 1947; Ace F-372; Prmd T2618; N3300;
SUBSPACE EXPLORERS (N) Canaveral 1965; Ace H-102; 79070;

FAMILY D'ALEMBERT SERIES (Sequels by S Goldin)
IMPERIAL STARS (N) (with Steve Goldin) Prmd V3839, 1976;
STRANGLER'S MOON (N) Prmd V4002, 1976;
THE CLOCKWORK TRAITOR (N) Prmd V4003, 1977;
GETAWAY WORLD (N) Prmd V4004, 1977;
APPOINTMENT AT BLOODSTAR (N) Jove 04005, 1978;

SMITH, EVELYN E.

THE PERFECT PLANET (N) Avalon 1962; Lanc 72-679;
UNPOPULAR PLANET (N) Dell 6153, 1975;

SMITH, G. H. = GEORGE HENRY SMITH

THE COMING OF THE RATS (N) Pike 203 1961;
DOOMSDAY WING (N) Mon 388, 1963;
DRUIDS WORLD (N) Avalon 1967;
THE FORGOTTEN PLANET (N) Avalon 1965;
THE FOUR DAY WEEKEND (N) Belm B50-699, 1966;
KAR KABALLA (N) Ace 42900, 1969;
THE SECOND WAR OF THE WORLDS (N) DAW 215, 1976;
1976 THE YEAR OF TERROR (N) Epic 103, 1961;
THE UNENDING NIGHT (N) Mon 464, 1964;
WITCH QUEEN OF LOCHLANN (N) Sig P4098, 1969;
THE ISLAND SNATCHERS (N) Daw 298, 1978; (fc 7/78)

SMITH, GEORGE OLIVER

FIRE IN THE HEAVENS (N) Avalon 1958; Ace D+375;
THE FOURTH R (N) BB 316K, 1959;
= THE BRAIN MACHINE (N) Lanc 74-936, 1968; Garland 1976;
HELLFLOWER (N) Abelard 1953; Prmd G298; X1957;
HIGHWAYS IN HIDING (N) Gnome 1955; (=); Lanc 73-636;
= SPACE PLAGUE (N) Avon T180, 1957; G1154;
LOST IN SPACE (N) Avalon 1959; Ace D+431;
NOMAD (N) Prime 1950;
OPERATION INTERSTELLAR (N) Century B-10; 1950;
THE PATH OF UNREASON (N) Gnome 1958; BB 24613;
PATTERN FOR CONQUEST (N) Gnome 1949; Gnome pb;
TROUBLED STAR (N) Avalon 1957; Galaxy 256;
VENUS EQUILATERAL (S10) Prime 1947; Prmd T1724; Garland 1976;
=+ THE COMPLETE VENUS EQUILATERAL (S13) BB 25551; 1976;

SMITH, H. ALLEN

THE AGE OF THE TAIL (N) Little-B. 1955; G+D 1956; Bant 1541;

SMITH, MARTIN

THE INDIANS WON (N) Belm B95-2045, 1970;

SMITH, PERRY MICHAEL

LAST RITES (N) Scrib 1971; Lanc 78716;

SMITH, WILBURN

THE SUNBIRD (N) Dday 1973; Sig J5973;

SNYDER, CECIL III

THE HAWKS OF ARCTURUS (N) DAW 103, 1974;

SNYDER, GUY

TESTAMENT XXI (N) DAW 64, 1973;

SOHL, JERRY

THE ALTERED EGO (N) Rinehart 1954; SFBC; Bant P-75;
THE ANOMALY (N) Curt 7151, 1971;
COSTIGAN'S NEEDLE (N) Rinehart 1953; SFBC; Bant 1278; Avon S349;
THE HAPLOIDS (N) Rinehart 1952; Lion 118;
I, ALEPPO (N) Laser 35, 1976;
THE MARS MONOPLY (N) Ace D+162, 1956;
NIGHT SLAVES (N) G-M d1561, 1965;
THE ODIOUS ONES (N) Rinehart 1959;
ONE AGAINST HERCULUM (N) Ace D+381, 1959;
POINT ULTIMATE (N) Rinehart 1955; SFBC; Bant A1952;
THE TIME DISSOLVER (N) Avon T186, 1957;
THE TRANSCENDENT MAN (N) Rinehart 1953; Bant A1971;

SOMERS, BART = GARDNER F. FOX

SOUTHWELL, SAMUEL

IF ALL THE REBELS DIE (N) Dday 1966; Avon N189

SOUZA, STEVEN M.

THE ESPERS (N) Lenox Hill, 1972;

SPIELBERG, STEPHEN

CLOSE ENCOUNTERS OF THE THIRD KIND (N) Delacorte 1977; Dell 11433;

SPINRAD, NORMAN

AGENT OF CHAOS (N) Belm 50-739, 1967; BT 40125; 75-2003; Unibook; Pop 04164;
BUG JACK BARRON (N) Walker 1969; Avon N206; 14365;
THE IRON DREAM (N) Avon N448, 1972; E 22509; Gregg 1977;
THE LAST HURRAH OF THE GOLDEN HORDE (C18) SFBC; 1970; Avon V2368;
THE MEN IN THE JUNGLE (N) Dday 1967; Avon N228; Leis LB454KK;
NO DIRECTION HOME (C11) Poc 78887, 1975;

RIDING THE TORCH (NA) Dell +10564, 1978; (fc 8/78)
THE SOLARIANS (N) PBL 52-985, 1966; B-T 50296; Leis LB 327;

SPRINGER, NANCY

THE BOOK OF SUNS (N) Poc 80920, 1977;

SPRUILL, STEPHEN G.

KEEPERS OF THE GATE (N) Dday 1977; Dell 14441;
THE PSYCHOPATH PLAGUE (N) Dday 1978;

STABLEFORD, BRIAN M.

DIES IRAE SERIES
THE DAYS OF GLORY (N) Ace 14000, 1971;
IN THE KINGDOM OF THE BEASTS (N) Ace 37106, 1971;
DAY OF WRATH (N) Ace 13972, 1971;

STAR PILOT GRAINGER
THE HALYCON DRIFT (N) DAW 32, 1972;
RHAPSODY IN BLACK (N) DAW 59, 1973;
PROMISED LAND (N) DAW 92, 1973;
THE PARADISE GAME (N) DAW 111, 1974;
THE FENRIS DEVICE (N) DAW 130, 1974;
SWAN SONG (N) Daw 149, 1975;

DAEDALUS
THE FLORIANS (N) DAW 211, 1976;
CRITICAL THRESHOLD (N) DAW 230, 1977;
WILDEBOODS EMPIRE (N) Daw 263, 1977;
THE CITY OF THE SUN (N) Daw 289, 1978;

THE BLIND WORM (N) ACE +06707, 1970;
CRADLE IN THE SUN (N) ACE +12140, 1969;
THE MIND—RIDERS (N) DAW 194, 1976;
TO CHALLENGE CHAOS (N) DAW 7, 1972;
MAN IN A CAGE (N) Dday 1976;
THE REALMS OF TARTARUS (N) DAW 248, 1977;

STANBURY, C. M.

ANTIMATER (N) Dustbook 1977;

STANLEY, JOHN

WORLD WAR III (N) Avon 26872, 1975;

STANTON, PAUL

VILLAGE OF STARS (N) Mills 1960; Perm M4230; (Borderline)

STAPLEDON, OLAF

LAST AND FIRST MEN (N) Cape & Smith 1931; Dover + T 1962;
LAST MEN IN LONDON (N) Penguin 3506, 1974; Gregg 1976;

ODD JOHN (N) Dutton 1936; GALX 8; 236; Berk F 1128; Dover +21133; Garland 1976;
SIRIUS (N) Dover +21133; Penguin 1999, 1974;
THE STARMAKER (N) Berk F563; Dover + T 1962; Penguin 3541;
DARKNESS & THE LIGHT (C2) Hyperion 1974;
WORLDS OF WONDER (C3) FPCI 1949;
TO THE END OF TIME (C5) Funk & W 1953; Gregg 1975;
= LAST & FIRST MEN, STARMAKER, ODD JOHN, THE FLAMES & SIRIUS

STARR, BILL

FARSTAR & SON
THE WAY TO DAWNWORLD (N) BB24643, 1976;
THE TREASURE OF WONDERWHAT (N) BB25157, 1976;

STARR, ROLAND

OPERATION OMINA (N) Lenox Hill, 1970;

STASHEFF, CHRISTOPHER

ROD GALLOWGLASS SERIES
THE WARLOCK IN SPITE OF HIMSELF (N) Ace 87300, 1969; Garland 1976;
KING KOBOLD (N) Ace 44485, 1971;

STATON, MARY

FROM THE LEGEND OF BIEL (N) Ace 25461, 1975;

STERLING, BRETT - See E. HAMILTON

STERLING, BRUCE

INVOLUTION OCEAN (N) Jove 04301, 1978;

STERN, STUART

THE MINO TOUR FACTOR (N) Playboy 1977;

STERNBERG, JACQUES

FUTURE WITHOUT FUTURE (C5) Seabury 1973;

STEVENS, FRANCIS = GERTRUDE BENNETT

CLAIMED (N) Avalon 1966;
THE CITADEL OF FEAR (N) PBL 65-401, 1970;
THE HEADS OF CERBERUS (N) Polaris 1952;

STEWART, FRED MUSTARD

THE METHUSELAH ENZYME (N) Arbor 1970; BC; Bant T6532;
STARCHILD (N) Arbor 1974; Bant X2101;

STEWART, GEORGE R.

EARTH ABIDES (N) Random 1949; Ace K-154; Crst M1551; (Hermes 1974); Crest 3252;

STEWART, WILL = JACK WILLIAMSON

STILSON, CHARLES B.

SERIES

POLARIS OF THE SNOWS (N) Avalon 1965;
MINOS OF SARDANES (N) Avalon 1966;
POLARIS AND THE IMMORTALS (N) Avalon 1968;

STOCTON, FRANK R.

THE GREAT STONE OF SARDIS (N) Harper 1898; BT 51103;

STONE, ALMA

THE BANISHMENT AND 3 STORIES (N+3) Dday 1973;

STONE, GEORGE

BLIZZARD (N) G&D 1977;
A LEGEND OF WOLF STONE (N) Dell 47322, 1976;

STONE, LESLIE F. = MRS. WILLIAM SILVERBERG

OUT OF THE VOID (N) Avalon 1967;
WHEN THE SUN WENT OUT (S) Stellar 4, 1930;

STRETE, CRAIG

THE BLEEDING MAN (C6) Greenwillow 1977;

STRICKGOLD, BOB

GLORY HITS (N) (with M. Noble) Del Rey 1978;

STRIKE, JEREMY

A PROMISING PLANET (N) Ace +24100, 1970;

STRUGATSKY, ARKADY & BORIS

DEFINITELY MAYBE (N) Macmil 1978;
THE FINAL CIRCLE OF PARADISE (N) Daw 218, 1976;
HARD TO BE A GOD (N) Seabury 1973; DAW 126;
MONDAY BEGINS ON SATURDAY (N) Daw 265, 1977;
PRISONERS OF POWER (N) Macmil 1977;
ROADSIDE PICNIC & TALE OF THE TROIKA (2N) MacMil 1977; Poc 81976, 1978;

STUART, W. J.

FORBIDDEN PLANET (N) F-S&C 1956; Bant A1443; PBL 52-572; Gregg 1978;

STURGEON, THEODORE

ALIENS 4 (C4) Avon T304, 1959; V2363;
..AND MY FEAR IS GREAT AND BABY IS THREE (2N) Magabook 3, 1963;
BEYOND (C6) Avon T439, 1960; V2349;
CASE AND THE DREAMER (C3) SFBC; 1974; Sig Q 6074; W7933;
CAVIAR (C8) BBHC 1955; BB F119; F562; 1829; BBDR 25783;
THE COSMIC RAPE (N) Dell B120, 1958; 1512; Gregg 1977; Poc 81414;
THE DREAMING JEWELS (N) Greenberg 1950; Dell 1980
= THE SYNTHETIC MAN (N) Prmd G247, 1957; G636; R1126; X1691; X2007; N3344;
IT (S) Prime pb 1948;

E PLURIBUS UNICORN (C13) Abelard 1953; BB179; U2247; 1827; Poc 81355;
MORE THAN HUMAN (S3) F-S&Y 1953; BB 46; 462; U2231; 72009; 1828; 2199; 2756; 22756; 24389; Garland 1975; SFBC;
SOME OF YOUR BLOOD (N) BB 458K, 1961; U2253; 25712; (Marginal)
STARSHINE (C6) Prmd X1543, 1966; X1977; T2658; Jove A4454;
STURGEON IN ORBIT (C5) Prmd F974, 1964; Jove 04477;
STURGEON IS ALIVE AND WELL (C12) Putnam 1971; SFBC; Berk S2045; Poc 81415;
A TOUCH OF STRANGE (C9) Dday 1958; SFBC; Berk G280; F1058; N1830; Daw 286;
VENUS PLUS X (N) Prmd G544, 1960; F732; X1773; T2134; T2552; Gregg 1976;
VOYAGE TO THE BOTTOM OF THE SEA (N) Prmd G622, 1961; R1068;
A WAY HOME (C11) F&W 1955; (C9) Prmd G184; F673; X1739; X2030; Jove 04467;
WITHOUT SORCERY (C13) Prime 1948;
= NOT WITHOUT SORCERY (C8) BB 506K, 1961; 24664;
THE WORLDS OF THEODORE STURGEON (C9) Ace 91060, 1972;

SUDAK, EUNICE

X (N) Lancer 70-052, 1963;

SUTHERLAND, JAMES

STORMTRACK (N) Prmd N 3297, 1974;

SUTTON, JEFF - MARRIED TO JEAN SUTTON

ALIEN FROM THE STARS (JN) Put 1970 (with Jean Sutton)
ALTON'S UNGUESSABLE (N) Ace +76096, 1970;
APOLLO AT GO (N) Putnam 1963; SFBC; Pop SP305; 2525;
THE ATOM CONSPIRACY (N) Avalon 1963; Ace F-374;
THE BEYOND (JN) (with Jean Sutton) Putnam 1967;
BEYOND APOLLO (JN) Putnam 1966;
BOMBS IN ORBIT (N) Ace D-377, 1959;
THE BOY WHO HAD THE POWER (JN) Putnam 1971; (with Jean Sutton)
FIRST ON THE MOON (N) Ace D-327, 1958; F-222;
H-BOMB OVER AMERICA (N) Ace H-18, 1967;
LORD OF THE STARS (JN) (with Jean Sutton) Putnam 1969;
THE MAN WHO SAW TOMORROW (N) Ace H+95, 1968;
THE MINDBLOCKED MAN (N) DAW 8, 1972;
THE PROGRAMED MAN (JN) (with Jean Sutton) Putnam 1968;
SPACEHIVE (N) Ace D-478, 1960;
WHISPER FROM THE STARS (N) Dell 9520, 1960;

SUTTON, HENRY = DAVID R. SLAVITT

VECTOR (N) Geis 1970; Dell 9388,

SWAIN, DWIGHT V.

THE TRANSPOSED MAN (N) Ace D+113, 1955;

SWANN, INGO

STAR FIRE (N) Dell 18219, 1978;

SWANN, THOMAS BURNETT

MELLONIA SERIES
GREEN PHOENIX (N) DAW 27, 1972; UY1222;
LADY OF THE BEES (N) Ace 46850, 1976;
*= WHERE IS THE BIRD OF FIRE (N+2) Ace 88270, 1970;

CRY SILVER BELLS (N) Daw 270, 1977;
DAY OF THE MINOTAUR (N) Ace F-407, 1966; 13921;
THE DOLPHIN AND THE DEEP (C3) Ace G-694, 1968;
THE FOREST OF FOREVER (N) Ace 24650, 1971;
THE GOAT WITHOUT HORNS (N) BB 2395, 1971;
THE GODS ABIDE (N) DAW 222, 1976;
HOW ARE THE MIGHTY FALLEN (N) DAW 94, 1974;
THE MINIKINS OF YAM (N) DAW 182, 1976;
MOONDUST (N) Ace G-758, 1968; 54201;
THE NOT-WORLD (N) DAW 140, 1975;
QUEENS WALK IN THE DUSK (N) Heritage 1976;
THE TOURNAMENT OF THORNS (N) Ace 81900, 1976;
THE WEIRWOODS (N) Ace G-640, 1967; 87941;
WOLFWINTER (N) BB 2905, 1972;

SZILARD, LEO

THE VOICE OF THE DOLPHINS (C6) S&S 1961;

T

TABORI, PAUL = PAUL TABOR

THE CLEFT (N) Byramid X1940, 1969;
THE DEMONS OF SANDORA(N) Award AS716, 1970;
THE GREEN RAIN (N) Pyramid G624, 1961; R1152; X1941;
THE TORTURE MACHINE (N) Pyramid X2057, 1969;

TAINE, JOHN = ERIC TEMPLE BELL

THE COSMIC GEOIDS (N+1) FPCI 1949; FPCI pb;
THE CRYSTRAL HORDE (N) Fantasy 1952;
= WHITE LILY (N) Dover T+1626, 1966;
THE FORBIDDEN GARDEN (N) Fantasy 1947;
G. O. G. 666 (N) Fantasy 1954;
THE GREATEST ADVENTURE (N) Dutton 1929; Ace D-473; Dover T+1180;
GREEN FIRE (N) Dutton 1928; FPCI 1952;
THE IRON STAR (N) Dutton 1930; FPCI 1952; Hyperion 1976;
SEEDS OF LIFE (N) Fantasy 1951; Galaxy 13; Dover T+1626;
THE TIME STREAM (N) Buffalo 1946; Dover T+1180; Garland 1976;
BEFORE THE DAWN (N) Williams and Wilkins, 1934;
THE GOLD TOOTH (N) Dutton 1927; Burr 1929;

QUAYLE'S INVENTION (N) Dutton 1927;
THE PURPLE SAPPHIRE (N) Dutton 1924; Dover T+1180;

TALL, STEPHEN = COMPTON N. CROOK

STARDUST SERIES

THE STARDUST VOYAGES (S6) Berk N2972, 1975;
THE RAMSGATE PARADOX (N) Berk Z3186, 1976;

TATE, PETER

COUNTRY LOVE AND POISON RAIN (N) Dday 1973;
FACES IN THE FLAMES (N) Dday 1976;
GARDENS ONE TO FIVE (N) Dday 1971;
MOON ON AN IRON MEADOW (N) Dday 1974;
SEAGULLS UNDER GLASS (C12) Dday 1975;
THE THINKING SEAT (N) Dday 1969; Curt 7208;

TAYLOR, ROBERT LEWIS

ADRIFT IN A BONE YARD (N) Dday 1947; Avon G1132;

TEMPLE, WILLIAM

THE AUTOMATED GOLIATH (N) Ace F+129, 1962;
BATTLE ON VENUS (N) Ace F+195, 1963; + 76380;
FOUR SIDED TRIANGLE (N) Fell 1951; Galaxy 9;
SHOOT AT THE MOON (N) S&S 1966; SFBC; M-B 60-239; 75-356;
THE THREE SUNS OF AMARA (N) Ace F+129, 1962; +76380;

TENN, WILLIAM = PHILLIP KLASS

THE HUMAN ANGLE (C8) BBHC 1956; BB 159; U2190; U6135;
A LAMP FOR MEDUSA (N) Belm B60+077, 1968;
OF ALL POSSIBLE WORLDS (C7) BBHC 1955; BB 99; 407K; U6136;
OF MEN AND MONSTERS (N) BB U6131, 1968; Walker 1969; BB24884;
THE SEVEN SEXES (C8) BB U6134, 1968;
THE SQUARE ROOT OF MAN (C9) BB U6132, 1968;
TIME IN ADVANCE (C4) Bant A1786, 1958;
THE WOODEN STAR (C11) BB U6133, 1968;

TERRAL, ROBERT

A KILLER IS LOOSE AMONG US (N) Duell-Sloane & Pearce, 1948;

TEVIS, WALTER

THE MAN WHO FELL TO EARTH (N) GM K 1276, 1963; Lanc 74650; Avon 27276;

THEOBOLD, ROBERT & SCOTT J. M.

TEG'S 1994 (N) Swallow 1972; Warn 76-150;

THOMAS, DAN = LEONARD M. SANDERS, JR.

THE SEED (N) BB U6115, 1968;

THOMAS, MARTIN = THOMAS A. MARTIN also Peter Saxon

BEYOND THE SPECTRUM (N) 52-554, 1967;

THOMAS, THEODORE

THE CLONE (N) (with K. Wilhelm) Berk F1169, 1965;
THE YEAR OF THE CLOUD (N) (with K. Wilhelm) Dday 1970; SFBC; Play 16150;

THOMPSON, HARLAN

SILENT RUNNING (N) SBS TK 2227, 1972; (Movie tie-in);

THOMPSON, JOYCE

THE BLUE CHAIR (N) Avon 33241, 1977;

TIERNEY, RICHARD

See D.C. SMITH
See ROBERT E. HOWARD

TILLEY, PATRICK

FADE-OUT (N) Morrow 1975; Dell 12232;

TIMLETT, PETER VALENTINE

SEEDBEARERS
THE POWER OF THE SERPENT (N) Bant 2370, 1976;
THE SEEDBEARERS (N) BantT2570, 1976;
TWILIGHT OF THE SERPENT (N) Bant 10081, 1977;

TIPTREE, JAMES JR. = ALICE SHELDON

TEN THOUSAND LIGHT-YEARS FROM HOME (C15) Ace 80180, 1973; Gregg 1976; Ace 80181;
UP THE WALLS OF THE WORLD (N) Berk/Put 1978; SFBC;
STAR SONGS OF AN OLD PRIMATE (C7) BBDR 25417, 1978;
WARM WORLDS AND OTHERWISE (C12) BB 24380, 1975;

TOFTE, ARTHUR

CRASH LANDING ON IDUNA (N) Laser 3, 1975;
SURVIVAL PLANET (N) Bobbs-M 1977;
WALLS WITHIN WALLS (N) Laser 5, 1975;

TOLKIEN, JOHN RONALD REVEL

LORD OF THE RINGS
THE FELLOWSHIP OF THE RING (N) Houghton-M, 1954; Ace A-3; BBu7040; 1533; 21533; 23509;; 25343;
THE TWO TOWERS (N) Houghton-M 1955; Ace A-4; BBU7041; 1534; 21534; 23510; 25344;
THE RETURN OF THE KING (N) Houghton M 1956; Ace A-5; BBU7042; 1535;) 21535; 23511; 25345;

FARMER GILES OF HAM (N) Houghton-M 1950;
THE HOBBIT (N) Houghton-M 1938; BBU7039; 1532; 21532; 23512; 24826; 25342; Abrams
THE TOLKIEN READER (C4) BBU7038, 1966; 1536; 21536; 24070; 25585;
SMITH OF WOOTAN MAJOR AND FARMET GILES OF HAM (2N) Houghton-M 1967; BB1538, 21538;; 24564;
THE SILMARILLION (N+C4) Houghton-M 1977;

TOMAS, ANDREW

ON THE SHORES OF ENDLESS WORLDS (N) Putnam 1974;

TOOMEY, ROBERT E. JR.

A WORLD OF TROUBLE (N) BB 3262, 1973;

TORRO, PEL See R.L. FANTHORPE

TRAIN, ARTHUR & WOOD, ROBERT W.

THE MAN WHO ROCKED THE EARTH (N) Dday 1915;
THE MOON MAKER (N) Krueger 1958; Dawn Press;

TRALINS, ROBERT

ANDROID ARMAGEDDON (N) Pinn 513, 1974;
THE COSMOZOIDS (N) Belm B50-692, 1966; Tower T060-5;

TRANSUE, JACOB = JOAN MATHESON

TWILIGHT OF THE BASILISKS (N) Berk N2476, 1973;

TREECE, HENRY

THE GREEN MAN (N) Putnam 1966; PBL 55-752;
GOLDEN STRANGERS (N) Random 1956;
= THE INVADERS (N) Avon T400, 1960;
JASON (N) Random 1961; Sig T2165; PBL 65-064;

TREIBICH, S. J. See L. JANIFER co-author

TRIMBLE, LOUIS

ANTHROPOL (N) Ace H+59, 1968; +81150;
THE BODELAN WAY (N) DAW 86, 1974;
THE CITY MACHINE (N) DAW 24, 1972;
GUARDIANS OF THE GATE (N) (with J. Trimble) Ace 30590, 1972;
THE NOBLEST EXPERIMENT IN THE GALAXY (N) Ace +11560, 1970;
THE WANDERING VARIABLES (N) DAW 34, 1972;

TROUT, KILGORE See P.J. FARMER

TUBB, E. C. also GREGORY KERN

DUMAREST OF TERRA
THE WINDS OF GATH (N) Ace H+27, 1967; + 89301;

DERAI (N) Ace H+77, 1968; +14260; +89301;
TOYMAN (N) Ace +23140, 1969;
KALIN (N) Ace +42800, 1969; 42801;
THE JESTER AT SCAR (N) Ace +81670, 1970;
LALLIA (N) Ace +71082, 1971;
TECHNOS (N) Ace +79975, 1972;
VERUCHIA (N) Ace 86180, 1973;
MAYENNE (N) DAW 54, 1973;
JONDELLE (N) DAW 74, 1973;
ZENYA (N) DAW 115, 1974;
ELOISE (N) DAW 143, 1975;
EYE OF THE ZODIAC (N) DAW 163, 1975;
JACK OF SWORDS (N) DAW 198, 1976;
SPECTRUM OF A FORGOTTEN SUN (N) DAW 219, 1976;
HAVEN OF DARKNESS (N) DAW 242, 1977;
PRISON OF NIGHT (N) Daw 271, 1977;
INCIDENT ON ATH (N) Daw 299, 1978;(fc 7/78)

ALIEN DUST (N) Avalon 1957;
CENTURY OF THE MANIKIN (N) DAW 18, 1972;
C. O. D. MARS (N) Ace H+40, 1968; +11500;
DEATH IS A DREAM (N) Ace H+34, 1967;
THE MECHANICAL MONARCH (N) Ace D+266, 1958;
MOON BASE (N) Ace F-293, 1964;
A SCATTER OF STARDUST (C8) Ace +79975, 1972;
S. T. A. R. FLIGHT (N) PBL 62-009, 1969; Warn 75-461;
THE SPACE BORN (N) Ace D+193, 1956; Avon E26260;

SEE ALSO CAP KENNEDY SERIES (as Gregory Kern)
SEE ALSO SPACE 1999 SERIES

TUCKER, WILSON =ARTHUR WILSON TUCKER also BOB TUCKER

THE CITY IN THE SEA (N) Rinehart 1951; Galx 11, 1952;
ICE AND IRON (N) Dday 1974; SFBC; (rev)BB 24660;
THE LINCOLN HUNTERS (N) Rinehart 1958; SFBC; Ace H-62; 48421;
THE LONG LOUD SILENCE (N) Rinehart 1952; SFBC; Dell 791; Lanc 74-600;
THE SCIENCE FICTION SUBTREASURY (C11) Rinehart 1954;
= TIME: X (C10) Bant 1400, 1955;
THE TIME MASTERS (N) Rinehart 1953; Sig 1127; Rev. SFBC; Lancer 75-290;
TIME BOMB (N) Rinehart 1955; SFBC;
= TOMORROW PLUS X (N) Avon T168, 1957;
TO THE TOMBAUGH STATION (N) Ace D+479, 1960;
WILD TALENT (N) Rinehart 1954; SFBC; (=); Avon G1301;
= MAN FROM TOMORROW (N) Bant 1343, 1955;
THE YEAR OF THE QUIET SUN IN) Sce 94200, 1970;
THE WARLOCK (N) Avon V2829, 1970; Marginal;
THIS WITCH (N) Dday 1971; Marginal

TURNER, FREDERICK

A DOUBLE SHADOW (N) Berk/Put 1978;

TYLER, THEODORE = EDWARD WILLIAM ZIEGLER

THE MAN WHOSE NAME WOULDN'T FIT (N) Dday 1968; Curt 7020;

U

UTLEY, BRIAN R.

MARTYR (N) Curt 7150, 1971;

V

VALE, RENA

BEYOND THE SEALED WORLD (N) PBL 52-811, 1965; 52-651;
TAURUS FOUR (N) PBL 63-253, 1970;
THE DAY AFTER DOOMSDAY (N) PBL 63-479, 1970;

VAN ARNAM, DAVID with T. WHITE = RON ARCHER

JAMNAR

STAR BARBARIAN (N) Lancer 74-509, 1969;
LORD OF BLOOD (N) Lancer 74-688, 1970;

ZANTAIN

THE PLAYERS OF HELL (N) Belmont B60+077, 1967;
WIZARD OF STORMS (N) Belmont B75-2015, 1970;

GREYLAND (N) B-T 50295, 1972; Leis 553;
LOST IN SPACE (N) (as Archer) Pyramid X1679, 1967;
STAR GLADIATOR (N) Belmont B50+788, 1967;
STARMIND (N) BB 1626, 1969;

VAN HERCK, PAUL

WHERE WERE YOU LAST PLUTERDAY (N) DAW 51, 1973;

VAN LIHN, ERIC = LESTER DEL REY

VAN LUSTBADER, ERIC

SHALLOW'S OF NIGHT (N) Dday 1978; (fc 6/78)
THE SUNSET WARRIOR (N) Dday 1977;

VAN SCYOC, SYDNEY

ASSIGNMENT NOR'DYREN (N) Avon 17160, 1973;
SALTFLOWER (N) Avon V2386, 1971;
STARMOTHER (N) Berk/Put 1976, SFBC; Berk 3345;
CLOUD CRY (N) Berk/Put 1977; SFBC; Berk 03651;

VAN VOGT, A. E. - Married to E. Mayne Hull

GILBERT GOSSEYN
THE WORLD OF NULL-A (N) S&S 1948; G&D 1950; Ace D+31; F-295; Berk S1802; N2558; D3322;
THE PAWNS OF NULL-A (N) Ace D-187, 1956;
=THE PLAYERS OF NULL-A (N) BERK F1195, 1966; N2559; 3368; Gregg 1977;

CLANE
EMPIRE OF THE ATOM (N) Shasta 1957; SFBC; Ace D+242; M-B 60-267; 75-387; 95320 Manor
THE WIZARD OF LINN (N) Ace F-154; 1962; M-B 60-366; Manor 12344

WEAPON SHOP SERIES
THE WEAPON SHOPS OF ISHER (N) Greenburg 1951; Ace D+53; D-482; 87855; Poc 81354;
THE WEAPON MAKERS (N) Hadley 1946; Greenberg 1952; (=); Ace M-153;
=ONE AGAINST ETERNITY (N) Ace D+94, 1955;

THE ANARCHISTIC COLOSSUS (N) Ace 02255, 1977;
AWAY AND BEYOND (C9) P&C 1952; Avon 548; (C7) Berk G215; F812; Jove M4426;
THE BATTLE OF FOREVER (N) Ace 04860, 1971;
THE BEAST (N) Dday 1963; SFBC; M-B 60-169; 60-343; Manor 75-479; 95-399; 15265;
THE BEST OF A. E. VAN VOGT, (C11) Poc 80546, 1976;
THE BOOK OF VAN VOGT (C7) DAW 4, 1972;
THE BOOK OF PTATH (N) Fantasy 1947; = 63-092; Garland 1976;
=200 MILLION A.D. (N) PBL 52-304, 1964; 52-406; 62-718; Zebra 357; (fc 8/78)
= PTATH (N) Zebra 172, 1976;
THE CHANGLING (N) (in Masters of Time) 1950; M-B 50-335; 60-416; Manor 75-421; 95421
CHILDREN OF TOMORROW (N) Ace 10410, 1970;
THE DARKNESS ON DIAMONDIA (N) Ace 13798, 1972;
DESTINATION: UNIVERSE (C10) P&C 1952; Sig 1007; 1558; Berk F893; S1912; Jove 04412;
THE FAR OUT WORLDS OF A. E. VAN VOGT (C12) Ace H-92, 1968; 22810;
=+THE WORLDS OF A. E. VAN VOGT (C15) Ace 22812, 1974;
FUTURE GLITTER (N) Ace 25980, 1973;
THE HOUSE THAT STOOD STILL (N) Greenberg 1950; (=); PBL 52-873; 63-016; 64603;
=THE MATING CRY (N) Galx 298, 1960;
THE MAN WITH A THOUSAND NAMES (N) DAW 114, 1974; UY1202;
MASTERS OF TIME (N+1) Fantasy 1950; (=); M-B 50-334; 60-406; 75-520; Manor 95-417;
= EARTH'S LAST FORTRESS (N) Ace D+431, 1960;
THE MIND CAGE (N) S&S 1957; SFBC; Avon T252; Belm B75-1093; Towr 43-503; Poc 81770;
THE MIXED MEN (N) Gnome 1952; SFBC;
=MISSION TO THE STARS (N) Berk 344; 1955; F704; S1973; Poc 81451;
M-33 IN ANDROMEDA (C6) PBL 65-584, 1971;
MONSTERS (C8) PBL 52-515, 1965; 52-555; 63-406;
= THE BLAL (C8) Zebra 200, 1972;
MORE THAN SUPERHUMAN (C6) Dell 5815, 1971;
OUT OF THE UNKNOWN (C6) (with Hull) FPCI 1948; (C7) Powl PP128, 1969;

PLANETS FOR SALE (N) See Hull co-author
THE PROXY INTELLIGENCE & OTHER MIND BENDERS (C6) PBL 64-512, 1971;
QUEST FOR THE FUTURE (N) Ace 69700 1970; SFBC;
ROGUE SHIP (N) Dday 1965; SFBC; Berk F1292;
THE SECRET GALACTICS (N) Reward #1; 1974;
= EARTH FACTOR X (N) DAW 206, 1976;
THE SILKIE (N) Ace 76500, 1969;
SLAN (N) Arkham 1946; S&S 1951; Dell 696; BB 511K; Berk X1543; S1930; N 2900; 3552; Garland 1976 SFBC;
SIEGE OF THE UNSEEN (N) Ace D+391, 1959;
THE TWISTED MEN (C3) Ace F+253, 1964;
THE VOYAGE OF THE SPACE BEAGLE (N) S&S 1950; (=); M-B 60-146; 60-318; Manor 12345;
= MISSION: INTERPLANETARY (N) Sig 914, 1952;
THE UNIVERSE MAKER (N) Ace D+31, 1953; G-660; 85481;
THE WAR AGAINST THE RULL (N) S&S 1959; SFBC; Ace 87180; Poc M4263;
THE WINGED MAN (N) (with Hull) Dday 1966; Berk X1403; S1946;
THE GRYB (C6) Zebra 182, 1976;
SUPERMIND (N) DAW 224, 1977;
THE VIOLENT MAN (N) FS&C 1962; Avon N258; (Not S.F.)
TRIAD (3N) SFBC 1955; = World of Null A, Voyage of Space Beagle, and Slan;

VANCE, JACK = JOHN HOLBROOK VANCE

KIRTH GERSON
THE STAR KING (N) Berk F905, 1964;
THE KILLING MACHINE (N) Berk F1003, 1964;
THE PALACE OF LOVE (N) Berk X1454, 1967;

PLANET OF ADVENTURE
CITY OF THE CHASCH (N) Ace G-688, 1968; Miller-Underwood 1978; (fc)
SERVANTS OF THE WANKH (N) Ace 66900, 1969; Miller-Undewood 1978; (fc)
THE DIRDIR (N) Ace 66901, 1969; Miller-Underwood 1978; (fc)
THE PNUME (N) Ace 66902, 1970; Miller-Undewood 1978; (fc)

DURDANE
THE ANOME (N) Dell 0441, 1973;
=THE FACELESS MAN (N) Ace 22500, 1978; (fc 7/78)
THE BRAVE FREE MEN (N) Dell 1708, 1973;
THE ASUTRA (N) Dell 3157, 1974;

ALASTOR CLUSTER
TRULLION: ALASTOR 2262 (N) BB 3308, 1973;
THE GRAY PRINCE (N) Bobbs-M 1974; Avon 26799;
MARUNE: ALASTOR 933 (N) BB24518, 1975;

DYING EARTH (See also M. Shea)
THE DYING EARTH (S6) Hillman #41, 1950; Lanc 74-807, 1962; 74547; 75373; Underwood & Miller 1976; Pocket 81092;
THE EYES OF THE OVERWORLD (N) Ace M-149, 1966; Poc 80904; Gregg 1977; Underwood-Miller 1978;

THE BEST OF JACK VANCE (C6) Poc 80510, 1976;
BIG PLANET (N) Avalon 1957; Ace D+295; Ace G-661; 06170; 06171; Miller-Underwood
THE BLUE WORLD (N) BB U2169, 1966; BBDR 25784;

THE BRAINS OF EARTH (N) Ace M+141, 1966;
THE DRAGON MASTERS (N) Ace F+185, 1963; +16640; +16641; Gregg 1976;
EMPHYRIO (N) Dday 1969; Dell 2345;
EIGHT FANTASMS AND MAGICS (C8) Macmil 1969; Coll 2598;
THE SPACE PIRATE (N) Toby 1953; (Mag size paperback);
=FIVE GOLD BANDS (N) Ace F+185, 1963; +16640;
FUTURE TENSE (C4) BB U2214, 1964;
THE HOUSES OF ISZM (N) Ace F+265, 1964; +77525;
THE LANGUAGES OF PAO (N) Avalon 1957; Ace F-390; 47041;
THE LAST CASTLE (N) Ace H+21, 1967; +16641; 47071;
MASKE: THAERY (N) Berk/Put 1976; SFBC; Berk 3503;
THE MANY WORLDS OF MAGNUS RIDOLPH (S6) Ace+141, 1966;
MONSTERS IN ORBIT (N) Ace M+125, 1965;
SLAVES OF THE KLAU (N) Ace D+295; 1958;
SON OF THE TREE (N) Ace F+265, 1964; + 77525;
SHOWBOAT WORLD (N) Prmd V3698, 1975;
SPACE OPERA (N) Prmd R1140, 1965;
TO LIVE FOREVER (N) BBHC 1956; BB167; U2346; 25198;
VANDALS OF THE VOID (JN) Winston 1953;
THE WORLD BETWEEN AND OTHER STORIES (C5) Ace M+125, 1965;
THE WORLDS OF JACK VANCE (C9) Ace 90955, 1974;
THE DOGTOWN TOURIST AGENCY (N) (in Epoch Berk/Put 1975)

VANCE, STEVE

PLANET OF GAWFS (N) Leis 545, 1978;

VARLEY, JOHN

THE OPHIUCHI HOTLINE (N) Dial 1977; SFBC; Dell 15890;
THE PERSISTENCE OF VISION ( ) Dial 1978; SFBC

VERNE, JULES (Partial Listing)

CAPTAIN NEMO

TWENTY THOUSAND LEAGUES UNDER THE SEA (N) Smith 1873; Heritage 1957; Fitzroy 1960; Bant F2458; Air CL12; Bant HP84; HP4448; Lanc 14-608; Prmd X1409; Bant SP5939; N8569;

THE MYSTERIOUS ISLAND (N) Scribners 1876; Heritage 1959; Perm M6002; Air CL77; Bant SP5439; N8652;

BARSAC MISSION

INTO THE NIGER BEN (N) Fitzroy 1960; Ace H-41; 37110;
THE CITY IN THE SAHARA (N) Fitzroy 1960; Ace H-43; 10560;

CAPTAIN HATTERAS

AT THE NORTH POLE (N) Fitzroy 1960; Aeonian 1975;
THE WILDERNESS OF ICE (N) Fitzroy 1961;
=THE DESERT OF ICE (N) Aeonian 1975;
Both =THE ADVENTURES OF CAPTAIN HATTERAS (N) Didier 1951;

MOON

FROM THE EARTH TO THE MOON (N) Scrib 1874; Fitzroy 1960; SFBC; SBS T619; Air CL142; Bant HP161; Aeonian 1975;

ROUND THE MOON (N) Air CL 182, 1968;

Both =FROM THE EARTH TO THE MOON & A TRIP AROUND IT (2N) Lippincott 1958; Crest S216;

Both =FROM THE EARTH TO THE MOON & ALL AROUND THE MOON (2N) Dover T633, 1960;

AN ANTARTIC MYSTERY (N) Lippincott 1900; Fitzroy 1960; Gregg 1976;

AROUND THE WORLD IN 80 DAYS (N) Osgood 1873; Avon T148; Lion LL90; Air CL24; Avon ZS135; Lanc 13-415; (Marginal)

THE CASTLE OF THE CARPATHIANS (N) Saalfield 1900;

=CARPATHIAN CASTLE (N) Fitzroy 1963; Ace H-60;

THE 500 MILLIONS OF THE BEGUM (N) Munro 1879;

=THE BEGUMS FORTUNE (N) Fitzroy 1958; Ace H-49; 05350;

FIVE WEEKS IN A BALLOON (N) Appleton 1869; Fitzroy 1958; Prmd F-753; Aeonian 1976;

FOR THE FLAG (N) Fitzroy 1961; Ace 24800;

THE GIANT RAFT (2Vol) Lovell 1882;

=& DOWN THE AMAZON (N) Fitzroy 1967;

=& THE CRYPTOGRAM (N) Fitzroy 1967;

Both =800 LEAGUES ON THE AMAZON (2N) Burt 1935;

HECTOR SERVADAC (N) Scrib 1878;

=* OFF ON A COMET (N) Ace D-245; Aeonian 1975;

=TO THE SUN & OFF ON A COMET (N) Dover T-634, 1960;

THE HUNT FOR THE METEOR (N) Fitzroy 1965; Ace H-78; 35350;

A JOURNEY TO THE CENTER OF THE EARTH (N) Shepard 1874; Wyn 1956; Ace D-155; D-397; Perm M4161; Fitzroy 1961; Ace F-191; M-119; SFBC; Air CL60; Lanc 13-409; Heritage 1967;

MASTER OF THE WORLD(& ROBUR THE CONQUEROR) (2N) Ace D-504, 1961; Fitzroy 1962 (2Vol); Air CL73; Lanc 13-425;

THE PURCHASE OF THE NORTH POLE (N) Once A Week 1891; Ace D-434; Fitzroy 1968;

THE STEAM HOUSE (2Vol) Scribners 1881;

=& THE DEMON OF CAWNPORE (N) Fitzroy 1959; Ace 14253; Aeonian 1976;

=& TIGERS & TRAITORS (N) Fitzroy 1959; Ace 80900; Aeonian 1976;

THE VILLAGE IN THE TREETOPS (N) Fitzroy 1964; Ace H-67; 86400;

YESTERDAY & TOMORROW (C8) Fitzroy 1965; Ace H-52; 94490;

VERNON, LEE

THE SPACE FRONTIERS (C9) Sig 1224, 1955;

ROBOT HUNT (N) Avalon 1959;

VERRILL, A. HYATT

THE BRIDGE OF LIGHT (N) Fantasy 1950;

VIDAL, GORE

MESSIAH (N) Dutton 1954; BB 94; 484K; U5022; 72005; Bant Q7139;

VIERECK, GEORGE SYLVESTER & ELDRIDGE, PAUL

WANDERING JEW

MY FIRST TWO THOUSAND YEARS (N) Maculey 1928; Crst s148; d425; R673;
SALOME-THE WANDERING JEWESS (N) Liveright 1930;
= SALOME 2000 YEARS OF LOVE (N) Ace D-43, 1953;
THE INVINCIBLE ADAM (N) Liveright 1932;

VINCENT, HARL = HARL VINCENT SCHOEPFLIN

THE DOOMSDAY PLANET (N) Towr 42-621, 1966; 42947;

VINGE, VERNOR

GRIMM'S WORLD (N) Berk X1750, 1969;
THE WITLING (N) DAW 179, 1976;

VIVIAN, E. CHARLES also JACK MANN

CITY OF WONDER (N) Moffat-Yard 1923; Centaur 1973;

VON BRAUN, WERNHER

FIRST MEN TO THE MOON (N) H-R-W 1960;

VON HARBOU, THEA

METROPOLIS (N) Hutchinson 1927; Ace F-246; Gregg 1975; Ace 52831;
THE ROCKET TO THE MOON (N) World 1930; Gregg 1977;

VONNEGUT, KURT

CANARY IN A CAT HOUSE (C12) G-M s1153, 1961;
CATS CRADLE (N) HRW 1963; Dell 1149; SFBC; Delacorte 1971;
GOD BLESS YOU MR. ROSEWATER (N) HRW 1965; Dell 2929; Delacorte 1971;
MOTHER NIGHT (N) H&R 1966; Delacorte 1966; Dell 5853;
PLAYER PIANO (N) Scrib 1952; SFBC; Avon N516; YW 287; H-R-W 1966; Delacorte 1971;
= UTOPIA 14; Bantam A1262, 1956;
SLAUGHTERHOUSE-FIVE (N) Delacorte 1969; BC; Dell 8029;
THE SIRENS OF TITAN (N) Dell B138, 1959; H-M 1961; Dell 7948, Delacorte 1968;
WELCOME TO THE MONKEY HOUSE (C25) Delacorte 1968; Dell 9478;
BETWEEN TIME AND TIMBUKTO ( ) Delacorte 1972; Delacorte pb;

WADEY, VICTOR

THE UNITED PLANETS (N) Arcadia 1967;

WAGNER, KARL EDWARD

KANE

DARKNESS WEAVES (N) Powell Pp213, 1970; (rev) Warn 89-598;
DEATH ANGEL'S SHADOW (S3) WPBL 75-102, 1973;
BLOODSTONE (N) WPBL 78-711, 1975; 88-285;
NIGHT WINDS (N) Warn 89-597, 1978;(fc 8/78);

DARK CRUSADE (N) Warn 88-154, 1976;

BRAN MAC MORN: (see R E Howard)
LEGION FROM THE SHADOWS (N) Zebra 177, 1976;

WAHLOO, PETER

INSPECTOR JENSEN SERIES
THE STEEL SPRING (N) Delacorte 1970;
THE THIRTY-FIRST FLOOR (N) Knopf 1967; Bant N5945

THE GENERALS (N) Pantheon 1974;

WALKER, DAVID

THE LORD'S PINK OCEAN (N) Houghton-M 1972; DAW 67;

WALKER, JERRY

MISSION ACCOMPLISHED (N) Cosmos 1947

WALLACE F.L.

ADDRESS CENTAURI (N) Gnome 1955; Galx 32;

WALLACE, IAN = JOHN PRITCHARD?

CROYD
CROYD (N) Putnam 1967; Berkley X1616;
DR. ORPHEUS (N) Putnam 1968; SFBC; Berkley X1767;
A VOYAGE TO DARI (N) DAW 127, 1974;

ST. CYR & U. TULI
DEATHSTAR VOYAGE (N) Putnam 1969; SFBC; Berkley S1924;
THE PURLOINED PRINCE (N) McCall 1971;
THE SIGN OF THE MUTE MEDUSA (N) Popular 3173, 1977;

THE WORLD ASUNDER (N) DAW 216, 1976;
PAN SAGITTARIUS (N) Putnam 1973; Berkley N2659;

WALLERSTEIN, JAMES

THE DEMON'S MIRROR (N) Bellamy 1951;

WALLING, WILLIAM

NO ONE GOES THERE NOW (N) Dday 1971;

WALLIS, DAVE

ONLY LOVERS LEFT ALIVE(N) Dutton 1964; Bant H3029; S5470;

WALLIS, G. McDONALD

LEGEND OF LOST EARTH (N) Ace F+187, 1963;
THE LIGHT OF LILITH (N) Ace F+108, 1961;

WALTER, W. GREY

THE CURVE OF THE SNOWFLAKE (N) Norton 1956

WALTON, BRYCE

SONS OF THE OCEAN DEEP (JN) Winston 1952;

WALTON, EVANGELINE

MABINOGI
THE VIRGIN AND THE SWINE (N) Willett-Clark 1936;
= THE ISLAND OF THE MIGHTY (N) BBAF 1959, 1970; 24211;
THE CHILDREN OF LLYR (N) BBAF 2332, 1971; 24210;
THE SONG OF RHIANNON (N) BBAF 2773, 1972; 22773; 24209;
PRINCE OF ANNWN (N) BBAF 24233, 1974; BBDR 27060;

WITCHHOUSE (N) Arkham 1945; Monarch 264; Award An1246;

WARNER, SYLVIA TOWNSEND

KINGDOMS OF ELFIN (C18) Viking 1977; Delta 54499, 1978;

WATERS, T. A.

CENTER FORCE (N) Dell 6101, 1975;
THE PROBABILITY PAD (N) Prmd T2206, 1970;

WATKINS, WILLIAM JON

CLICKWHISTLE (N) Dday 1973;

ECODEATH (N) (with E. V. Snyder) Dday 1972;
THE GOD MACHINE (N) Dday 1973;
THE LITANY OF SH'REEV (N) (with Gene Snyder) Dday 1976;

WATSON, IAN

ALIEN EMBASSY (N) Ace 01475, 1978;(fc 7/78)
THE EMBEDDING (N) Scribners 1975; Bant 2311;
THE JOHAH KIT (N) Scribners 1976; Ban 10879;
THE MARTIAN INCA (N) Scrib 1977;

WAYMAN, TONY RUSSELL

ADS INFINITUM (N) Curt 7130, 1971;
DUNES OF PRADAI (N) Curt 7178, 1971;
WORLD OF THE SLEEPER (N) Ace H+21, 1967;

WEINBAUM, STANLEY G.

THE BEST OF STANLEY G. WEINBAUM (C12) BB 23890, 1974;
THE BLACK FLAME (N) Fantasy 1948; Avon V2280;
THE DARK OTHER (N) FPCI 1950;
DAWN OF FLAME AND OTHER STORIES (C7) Milwaukee Fictioneers 1936;
A MARTIAN ODYSSEY (C12)Fantasy 1949; (C5) Lanc 74-808; 72-146; 75-399;
THE NEW ADAM (N) Ziff-Davis 1939; Avon V2288;
THE RED PERI (C8) Fantasy 1952; GSFL4;

WELLMAN, MANLY WADE

THE BEYONDERS (N) Warn 88-202, 1977;
THE DARK DESTROYERS (N) Avalon 1959; Ace D+443;
THE INVADING ASTEROID (N) Stellar 15, 1932;
ISLAND IN THE SKY (N) Avalon 1961;
GIANTS FROM ETERNITY (N) Avalon 1959;
SHERLOCK HOLMES WAR OF THE WORLDS (N) (with Wade Wellman) WPBL 76-982; 1975;
SOJAR OF TITAN (N) Crestwood Prize 11, 1949;
THE SOLAR INVASION (N) Popular 2346, 1967; (Captain Future Series- See E. Hamilton)
TWICE IN TIME (N) Avalon 1957; Galaxy 34;
WHO FEARS THE DEVIL (C11) Arkham 1963; BB U2222;
WORSE THINGS WAITING (C29) Carcosa 1973;

WELLEN, EDWARD

HIJACK (N) Begl 95070, 1971;

WELLS, BARRY

THE DAY THE EARTH CAUGHT FIRE (N) BB F602, 1962;

WELLS, BASIL

DOORWAYS TO SPACE (C15) FPCI 1951;
PLANETS OF ADVENTURE (C15) FPCI 1949;

WELLS, HERBERT GEORGE (Partial Listing)

THE BEST STORIES OF H. G. WELLS (C16) BB S414K, 1960; S742;
BEST SCIENCE FICTION STORIES OF H.G. WELLS (C18) Dover pb 1966;
THE COMPLETE SHORT STORIES OF H.G. WELLS (C64) Wehman Bros, 1965;
1. FIRST MEN IN THE MOON (N) (Brit 1901) Dell 201; BB F687; U2232; Berk F1398; +
2. THE FOOD OF THE GODS (N) Macmil 1904; BB F725; Air CL59; Berk X1407; Pop SP286; +
THE HOLY TERROR (N) S & S 1939;
3. IN THE DAYS OF THE COMET (N) Century 1906; Berk X1440;
4. THE INVISIBLE MAN (N) Arnold 1897; Dell 269; Poc 1140; Pop K-71; Chariot 128; Berk F934; F1256; S2989; Lanc 13424; Bant FP S732; BT50537; Pop 1503; GM + Berk 3438; M+491;
5. THE ISLAND OF DR. MOREAU (N) Stone & Kimball 1896; Ace D-309; D-537; BB F761; Berk F1363; Lanc 13-435; Leis LB 211NK; SFBC 1977 (Movie Tie in) Temp 141361+
6. MEN LIKE GODS (N) Macmil 1923; Leis LB 16;
7. WHEN THE SLEEPER WAKES (N) Harper 1899; Ace D-388; F-240; 88091;
8. STAR-BEGOTTEN (N) Viking 1937; Leis LB 004, 1971; Manor 95394;
9. THE TIME MACHINE (N) Holt 1895; Berk 380; G445; F1063; F1361; N2853; GM+M 491; Prmd X1414; Bant FP 4063; S8783; Dolphin C+304; Berk 3440;
10. THE WAR OF THE WORLDS (N) Harper 1898; Poc 947; Pop SP 170; Berk F1255; S2694: Lanc 13-410; Dolphin C+304: Berk 3439
SEVEN FAMOUS NOVELS (7N) Knopf 1934 = 1,2,3,4,5,9&10;
= SEVEN SCIENCE FICTION NOVELS OF H.G. WELLS (7N) Dover, 1949;

THREE PROPHETIC NOVELS (3N) Dover pb 7, 9 & Story of the Days to Come;
28 STORIES (2N+C26) Dover 1952; Novel =8.&6.
THE WAR IN THE AIR (3N) Dover 1963 =Title +3 +2
THE TIME MACHINE AND THE WAR OF THE WORLDS (2N) Heritage 1964;
THE WAR OF THE WORLDS, THE TIME MACHINE AND SELECTED SHORT STORIES (2N+C8) Platt 1963;
THE CROQUET PLAYER (N) Viking 1937;
EMPIRE OF THE ANTS & 8 OTHER S.F. STORIES (N+C8) Tempo 14455, 1977;
THE SEA LADY (N) APPLETON 1902; Hyperion 1976;
THE SHAPE OF THINGS TO COME (N) Macmil 1933;
THE UNDYING FIRE (N) Macmil 1919;
THE WORLD SET FREE (N) Dutton 1914; Leis 13X;

WELLS, ROBERT

CANDLE IN THE SUN (N) Berk S2016, 1971;
THE PARASAURIANS (N) Berk X1779, 1969;
RIGHT HANDED WILDERNESS (N) BB 3355, 1973;
THE SPACEJACKS (N) Berk N2847, 1975;

WERFEL, FRANZ

STAR OF THE UNBORN (N) Viking 1946; Bant Y7915, 1976;

WERPER, BARTON =PETER T. SCOTT

UNAUTHORIZED TARZAN NOVELS
TARZAN AND THE SILVER GLOBE (N) Gold Star 1964;
TARZAN AND THE CAVE CITY (N) Gold Star 1964;
TARZAN AND THE SNAKE PEOPLE (N) Gold Star 1964(by Peg O'Neill Scott);
TARZAN AND THE ABDOMINABLE SNOWMAN (N) Gold Star 1965;
TARZAN AND THE WINGED INVADERS (N) Gold Star 1965;

WESLEY, MARY

THE SIXTH SEAL (N) Stein & Day 1971;

WEST, PAUL

COLONEL MINT, (N) Dutton, 1972;

WEST, JESSAMYN

THE CHILEKINGS (N) BB U2845, 1968;

WEST, WALLACE

THE BIRD OF TIME (N) Gnome 1959; Ace F-114;
THE EVERLASTING EXILES (N) Avalon 1967;
LORDS OF ATLANTIS (N) Avalon 1960; Air SF3;
THE MEMORY BANK (N) Avalon 1961; Air SF1;
RIVER OF TIME (N) Avalon 1963;
THE TIME LOCKERS (N) Avalon 1964;
OUTPOSTS IN SPACE (N) Avalon 1962;

WESTON, GEORGE

HIS FIRST MILLION WOMEN (N) Farrar & Rinehart 1934; Avon 396;

WETHERELL, JUNE

BLUEPRINT FOR YESTERDAY (N) Walker 1971;

WHEATLEY, DENNIS (partial listing)

THEY FOUND ATLANTIS (N) Lipp 1936; BB 3080;

WHITE, JAMES

SECTOR GENERAL
HOSPITAL STATION (S5) BB595, 1962; 2027;
STAR SURGEON (N) BB F709, 1963; U2866;2028;
MAJOR OPERATION (S6) BB 2149, 1971; 24229;

ALL JUDGEMENT FLED (N) Walker 1969; BB 2016;
THE ALIENS AMONG US (C7) BB 1545, 1969;
DEADLY LITTER (C4) BB U2224, 1964; 2029;
THE DREAM MILLENNIUM (N) BB 24012, 1974;
THE ESCAPE ORBIT (N) Ace F-317, 1965;
LIFEBOAT (N) BB 2797, 1972;
MONSTERS AND MEDICS (C8) BBDR 25623, 1977;
= & SECOND ENDING (N) Ace F+173, 1962;
THE SECRET VISITORS (N) Ace D+237, 1957; G-675; 75870;
TOMORROW IS TO FAR (N) BB 2150, 1971;
THE WATCH BELOW (N) BB U2285, 1966; Walker 1969; BB 2795;

WHITE, JANE

COMET (N) H&R 1975;

WHITE, TED with T. CARR = NORMAN EDWARDS

WITH D. VAN ARNAM = RON ARCHER

MAXIMILLION QUEST ON QANAR
PHOENIX PRIME (N) Lancer 73-476, 1966; 74-593;
THE SORCERESS OF QAR (N) Lancer 73-528, 1966; 74-592;
STAR WOLF (N) Lancer 75252, 1971;

TANNER
ANDROID AVENGER (N) Ace M+123, 1965;
THE SPAWN OF THE DEATH MACHINE (N) PBL 53-680, 1968; WPBL 75-532;

BY FURIES POSSESSED (N) Signet T4275, 1970;
INVASION FROM 2500 (N) (as Edwards) Monarch 453, 1964;
THE JEWELS OF ELSEWHEN (N) Belmont B50-751, 1967;
NO TIME LIKE TOMORROW (JN) Crown 1969;
SECRET OF THE MARAUDER SATELLITE (JN) Westminister 1967;
SIDESLIP (N) (with Van Arnam) Prmd X1787, 1968;

TROUBLE ON PROJECT CERES (JN) Westminister 1971;
CAPTAIN AMERICA -THE GREAT GOLD STEAL (N) Bant F3780, 1968;
THE OZ ENCOUNTER (N) (with M. Woldman) Prmd; 4036 Doc Phoenix Book 1;
LOST IN SPACE (N) (as Archer) Pyramid X1679, 1967;

WHITE, TERENCE HANSBURY

CAMELOT
THE SWORD IN THE STONE (N) Putnam 1939; Dell 8445;
THE WITCH IN THE WOOD (N) Putnam 1939;
THE ILL-MADE KNIGHT (N) Putnam 1940;
ALL =+ THE ONCE AND FUTURE KING (N) Putnam 1958; Dell Y001, Berk T2678;
= CAMELOT (N) Berk D1662;
THE BOOK OF MERLYN (N) Texas Press 1977;
THE MASTER (N) Putnam 1957; Avon ZS118, 1967;
THE ELEPHANT AND THE KANGAROO (N) Putnam 1947;

WHYTE, H. WALTER

DEEP FREEZE (N) Manor 12527, 1977;

WIBBERLEY, LEONARD

HOMEWARD TO ITHAKA (N) Morrow 1978;
ONE IN FOUR (N) Morrow 1976;
THE QUEST OF EXCALIBUR (N) Putnam 1959;

WILDER, CHERRY

THE LUCK OF BRIN'S FIVE (N) Atheneum 1977;

WILHELM, KATE MARRIED TO DAMON KNIGHT

ABYSS (2N) Dday 1971; Bant N7234;
CITY OF OF CAIN (N) Little-B 1974;
THE CLEWISTON TEST (N) FS&G 1976; Pocket 80888;
THE CLONE (See T. Thomas co-author)
THE DOWNSTAIRS ROOM (C14) Dday 1967; Dell 2129;
THE KILLER THING (N) Dday 1967; SFBC; Dell 4496;
LET THE FIRE FALL (N) Dday 1969; Lanc 74-586;
MARGARET AND I (N) Little-B. 1971; BB 2660; Poc 81449;
THE MILE LONG SPACESHIP (C11) Berk F862, 1963;
MORE BITTER THAN DEATH (N) Tower 42-558, 1966;
THE INFINITY BOX (C9) H&R 1975; Pocket 80955;
THE NEVERMORE AFFAIR (N) Dday 1966; Curt 7011;
SOMERSET DREAMS & OTHER FICTIONS (C8) H&R 1978;
WHERE LATE THE SWEET BIRDS SAND (N) H&R 1976; SFBC; Poc 80912;
THE YEAR OF THE CLOUD (see T. Thomas Co-author)

WILKINS, VAUGHN

THE CITY OF FROZEN FIRE (N) Macmil 1951;
VALLEY BEYOND TIME (N) St. Martin's 1955;

WILLIAMS, FRANCIS

IT HAPPENED TOMORROW (N) Abeland 1952

WILLIAMS, GORDON

THE MICRONAUTS (N) BANTAM 11139, 1977;

WILLIAMS, NICK BODIE

THE ATOM CURTAIN (N) Ace D+139, 1956;

WILLIAMS, ROBERT MOORE

JONGOR
JONGOR OF LOST LAND (N) Pop 2498, 1970;
THE RETURN OF JONGOR (N) Pop 2511, 1970;
JONGOR FIGHTS BACK (N) Pop 2540, 1970;
ZANTHAR
ZANTHAR OF THE MANY WORLDS (N) Lanc 73-694, 1967;
ZANTHAR AT THE EDGE OF NEVER (N) Lanc 74-941, 1968;
ZANTHAR AT MOON'S MADNESS (N) Lanc 73-805, 1968;
ZANTHAR AT TRIPS END (N) Lanc 73-836, 1969;

BEACHHEAD PLANET (N) Dell 0462, 1970;
THE BELL FROM INFINITY (N) Lanc 73-766, 1968;
THE BLUE ATOM (N) Ace D+322, 1958;
THE CHAOS FIGHTERS (N) Ace S-90, 1955;
CONQUEST OF THE SPACE SEA (N) Ace D+99, 1955;
THE DAY THEY H-BOMBED LOS ANGELES (N) Ace D-530, 1961;
THE DARKNESS BEFORE TOMORROW (N) Ace F+141, 1962;
DOOMSDAY EVE (N) Ace D+215, 1957;
FLIGHT FROM YESTERDAY (N) Ace F+223, 1963;
KING OF THE FOURTH PLANET (N) Ace F+149, 1962;
LOVE IS FOREVER, WE ARE FOR TONIGHT (N) Curt 6101, 1970;
THE LUNAR EYE (N) Ace F+261, 1964;
NOW COMES TOMORROW (N) Curt 7115, 1971;
THE SECOND ATLANTIS (N) Ace F-335, 1965;
THE STAR WASPS (N) Ace F+177, 1963;
TO THE END OF TIME (C5) Ace D+427, 1960;
VIGILANTE -21ST CENTURY (N) Lanc 73-644, 1967;
THE VOID BEYOND (C6) Ace D+322, 1958;
WHEN TWO WORLDS MEET (C6) Curt 7081, 1970;
WALK UP THE SKY (N) Avalon 1962;
WORLD OF THE MASTERMINDS (N) Ace D+427, 1960;

WILLIAMS, THOMAS

TSUGA'S CHILDREN (N) Random 1977;

WILLIAMS, T. OWEN

A MONTH FOR MANKIND (N) Lenox Hill 1971;

WILLIAMSON, JACK - also WILL STEWART

GILES HABIBULA

THE LEGION OF SPACE (N) Fantasy 1947; Galx 2; Prmd X1576; T2022; Garland 1976; Poc 81450;
THE COMETEERS (N+1)Fantasy 1950; Prmd X1634; Poc 81652;
ONE AGAINST THE LEGION (S2) Prmd X1657, 1967;

CONTRA TERRENE MATTER (as Stewart)

SEETEE SHIP (N) Gnome 1951; Lanc 73-732;
SEETEE SHOCK (N) S&S 1949; Lanc 73-733;
= SEETEE SHOCK - SEETEE SHIP (2N) (as Williamson) Lancer 78-706, 1972;

BEST OF JACK WILLIAMSON (C) BBDR 27335, 1978;
BRIGHT NEW UNIVERSE (N) Ace G-641, 1967;
BROTHER TO THE GODS (N) Pinn (fc 1978)
DARKER THAN YOU THINK (N) Fantasy 1948; Lanc 73-421; Berk X1751; Garland 1976;
DRAGON'S ISLAND (N) S&S 1951; Pop 447; Tower 43-531;
= THE NOT MEN (N) Tower 43-957, 1968;
DOME AROUND AMERICA (N) Ace D+118, 1955;
THE EARLY WILLIAMSON (C11) Dday 1975;
GOLDEN BLOOD (N) Lanc 72-740, 1964; 73-630;
THE GREEN GIRL (N) Avon FN2, 1950;
THE LEGION OF TIME (2N) Fantasy 1953; Prmd X1586;
=AFTER WORLDS END & THE LEGION OF TIME (2N) Magabook 2, 1963;
THE MOON CHILDREN (N) Putnam 1972; Berk S2432;
THE PANDORA EFFECT (C7) Ace 65125, 1969;
PEOPLE MACHINES (C9) Ace 65890, 1971;
THE POWER OF BLACKNESS (N) Berk/Put 1976; Berk D3260;
THE HUMANIODS (N) S&S 1949; G&D 1950; Galx 21; Lanc 74-812; 72-129; 74-519; 75-362; Avon E26278;
THE REIGN OF WIZARDRY (N) Lanc 72-761, 1964; 73-748;
STAR BRIDGE (N) (with J. Gunn) Gnome 1955; Ace D-169; F-241; Berk 3294;
THE TRIAL OF TERRA (N) Ace D-555, 1962;
TRAPPED IN SPACE (JN) Dday 1968; Semaphore P6; SBS TX 1749
AFTER WORLDS END (N) Galaxy Magabook +2, 1963;
THE GIRL FROM MARS (N) (with M. J. Breuer) Stellar 1, 1930;

WILSON, COLIN

THE MIND PARASITES (N) Arkham 1967; Bant F3905;
THE PHILOSOPHERS STONE (N) Crown 1971; Warn 59213; 89442;
THE SPACE VAMPIRES (N) Random 1976; Poc 80916;

WILSON, F. PAUL

HEALER (N) Dday 1976; Dell 13569;

WILSON, RICHARD

THE GIRLS FROM PLANET 5 (N) BBHC 1955; BB 117; Lancer 75-550;
AND THEN THE TOWN TOOK OFF (N) Ace D+437, 1960;
TIME OUT FOR TOMORROW (C12) BB F658, 1962;

THOSE IDIOTS FROM EARTH (C10) BB 237, 1957;
30 DAY WONDER (N) BB 434K, 1960;

WILSON, STEVE

THE LOST TRAVELER (N) St. Martins 1977;

WINTERBOTHAM, RUSS - also J. HARVEY BOND AND FRANKLIN HADLEY

PLANET BIG ZERO (N)(as Hadley) Monarch 431, 1964;
THE LORD OF NARDOS (N) Avalon 1966;
THE MEN FROM ARCTURUS (N) Avalon 1963;
THE OTHER WORLD (N) (as Bond) Avalon 1963;
THE PUPPET PLANET (N) Avalon 1964;
THE RED PLANET (N) Mon 270, 1962;
THE SPACE EGG (N) Avalon 1958; Mon 252;

WINTERFELD, HENRY

STARGIRL (N) Harcorte-B 1957; Avon Camelot 28506; (Juvenile)

WOBIG, ELLEN

THE YOUTH MONOPOLY (N) Ace H+48, 1968;

WODHAMS, JACK

THE AUTHENTIC TOUCH (N) Curt 7142, 1971;

WOLFE, AARON

INVASION (N) Laser 9, 1975;

WOLFE, BERNARD

LIMBO (N) Random 1952; Ace A-3;

WOLF, GARY

KILLERBOWL (N) Dday 1975;
A GENERATION REMOVED (N) Dday 1977;

WOLFE, GENE

THE FIFTH HEAD OF CERBERUS (C3) Scrib 1972; Ace 23500;
OPERATION ARES (N) Berk S1858, 1970;
THE DEVIL IN A FOREST (N) Follett 1976; Ace 14288; (Marginal)

WOLFE, LOUIS

JOURNEY OF THE OCEANAUTS (N) Norton, 1968; Prmd T2299; (Juvenile)

WOLLHEIM, DONALD also DAVID GRINNELL

MIKE MARS

MIKE MARS, ASTRONAUT (JN) Dday 1961; PBL 56-968;
MIKE MARS FLIES THE X-15 (JN) Dday 1961; PBL 56-972;
MIKE MARS AT CAPE CANAVERAL (JN) Dday 1961;
= MIKE MARS AT CAPE KENNEDY (JN) PBL 56-981, 1966;

MIKE MARS IN ORBIT (JN) Dday 1961; PBL 56-998;
MIKE MARS FLIES THE DYNASOAR ((JN) Dday 1962; PBL 56-340;
MIKE MARS, SOUTH POLE SPACEMAN (JN) Dday 1962; PBL 56-358;
MIKE MARS AND THE MYSTERY SATELITE (JN) Dday 1963; PBL 56-369;
MIKE MARS AROUND THE MOON (JN) Dday 1964; PBL 56-383;

ONE AGAINST THE MOON (JN) World 1956;
THE SECRET OF SATURN'S RINGS (JN) Winston 1954; PBL 52-996;
SECRET OF THE MARTIAN MOONS (JN) Winston 1955; Tempo T28;
SECRET OF THE NINTH PLANET (JN) Winston 1959; PBL 52-874; Warn 64-753;
TWO DOZEN DRAGON EGGS (C24) Powell PP 181, 1969;

AS GRINNELL SERIES

DESTINY'S ORBIT (N) Avalon 1961; Ace F+161;

DESTINATION: SATURN (N) (with Carter) Avalon 1967; Ace H+85; +14280;

AS GRINNELL

ACROSS TIME (N) Avalon 1957; Ace D+286; G-728; 00300;
EDGE OF TIME (N) Avalon 1958; Ace D+362; M-162;
THE MARTIAN MISSILE (N) Avalon 1959; Ace D+465;
TO VENUS; TO VENUS (N) Ace +81610, 1970;

WOODBURY, DAVID A.

MR. FARADAYS FORMULA (N) Devin-Adair 1965;

WOODCOTT, KEITH see JOHN BRUNNER

WOODHOUSE, MARTIN

BLUE BONE (N) Coward 1973;
BUSHBABY (N) Coward 1968; BC; Berkley S1726;
MAMA DOLL (N) Coward 1972;
MOONHILL (N) Coward 1974;

WORMSER, RICHARD

PAN SATYRUS (N) Avon G1191, 1963;

WOUK, HERMAN

THE LOMOKOME PAPERS (N) S&S 1956; Poc 75226;

WRIGHT, AUSTIN TAPPAN

ISLANDIA (N) Farrar & Rinehart 1942; pb 1956; Sig Y2870; E4621; Plume Z5099;

WRIGHT, KENNETH (see Lester del Rey)

WRIGHT, LAN = LIONEL P. WRIGHT

EXILE FROM XANADU (N) Ace M+103, 1964;
THE LAST HOPE OF EARTH (N) Ace F-347, 1965;
A MAN CALLED DESTINY (N) Ace D+311, 1958;
THE PICTURES OF PAVANNE (N) Ace H+48, 1968; +66280
WHO SPEAKS OF CONQUEST (N) Ace Dd=02205, 1957;

WRIGHT, S. FOWLER

DELUGE: A ROMANCE (N) Cosmopolitan 1928; G&D 1929;
DAWN (N) Cosmopolitan 1929; G&D 1929;

THE ISLAND OF CAPTAIN SPARROW (N) Cosmopolitan 1928; G&D 1950;
THE WORLD BELOW (AND THE AMPHIBIANS) (N) Longmans-G 1930; Shasta 1949; Hyperion 1975;
=& THE WORLD BELOW (N) Galx 4, 1951;
=& THE AMPHIBIANS (N) Galx 5, 1951;
SPIDER'S WAR (N) Abelard 1954;
THE THRONE OF SATURN (C12) Arkham 1949;

WUL, STEFAN

THE TEMPLE OF THE PAST (N) Seabury 1973;

WYLIE, PHILIP

WITH E. BALMER
WHEN WORLDS COLLIDE (N) Stokes 1933; Burt 1935; Dell 627; PBL 52-180; 52-521; 64-360; Warn 76-881; 88-206;
AFTER WORLDS COLLIDE (N) Stokes 1934; Burt 1935; PBL 52-255; 64-361; Warn 74-219; 76-873;
Both =WHEN WORLDS COLLIDE (2N) Lippincott 1951;

THE ANSWER (N) Rinehart 1956; PBL 52-205;
THE DISAPPEARANCE (N) Rinehart 1951; Poc C-40; 75147; 77417; Warn 82-837-3;
THE END OF THE DREAM (N) Dday 1972; DAW 77; UY1139; UW1319;
GLADIATOR (N) Knopf 1930; Avon 216; Shakespear 1951; Lan 72-937; 73-562; 78-686; Hyperion 1975; Manor 15210;
LOS ANGELES AD 2017 (N) Popular 272, 1971;
THE MURDERER INVISIBLE (N) Farrar-R 1931; Burt 1932; Pop 2209; Hyperion 1976;
THE SMUGGLED ATOM BOMB (N) Avon 727, 1957; Lancer 72-976;
THE SPY WHO SPOKE PORPOISE (N) Dday 1969; Pyramid N2315;
TOMORROW (N) Rinehart 1954; Pop G156; PC1005; M2035;
TRIUMPH (N) Dday 1963; Crest R675;

WYNDHAM, JOHN = JOHN BEYNON HARRIS

Also JOHN BEYNON and LUCAS PARKES
CHOCKY (N) BB U6119, 1968; SFBC;
THE DAY OF THE TRIFFIDS (N) Dday 1951; (=); SFBC; Crst D531; D741; R1049; 1322;
= REVOLT OF THE TRIFFIDS (N) Pop 411, 1952;
THE INFINITE MOMENT (C6) BB 546, 1961;
OUT OF THE DEEPS (N) BBHC 1953; BB50; 545; U2814; 1639; BBDR 27217;
THE MIDWICH CUCKOOS (N) BBHC 1958; BB299K;U2840; (=); Walker 1969; BB 2763; 22763;
= VILLAGE OF THE DAMNED (N) BB 453K, 1960;
THE OUTWARD URGE (N) (with Parkes) BB 341K, 1959; U2809;
RE-BIRTH (N) BBHC 1955; BB 104; 423K; U2820; BB 1638; Walker 1970; BBDR 27450;

THE SECRET PEOPLE (N) (as Beynon) Lanc 72-701, 1964; 72-155; G-M M2890;
TALES OF GOOSEFLESH AND LAUGHTER (C11) BB 182, 1956; U2832;
TROUBLE WITH LICHEN (N) BB 449K, 1960; Walker 1969; BBDR 25847;
STOWAWAY TO MARS (N) (as Beynon) G-M T2646, 1972;
THE JOHN WYNDHAM ONMIBUS (C3) S&S 1964;

Y

YARBRO, CHELSEA Q.

FALSE DAWN (N) Dday 1978;
HOTEL TRANSYLVANIA (N) St Martin's 1978;
THE TIME OF THE FOURTH HORSEMAN (N) Dday 1976; Ace 81180

YATES, ALLAN

CORIOLANUS, THE CHARIOT (N) Ace 11739, 1978(fc 7/78)

YEP, LAWRENCE

SEA DEMONS (N) Harper 1977;
SWEETWATER (JN) H&R 1973; Camelot 21907;

YOUNG, ROBERT F.

THE WORLDS OF ROBERT F. YOUNG (C16) S&S 1965;
A GLASS OF STARS(C13)Harris-Wolfe 1968;

Z

ZAGAT, ARTHUR LEO

SEVEN OUT OF TIME (N) Fantasy 1949;

ZAMYATIN, EVGENII IVANOVICH

WE (N) Dutton 1924; Viking 1972; Bant X7271; Dutton pb; Gregg 1975;

ZAREM LEWIS

GREEN MEN FROM SPACE (N) Dutton 1955;

ZEBROWSKI, GEORGE

OMEGA SERIES
ASHES AND STARS (N) Ace 87269, 1977;
THE OMEGA POINT (N) 62380, 1972;
MIRROR OF MINDS (   ) Tentative Title

THE STAR WEB (N) Laser 15, 1975;
THE MONADIC UNIVERSE (C12) Ace 53540, 1977;

ZELAZNY, ROGER

AMBER SERIES
NINE PRINCES IN AMBER (N) Dday 1970; Avon V2444; 4291; 27664; 35527;
GUNS OF AVALONE (N) Dday 1972; Avon 20032; 24695; 31112;
THE SIGN OF THE UNICORN (N) Dday 1975; Avon 30973;
THE HAND OF OBERON (N) Dday 1976; Avon 33324;
THE COURTS OF CHAOS (N) (fc 10/78)

BRIDGE OF ASHES (N) Sig Y7080, 1976;
CREATURES OF LIGHT AND DARKNESS (N) Dday 1969; Avon V2362; 3525; 27821; 35956;
DAMNATION ALLEY (N) Putnam 1969; Berk S1846; Z3123; 3641;
DEUS IRAE (N) (see P. Dick co-author)
THE DOORS OF HIS FACE: THE LAMPS OF HIS MOUTH AND OTHER STORIES (C15) Dday 1971; Avon 18846;
DOORWAYS IN THE SAND (N) H&R 1976; SFBC; Avon 32086;
THE DREAM MASTER (N) Ace F-403, 1966; 16700; Gregg 1976;
FOUR FOR TOMORROW (C4) Ace M-155, 1966; 24900; Garland 1976;
THE ILLUSTRATED ROGER ZELAZNY (C) Baronet 1978;
ISLE OF THE DEAD (N) Ace 37465, 1969; Gregg 1976;
JACK OF SHADOWS (N) Walker 1971; SFBC; Sig Q5140, 1972; Y6283;
LORD OF LIGHT (N) Dday 1967; SFBC; Avon N187; 5652; 24687; 33985;
MY NAME IS LEGION (S3) BB 24867, 1976;
THIS IMMORTAL (N) Ace F-393, 1966; 80690; Garland 1976;
TODAY WE CHOOSE FACES (N) Sig Q5435, 1973; Gregg 1978;
TO DIE IN ITALBAR (N) Dday 1973; SFBC; DAW 117; UY1203;

ZERWICK, CHLOE AND HARRISON BROWN

THE CASSIOPEIA AFFAIR (N) Dday 1968; Curt 7037;

ZIEROLD, NORMAN

THE SKYSCRAPER DOOM (N) Lenox Hill 1972;

NUMBERED and MULTI-AUTHOR SERIES

ATTAR THE MERMAN by ROBERT GRAHAM = JOE HALDEMAN

1. ATTAR'S REVENGE (N) Pocket 77988, 1975
2. WAR OF NERVES (N) Pocket 77989, 1975

BALZAN OF THE CAT PEOPLE by WALLACE MOORE = GERALD CONWAY

1. - THE BLOODSTONE (N) Pyramid
2. THE CAVES OF MADNESS (N) Pyramid V3714, 1975
3. THE LIGHTS OF ZETAR (N) Pyramid V3934, 1975

BIG BRAIN by GARY BRADNER

1. THE AARDVARK AFFAIR (N) Zebra 108, 1975
2. THE BEELZEBUB BUSINESS (N) Zebra 128, 1975;
3. ENERGY ZERO (N) Zebra 159, 1976

BIONIC WOMAN From T.V. SERIES

1. LOTTMAN, EILEEN -WELCOME HOME, JAIME (N) Berk Z3230, 1976;
2. LOTTMAN, EILEEN - EXTRACURRICULAR ACTIVITIES (N) Berk Z3326, 1977;

CAP KENNEDY by "GREGORY KERN" = E.C. TUBB?

1. GALAXY OF THE LOST (N) DAW UT1073, 1973
2. SLAVE SHIP FROM SERGAN (N) DAW UT1078, 1973
3. MONSTER OF METELAZE (N) DAW UT1084, 1973
4. ENEMY WITHIN THE SKULL (N) DAW UT1093, 1974
5. JEWEL OF JARHEN (N) DAW UQ1098, 1974
6. SEETEE ALERT (N) DAW UQ1103, 1974
7. THE GHOLAN GATE (N) DAW UQ1108, 1974
8. THE EATER OF WORLDS (N) DAW UQ1113, 1974;
9. EARTH ENSLAVED (N) DAW UQ1118, 1974;
10. PLANET OF DREAD (N) DAW UQ1123, 1974;
11. SPAWN OF LABAN (N) DAW UQ1133, 1974;
12. THE GENETIC BUCCANEER (N) DAW UQ1138, 1974;
13. A WORLD AFLAME (N) DAW UQ1144, 1974;
14. THE GHOSTS OF EPIDORIS (N) Daw UQ1159, 1975;
15. MIMICS OF DEPHENE (N) DAW UY1168, 1975;
16. BEYOND THE GALACTIC LENS (N) DAW UY1211: #176, 1975;

DRACULA by ROBERT LORY

1. DRACULA RETURNS (N) Pinn 184, 1973;
2. THE HAND OF DRACULA (N) Pinn 200, 1973;
3. DRACULA'S BROTHERS (N) Pinn 225, 1973;
4. DRACULA'S GOLD (N) Pinn 256, 1973;
5. DRUMS OF DRACULA (N) Pinn 322, 1974;

6. THE WITCHING OF DRACULA (N) Pinn 398, 1974;
7. DRACULA'S LOST WORLD (N) Pinn 508, 1974
8. DRACULA'S DISCIPLE (N) Pinn 581, 1975;

THE DREAM LORDS ADRIAN COLE

1. A PLAGUE OF NIGHTMARES (N) Zebra 111, 1975; 279;
2. LORD OF NIGHTMARES (N) Zebra 148, 1975;
3. BANE OF NIGHTMARES (N) Zebra 224, 1976;

THE EXPENDABLES by RICHARD AVERY = EDMUND COOPER

1. THE DEATH WORMS OF KRATOS (N) G-M P3306, 1975;
2. THE RINGS OF TANTALUS (N) G-M P3307, 1975;
3. THE WARGAMES OF ZELOS (N) G-M P3430, 1975;
4. THE VENOM OF ARGUS (N) G-M 3586, 1976;

FLASH GORDON from THE ORIGINAL COMIC STRIPS by ALEX RAYMOND

1. THE LION MEN OF MONGO (N) Avon 18515, 1974 Adapted by Steffanson;
2. THE PLAGUE OF SOUND (N) Avon 19166, 1974; Adapted by Steffanson;
3. THE SPACE CIRCUS (N) Avon 19695, 1974; Adapted by Steffanson;
4. THE TIME TRAP OF MING XIII (N) Avon 20446, 1974; Adapted by Steffanson;
5. THE WITCH QUEEN OF MONGO (N) Avon 21378, 1974; Adapted by Bingham;
6. THE WAR OF THE CYBERNAUTS (N) Avon 22335, 1975; Adapted by Bingham;

THE INVADERS (from T.V. SERIES)

1. LAUMER- THE INVADERS (N) Pyramid R1664, 1967;
2. LAUMER - ENEMIES FROM BEYOND (N) Pyramid X1689, 1967;
3. RAFE' BERNARD - ARMY OF THE UNDEAD (N) Pyramid R1711, 1967;

LAND OF THE GIANTS (from T.V. SERIES)

1. LEINSTER - LAND OF THE GIANTS (N) Pyramid S1846, 1968;
2. LEINSTER - THE HOT SPOT (N) Pyramid 1921, 1969;
3. LEINSTER - UNKNOWN DANGER (N) Pyramid 2105, 1969;

RATH, C. H. -FLIGHT OF FEAR (N) Whitman 1516, 1969;

PLANET OF THE APES From MOTION PICTURES (*Original Novel-Basis of Series)

*BOULLE -PLANET OF THE APES (N) See Author Entry-
AVALLONE - BENEATH THE PLANET OF THE APES (N) Bant S5674, 1970;
GERROLD - BATTLE FOR THE PLANET OF THE APES (N) Award AN 1139, 1973;
POURNELLE - ESCAPE FROM THE PLANET OF THE APES (N) Award AN 1240, 1973;
JAKES -CONQUEST OF THE PLANET OF THE APES (N) Award AN 1241, 1974;

PLANET OF THE APES (from T.V. Series) by George A. Effinger

1. MAN THE FUGITIVE (S3) Award AN 1373; 1974;
2. ESCAPE TO TOMORROW (S2) Award AN 1407; 1975;

3. JOURNEY INTO TERROR (S2) Award (no number) 1975;
4. LORD OF THE APES (N) Award AN 1488, 1976;

RETURN TO PLANET OF THE APES by "WILLIAM ARROW"

1. VISIONS OF NOWHERE (N) BB 25122, 1976; (Actually by William Rotsler)
2. ESCAPE FROM TERROR LAGOON (N) BB 25167, 1976; (Actually by Don Pfeil)
3. MAN THE HUNTED ANIMAL (N) BB 25211, 1976; (Actually by William Rotsler)

RACK by LAWRENCE JAMES

1. EARTH LIES SLEEPING (N) Zebra 7, 1974;
2. WAR ON ALEPH (N) Zebra 35, 1974;
3. BACKFLASH (N) Pinn 555, 1975;
4. PLANET OF THE BLIND (N) Pinn 675, 1975;

RICHARD BLADE by JEFFREY LORD = House Pseud.

1. THE BRONZE AXE (N) M-B 60-376, 1969; Pinn 201, 1973;
2. THE JADE WARRIOR (N) MB75-246, 1969; Pinn 202, 1973;
3. JEWEL OF THARN (N) M-B 75-272, 1969; Pinn 203, 1973;
4. SLAVE OF SARMA (N) M-B 75-305, 1970; Pinn 204, 1973;
5. LIBERATOR OF JEDD (N) MB75-408, 1971; Pinn 205, 1973;
6. MONSTER OF THE MAZE (N) MB95-168, 1972; Pinn 206, 1973;
7. PEARL OF PATMOS (N) Pinn 207, 1973;
8. UNDYING WORLD (N) Pinn 208, 1973;
9. KINGDOM OF ROYTH (N) Pinn 295, 1974;
10. ICE DRAGON (N) Pinn 355, 1974;
11. DIMENSION OF DREAMS (N) Pinn 474, 1974;
12. KING OF ZUNGA (N) Pinn 523, 1975;
13. THE GOLDEN STEED (N) Pinn 559, 1975;
14. THE TEMPLES OF AYOCAN (N) Pinn 295, 1974
15. THE TOWERS OF MELNON (N) Pinn 688, 1975;
16. THE CRYSTAL SEAS (N) Pinn 780, 1975;
17. THE MOUNTAINS OF BREGA (N) Pinn 812, 1976;
18. WARLORDS OF GAIKON(N) Pinn 822, 1976;
19. LOOTERS OF THARN (N) Pinn 855, 1976;
20. GUARDIANS OF THE CORAL THRONE (N) Pinn 881, 1976;
21. CHAMPION OF THE GODS (N) Pinn 949, 1976;
22. THE FORESTS OF GLEOR (N) Pinn 993, 1977;
23. EMPIRE OF BLOOD (N) Pinn 018, 1977;
24. THE DRAGONS OF ENGLOR (N) Pinn 042, 1977;
25. THE TORIAN PEARLS (N) Pinn 40-111-0 1977;
26. CITY OF THE LIVING DEAD (N) Pinn 40-193-0, 1978;
27. MASTER OF THE HASHOMI (N) Pinn 40-205-8, 1978;
28. WIZARD OF RENTORO (N) Pinn 206, 1978;(fc 8/78)

RYDER HOOK by TULLY ZETFORD = KEN BULMER

1. WHIRLPOOL OF STARS (N) Pinn 528, 1975;
2. THE BOOSTED MAN (N) Pinn 630, 1975;

3. STAR CITY (N) Pinn 712, 1975;
4. THE VIRILITY GENE (N) Pinn 800, 1976;

SIX MILLION DOLLAR MAN From T.V. SERIES

1. JAHN, MICHAEL - - WINE, WOMEN AND WARS (N) WPBL 76-833, 1975;
2. RICHARDS, EVAN - THE SOLID GOLD KIDNAPPING (N) WPBL 76-834, 1975;
3. CAIDIN - HIGH CRYSTAL (N) see Author Entry;
4. BARBREE, JAY -PILOT ERROR (N) WPBL 76-835, 1975;
5. JAHN - THE RESCUE OF THE ATHENA ONE (N) WPBL 76-836, 1977;
6. CAIDIN - CYBORG IV (N) see Author Entry
7. JAHN, MICHAEL - THE SECRET OF BIG FOOT PASS (N) Berk Z3307, 1976;

2. JAHN -INTERNATIONAL INCIDENTS (N) Berkley 3331, 1977;

SPACE 1999 From T. V. SERIES

1. TUBB - BREAKAWAY (N) Poc 80184, 1975;
2. RANKINE - MOON ODYSSEY (N) Poc 80185, 1975;
3. BALL - THE SPACE GUARDIANS (N) Poc 80198, 1975;
4. TUBB - COLLISION COURSE (N) Poc 80274, 1976;
5. RANKINE -LUNAR ATTACK (N) Poc 80305, 1976;
6. RANKINE - ASTRAL QUEST (N) Poc 80392, 1976;
7. TUBB - ALIEN SEED (N) Poc 80520, 1976;
8. RANKINE - ANDROID PLANET (N) Poc 80706, 1976;
9. TUBB - ROGUE PLANET (N) Poc 80710, 1976;
10. RANKINE - PHOENIX OF MEGARION (N) Poc 80764, 1976;

YEAR 2

1. BUTTERWORTH - PLANET OF PERIL (N) Warn 88-341, 1977;
2. BUTTERWORTH - MIND BREAKS OF SPACE (N) Warn 88-342; 1977;
3. BUTTERWORTH - THE SPACE JACKERS (N) Warn 88-343; 1977;
4. BUTTERWORTH - THE PSYCHOMORPH (N) Warn; 88-344; 1977;
5. BUTTERWORTH - THE TIME FIGHTERS (N) Warn; 88-345, 1977;
6. BUTTERWORTH - THE EDGE OF THE INFINITE (N) Warn 88-346, 1977;

SPACE PROBE 6 by CHARLES HUNTINGTON

1. THE SOUL STEALERS (N) Awrd AS 1044, 1972;
2. NIGHTMARE ON VEGA 3 (N) Awrd AS 1045, 1972;

STAR TREK STORIES FROM ORIGINAL TV SERIES Adapted by JAMES BLISH

01. BLISH -STAR TREK (S7) Bant F3459, 1967, Q2114;
2. BLISH - STAR TREK 2 (S8) Bant F3439, 1968, N8066; Q2171;
3. BLISH - STAR TREK 3 (S7) Bant F4371, 1969, N8683;
4. BLISH - STAR TREK 4 (S7) Bant S7009, 1971, Q2172;
5. BLISH - STAR TREK 5 (S7) Bant S7300, 1972, N8180;
6. BLISH - STAR TREK 6 (S6) Bant S7364, 1972, N8184;
7. BLISH - STAR TREK 7 (S6) Bant S7480, 1972;

8. BLISH - STAR TREK 8 (S6) Bant SP7500, 1972, N8170;
9. BLISH - STAR TREK 9 (S6) Bant SP7808, 1973;
10. BLISH - STAR TREK 10 (S6) Bant SP8401, 1974;
11. BLISH - STAR TREK 11 (S6) Bant Q8711, 1975;
12. BLISH & LAWRENCE - STAR TREK 12 (S5) Bant 11382, 1977;

BLISH - THE STARTREK READER (S21) Dutton 1976; SFBC = 2,3&8
BLISH - THE STARTREK READER II (S19) Dutton 1977; SFBC== 1, 4 & 9
BLISH - STAR TREK READER III (S19) Dutton 1977; = 5, 6 & 7
BLISH - STAR TREK READER IV (S12+N) Dutton 1978; = 10, 12 & Spock Must Die!

STAR TREK FOTO-NOVELS

1. CITY ON THE EDGE OF FOREVER (N) Bant 11345, 1977;
2. WHERE NO MAN HAS GONE BEFORE (N) Bant 11346, 1977;
3. THE TROUBLE WITH TRIBBLES (N) Bant 11347, 1977;
4. A TASTE OF ARMAGEDDON (N) Bant 11348, 1978;
5. METAMORPHOSIS (N) Bant 11349, 1978;
6. ALL OUR YESTERDAYS (N) Bant 11350, 1978;
7. THE GALILEO 7 (N) Bant 12041, 1978;
8. A PIECE OF THE ACTION (N) Bant 12022, 1978;
9. THE DEVIL IN THE DARK (N) Bant 12021, 1978, (fc 7/78)
10. DAY OF THE DOVE (N) Bant 12017, 1978; (fc 8/78)
11. THE DEADLY YEARS (N) Bant 12028, 1978; (fc 9/78)
12. AMOK TIME (N) Bant 12012, 1978; (fc 10/78)

STAR TREK -NEW NOVELS AND STORIES

BLISH -SPOCK MUST DIE (N) Bantam H5515, 1970; 10749;
LAWRENCE, J.A. - MUDD'S ANGELS (N) Bant 11802, 1978;
MARSHAK & CULBREATH ED. -STAR TREK: THE NEW VOYAGES (S8) Bant S2719, 1976;
MARSHALK & CULBREATH (ed.) - STAR TREK THE NEW VOYAGES, VOL. 2 (S10) Bant 11392, 1978;
COGSWELL & SPANE -SPOCK, MESSIAH (N) Bantam 10159, 1976;
STEINER, D.T. - SPOCK ENSLAVED! (N) Love Child Press pb 1974;
LORRAH, JEAN - THE NIGHT OF THE TWIN MOONS (N) Lorrah pb 1976;
LORRAH, JEAN - FULL MOON RISING (S4);
BARTELS, MARTIN - SECRET AGENT: ENTERPRISE (N);
MARSHAK & CULBREATH - THE PRICE OF THE PHOENIX (N) Bant 10978, 1977;

KIRLIN - THE CASTAWAYS (N)
KERN, TRINETTE - THE CLIMB (N)
HALDEMAN - PLANET OF JUDGEMENT (N) Bant 11175, 1977;
SKY, KATHLEEN - VULCAN (N) Bant 12137, 1978; (fc 9/78)

STAR TREK -STORIES FROM ANIMATED T.V. SERIES by ALLAN DEAN FOSTER

1. STAR TREK LOG ONE (S3) BB Z4014, 1974, Aeonian 1975 BB25042, 25811;
2. STAR TREK LOG TWO (S3) BB 24184, 1974; Aconian 1975 BB25043; 25812;
3. STAR TREK LOG THREE (S3) BB 24366, 1975; Aconian 1975 BB25044; 25813;
4. STAR TREK LOG FOUR (S3) BB 24435, 1975; Aeonian 1975; BB25044; 25813;
5. STAR TREK LOG FIVE (S3) BB 24532, 1975; Aeonian 1975; BB25046; 25815;
6. STAR TREK LOG SIX (S3) BB24655, 1976; Aeonian 1976; BB25816;

7. STAR TREK LOG SEVEN (N) BB24965, 1976;
8. STAR TREK LOG EIGHT (N) BB25141, 1976;
9. STAR TREK LOG NINE (N) BB25557, 1977;
10. STAR TREK LOG TEN (N) BBDR 27212, 1978;

THE TIME TUNNEL (from T. V. SERIES)

1. LEINSTER - THE TIME TUNNEL (N) Pyramid R1522, 1967;
2. LEINSTER - TIME SLIP (N) Pyramid R1680, 1967;

VAMPIRELLA by RON GOULART

1. BLOODSTALK (N) WPBL 76-928, 1975;
2. ON ALIEN WINGS (N) WPBL 76-929, 1975;
3. DEAD WALK (N) WPBL 76-930, 1976;
4. BLOOD WEDDING (N) WPBL 86-088;
5. DEATHGAME (N) WPBL 86-089, 1976;
6. SNAKEGOD (N) WPBL 86-090, 1976;

AWARD WINNING SCIENCE FICTION TITLES

Note: "Novels" in this list includes all seperately published titles even though some are collections or novelettes or whatever.

Note: "Nom." lists nominated novels in alphabetical order by Author. This list is to guide readers and collectors -It is not a History of the various awards. For such a history see bibliography section.

A. INTERNATIONAL FANTASY AWARD - NOVELS

1951 1st. STEWART - EARTH ABIDES

1952 1st. COLLIER - FANCIES AND GOODNIGHTS (Collection)
2nd. WYNDHAM - THE DAY OF THE TRIFFIDS
3rd. BRADBURY - THE ILLUSTRATED MAN

1953 1st. SIMAK - CITY
2nd. KORNBLUTH - TAKEOFF
3rd. VONNEGUT - PLAYER PIANO

1954 1st. STURGEON - MORE THAN HUMAN
2nd. BESTER - THE DEMOLISHED MAN

1955 1st. PANGBORN - A MIRROR FOR OBSERVERS
2nd. CLEMENT - MISSION OF GRAVITY

1957 1st. TOLKIEN - THE LORD OF THE RINGS

B. HUGO AWARD - NOVELS

1953 1st. BESTER — THE DEMOLISHED MAN

1954 NO AWARDS

1955 1st. CLIFTON & RILEY —THEY'D RATHER BE RIGHT = The Forever Machine

1956 1st. HEINLEIN - DOUBLE STAR

1957 NO AWARDS FOR SPECIFIC FICTION

1958 1st. LEIBER — THE BIG TIME

1959 1st. BLISH —A CASE OF CONSCIENCE
NOM. ANDERSON - THE ENEMY STARS
BUDRYS - WHO?
HEINLEIN -HAVE SPACESUIT, WILL TRAVEL
SHECKLEY - IMMORTALITY, INC. (= Immortality Delivered)

1960 1st. HEINLEIN - STARSHIP TROOPERS
NOM. DICKSON — THE GENETIC GENERAL
LEINSTER - THE PIRATES OF ZAN
PHILLIPS - BRAIN TWISTER
VONNEGUT - THE SIRENS OF TITAN

1961 1st. MILLER - A CANTICLE FOR LEIBOWITZ
NOM. ANDERSON - THE HIGH CRUSADE
BUDRYS - ROGUE MOON
HARRISON - DEATHWORLD
STURGEON - VENUS PLUS X

1962 1st. HEINLEIN - STRANGER IN A STRANGE LAND
NOM. GALOUYE - DARK UNIVERSE
HARRISON - SENSE OF OBLIGATION (= Planet of the Damned)
SIMAK - TIME IS THE SIMPLEST THING
WHITE - SECOND ENDING
SHORT 1st. ALDISS - HOTHOUSE (= The Long Afternoon of Earth)

1963 1st.DICK - THE MAN IN THE HIGH CASTLE
NOM. BRADLEY - THE SWORD OF ALDONES
CLARKE - A FALL OF MOONDUST
PIPER - LITTLE FUZZY
VERCORS - SYLVA
N/ette 1st VANCE - THE DRAGON MASTERS

1964 1st. SIMAK - WAY STATION
NOM. HEINLEIN - GLORY ROAD
NORTON - WITCH WORLD
VONNEGUT - CAT'S CRADLE

1965 1st. LEIBER - THE WANDERER
NOM. BRUNNER - THE WHOLE MAN
PANGBORN - DAVY
SMITH C. - THE PLANET BUYER
Short 1st. DICKSON - SOLDIER ASK NOT

1966 1st.HERBERT - DUNE
TIE ZELAZNY - AND CALL ME CONRAD (= This Immortal)
NOM. BRUNNER - THE SQUARES OF THE CITY
SMITH E. E. - SKYLARK DUQUESNE
BEST ALL TIME SERIES:
1st. ASIMOV - FOUNDATION SERIES
NOM. BURROUGHS - MARS SERIES
HEINLEIN -FUTURE HISTORY SERIES
SMITH - LENSMEN SERIES
TOLKIEN - LORD OF THE RINGS

1967 1st. HEINLEIN -THE MOON IS A HARSH MISTRESS
NOM. DELANY - BABEL 17

GARRETT - TOO MANY MAGICIANS
KEYES - FLOWERS FOR ALGERNON
SCHMITZ - THE WITCHES OF KARRES
SWANN - DAY OF THE MINOTAUR
N/ETTE 1st. VANCE - THE LAST CASTLE

1968 1st. ZELAZNY - LORD OF LIGHT
NOM. ANTHONY - CHTHON
ANDERSON C. - THE BUTTERFLY KID
DELANY - EINSTEIN INTERSECTION
SILVERBERG - THORNS

1969 1st. BRUNNER - STAND ON ZANZIBAR
NOM. DELANY - NOVA
LAFFERTY - PAST MASTER
PANSHIN - RITE OF PASSAGE
SIMAK - THE GOBLIN RESERVATION

Note: Seperate parts of McCaffrey-Dragonflight were nominated for Hugo's in short fiction catageories in 1968 & 1969. In 1968 the Novella Weyr Search tied for 1st.

1970 1st. LEGUIN - THE LEFT HAND OF DARKNESS
NOM. ANTHONY - MACROSCOPE
SILVERBERG -UP THE LINE
SPINRAD - BUG JACK BARRON
VONNEGUT - SLAUGHTERHOUSE 5

1971 1st. NIVEN - RINGWORLD
NOM. ANDERSON - TAU ZERO
CLEMENT - STARLIGHT
SILVERBERG - TOWER OF GLASS
TUCKER - THE YEAR OF THE QUIET SUN

1972 1st. FARMER - TO YOUR SCATTERED BODIES GO
NOM. LE GUIN - THE LATHE OF HEAVEN
MCCAFFREY -DRAGONQUEST
SILVERBERG - A TIME OF CHANGES
ZELAZNY — JACK OF SHADOWS

1973 1st. ASIMOV - THE GODS THEMSELVES
NOM. ANDERSON- THERE WILL BE TIME
GERROLD - WHEN HARLIE WAS ONE
SILVERBERG -THE BOOK OF SKULLS
SILVERBERT -DYING INSIDE
SIMAK - A CHOICE OF GODS
N/lla 1st. LE GUIN - THE WORD FOR WORLD IS FOREST

1974 1st. CLARKE - RENDEZVOUS WITH RAMA
NOM. ANDERSON - PEOPLE OF THE WIND
GERROLD - THE MAN WHO FOLDED HIMSELF
HEINLEIN - TIME ENOUGH FOR LOVE
NIVEN - PROTECTOR

1975 1st. LEGUIN - THE DISPOSSESSED
NOM. ANDERSON - FIRE TIME
DICK - FLOW MY TEARS THE POLICEMAN SAID
NIVEN & POURNELLE - THE MOTE IN GODS EYE
PRIEST - THE INVERTED WORLD

1976 1st. HALDEMAN -THE FOREVER WAR
NOM. BESTER -THE COMPUTER CONNECTION
NIVEN & POURNELLE - INFERNO
SILVERBERG - THE STOCHASTIC MAN
ZELAZNY - DOORWAYS IN THE SAND

1977 1st WILHELM - WHERE LATE THE SWEET BIRDS SANG
NOM. HALDEMAN - MINDBRIDGE
HERBERT - CHILDREN OF DUNE
POHL - MAN PLUS
SILVERBERG - SHADRACH IN THE FURNACE

1978 NOM. BRADLEY - THE FORBIDDEN TOWER
DICKSON - TIME STORM
MARTIN - DYING OF THE LIGHT
NIVEN - LUCIFER'S HAMMER
POHL - GATEWAY

C. NEBULA AWARD

1965 1st. HERBERT -DUNE
NOM. DICK - THE THREE STIGMATA OF PLAMER ELDRIDGE
DAVIDSON - ROGUE DRAGON
DISCH - THE GENOCIDES
DICK - DR. BLOODMONEY
EDMONDSON -THE SHIP THAT SAILED THE TIME STREAM
LAUMER - A PLAGUE OF DEMONS
ANDERSON - THE STAR FOX
SIMAK -ALL FLESH IS GRASS
THOMAS & WILHELM - THE CLONE
WHITE - ESCAPE ORBIT

1966 1st. DELANY - BABEL -17
TIE KEYES - FLOWERS FOR ALGERNON
NOM. HEINLEIN - THE MOON IS A HARSH MISTRESS
N/Ila 1st.VANCE - THE LAST CASTLE

1967 1st. DELANY - THE EINSTEIN INTERSECTION
NOM. ANTHONY - CHTHON
HAYDEN - THE ESKIMO INVASION
SILVERBERG - THORNS
ZELAZNY - LORD OF LIGHT
N/Ila 1st. MOORCOCK - BEHOLD THE MAN

1968 1st.PANSHIN -RITE OF PASSAGE
NOM. BLISH - BLACK EASTER OR FAUST ALEPH NULL
BRUNNER - STAND ON ZANZIBAR
DICK - DO ANDROIDS DREAM OF ELECTRIC SHEEP
LAFFERTY - PAST MASTER
RUSS - PICNIC ON PARADISE
SILVERBERG - MASKS OF TIME
N/lla 1st. MCCAFFREY - DRAGONRIDER (part of novel)

1969 1st. LEGUIN - THE LEFT HAND OF DARKNESS
NOM. BRUNNER - JAGGED ORBIT
SILVERBERG - UP THE LINE
SPINRAD - BUG JACK BARRON
VONNEGUT - SLAUGHTERHOUSE 5
ZELAZNY - ISLE OF THE DEAD

1970 1st. NIVEN - RINGWORLD
NOM. COMPTON - THE STEEL CROCODILE
LAFFERTY - FOURTH MANSIONS
RUSS - AND CHAOS DIED
SILVERBERG - TOWER OF GLASS
TUCKER - THE YEAR OF THE QUIET SUN

1971 1st. SILVERBERG - A TIME OF CHANGES
NOM. ANDERSON - THE BY-WORLDER
BASS - HALF PAST HUMAN
LAFFERTY - THE DEVIL IS DEAD
LEGUIN - THE LATHE OF HEAVEN
WILHELM - MARGARET AND I

1972 1st.ASIMOV - THE GODS THEMSELVES
NOM. BRUNNER - THE SHEEP LOOK UP
EFFINGER - WHAT ENTROPY MEANS TO ME
GERROLD - WHEN HARLIE WAS ONE
SILVERBERG - THE BOOK OF SKULLS
SILVERBERG - DYING INSIDE
SPINRAD - THE IRON DREAM

1973 1st. CLARKE - RENDEZVOUS WITH RAMA
NOM. ANDERSON - THE PEOPLE OF THE WIND
HEINLEIN - TIME ENOUGH FOR LOVE
GERROLD - THE MAN WHO FOLDED HIMSELF
PYNCHON - GRAVITY'S RAINBOW

1974 1st. LEGUIN - THE DISPOSSESSED
NOM. DICK - FLOW MY TEARS THE POLICEMAN SAID
DISCH - 334
BASS - THE GODWHALE
MCKEE - WALK TO THE END OF THE WORLD

1975 1st. HALDEMAN - THE FOREVER WAR
NOM. DELANY - DHALGREN
CALVINO - INVISIBLE CITIES
MCINTYRE - THE EXILE WAITING
NIVEN & POURNELLE - THE MOTE IN GOD'S EYE
RUSS - THE FEMALE MAN
SILVERBERG - THE STOCHASTIC MAN

1976 1st. POHL - MAN PLUS
NOM. DELANY - TRITON
NIVEN & POURNELLE - INFERNO
RANDALL - ISLANDS
SILVERBERG - SHADRACH IN THE FURNACE
WILHELM - WHERE LATE THE SWEET BIRDS SANG

1977 NOM. BENFORD- IN THE OCEAN OF NIGHT
POHL - GATEWAY
GERROLD - MOONSTAR ODYSSEY
CARR - CIRQUE
LUPOFF - SWORD OF THE DEMON

IX A. Comments

1. Certain paperback publishers (chiefly Ace and Dell) use a code number which is computer generated and is based on where the computer estimates the title would fall in an alphabetical list. Subsequent printings use the same number or in the case of Ace, the next consecutive number. Such later printings are omitted.
2. I have included information on spouses where both wrote titles included in this compilation. This is to explain collaborations since many husband and wife teams combined to write books and one or the other may not be credited. In some cases one spouse is dead or the authors are divorced and remarried, etc. My information is supplied for bibliographic purposes only and is not to be considered current information on the authors private lives. My appologies to any current spouse other than those listed (and to any I may have missed who were doubtless the true inspiration behind the works and ought to be so credited)
3. I tried to maintain a uniform format, but in some cases this was not possible. In others, variations in format such as separating titles co-authored by others or separating titles authored under a pseudonym seem to be the best way to order the material. I used whatever format worked best and did not adhere to alphabetical listing as the only way to list non-series works by an author. Some series were moved to the back for paging purposes. Certain titles appear out of alphabetical order thru late inclusion in the list or simple error.
4. I have excluded titles published by"vanity' publishers such as Vantage and Exposition for two reasons: I have been unable to obtain any comprehensive information on these titles and none have ever appeared in paperback. So far as I know, no author has had Science Fiction titles published by both commercial and vanity publishers.
5. Contents of a few omnibus works are listed where the work includes other separately published titles.
6. A few notable non-SF titles are included for completeness. This is done on a completely subjective basis and only for the most prolific authors where they have written only a few such titles.
7. I considered (fleetingly) including a title-author cross index. I rejected this idea on the grounds that the extra 150 pages necessary would have added too much to the price of the publication.
8. Information such as pseudonyms which cannot be obtained from original sources is not included in this index unless I have been able to verify it from at least two sources. This does not insure that the information is correct, of course. I have tried to omit information that was doubtful or unverifiable.

IX B. Notes

1. Del Rey. Paul Fairman is credited with being an uncredited co-author of several titles. This information comes from Reginald-Contemporary Science Fiction Authors, and I have no reason to disbelieve it although I have not been able to verify it either.

2. Ivar Jorgenson — Ivar Jorgensen. So far I can determine, Paul Fairman wrote the stories where the name appeared with and **e** and Robert Silverberg wrote the stories where an **o** was used in the name. There is certainly the possibility that some other author wrote some of the titles attributed to Fairman.

3. Will Garth - Dr. Cyclops. Garth was house Psuedonym used by Kuttner, Hamilton & Wellman and others. Dr. Cyclops was a movie tie-in novel. A short version of the story under the same title was reprinted from the pulps in Popular 2485, 1969 and attributed to Henry Kuttner. Tuck, in the 1959 version of his encyclopedia attributes the novel to Manly Wade Wellman. His 1978 edition omits this reference. I have copies of the original novel and the recent paperback and neither gives any clue as to the true author.

4. When Worlds Collide & After Worlds Collide. Edward Balmer is actually the first listed author on the original hardcover editions. Philip Wylie is now the more famous author and is listed first on the paperback editions. I have listed them under Wylie since that seems to be the modern practice.

Partial Bibliography of Recommended Works

Bleiler, Everett F.
The Checklist of Fantastic Literature
Shasta 1948; Fax Collector's Editions 1972
Through 1947; The essential reference work for early Science Fiction.

Burger, Joanne
SF published in 1971; SF published in 1972; SF published in 1973; SF published in 1974; SF published in 1975; SF published in 1976; Published by the author 55 Blue Bonnet Ct., Lake Jackson, Texas 77566.

Day, Bradford M.
The Supplemental Checklist of Fantastic Literature
Science Fiction and Fantasy Publications 1963; Arno 1975 through 1963; Supplement to Bleiler

Day, Bradford M.
The Checklist of Fantastic Literature in Paperbound Books
Science Fiction and Fantasy Publication 1965; Arno 1975 through 1965

Reginald R.
Stella Nova: The Contemporary Science Fiction Authors
Unicorn and Sons 1970
Contemporary Science Fiction Authors; Arno 1975 through 1969; Chronological list of works by authors active between 1960-68

Tuck, Donald H.
The Encyclopedia of Science Fiction & Fantasy Vol 1
Advent 1974;
Authors A-L through 1968;

The Encylopedia of Science Fiction & Fantasy, Vol. 2.
Advent 1978;
Authors M-Z through 1968; plus cross reference by title

SPECIAL PURPOSE WORKS

Reginald, R. & Burgess, M.R.
Cumulative Paperback Index 1939-1959; Gale Research 1973
Covers all paperbacks - not just Science Fiction; lists publishers code numbers. Comprehensive but expensive for one interested only in S.F.

Spelman, Dick
Preliminary Checklist of S.F. & F. published by Ballantine Books. 1953-74
Institute For Specialized Literature 1976
The compiler has published other similar works

McGhan, Barry
Science Fiction and Fantasy Pseudonyms
Misfit Press, June 1975, 4705 Weddels St., Dearborn, Mich. 48125

Franson, Donald & DeVore, Howard
A History of the Hugo, Nebula and International Fantasy Awards
Published by the Authors, September 1976, 4705 Weddel St., Dearborn, Michigan 48125

The above reference works are recommended for quality and availability. This is not to say that copies are easy to locate, only that other works of importance are harder to find.

I cross-checked this index with all of the above numerous other publications including particularly an entire run of LUNA by Franklin and Ann Dietz; and A Handbook of Science Fiction and Fantasy, 2nd Edition 1959 by Donald A. Tuck. I am indebted to these sources for countless leads and items of information. However, this index is primarily based upon original sources ie. the books themselves.

Special Notice To All Readers

If after studying this index you have verifiable knowledge of errors in commission or omission in this book; or you know of authors that should be included, but are not; or you know of titles that should be included, but are not please detail your information the same as in the book (listing author, title, type, publisher, publisher number, and subsequent editions) and send this information to Purple Unicorn Books, 4532 London Road, Duluth, Minnesota 55804. If your report is used in a revised edition of this index, credit will be given to you in that edition. Thanks.

ADDENDUM

BAXTER, JOHN

THE HERMES FALL (N) S&S 1978;

BERGIN PAUL A.

XUAN AND THE GIRL FROM THE OTHERSIDE (N) Tower T-060-8, 1969; (marginal-sex oriented)

BREBNER, WINSTON

DOUBTING THOMAS (N) Rinehart 1956;

BROOKE, JOCELYN

THE IMAGE OF A DRAWN SWORD (N) Knopf 1951;

CHAPMAN, VERA

THE GREEN KNIGHT (N) Avon 33795, 1978;
THE KING'S DAMOSEL (N) Avon 37606, 1978;

CHRISTOPHER, JOHN

EMPTY WORLD (JN) Dutton, 1978;

CLEMENS, RODGERS

THE PRESENCE (N) GM 3890, 1977;

DE MARINIS, RICK

A LOVELY MONSTER (N) S&S 1975; Dell 14900;

DICK, PHILIP K.

A HANDFUL OF DARKNESS (C) Gregg 1978;

DICKSON, GORDON

HOME FROM THE SHORE (N) Sunridge(div of Ace) 1978; pb illustrated

ELLIOTT, JOHN

DRAGON FEAST (N) Belm B95-2009, 1970;

GRIFFITH, MARY

THREE HUNDRED YEARS HENCE (N) Prime 1950; Gregg 1976;

HALES, E.E.Y.

CHARIOT OF FIRE (N) Avon 36569, 1978;

HAY, JACOB

AUTOPSY FOR A COSMONAUT (N) (with J. Keshishian) Little-B 1969; Pop 1342;

HOWARD, ROBERT E

THE LAST RIDE (C) (Western) Berk 03754, 1978;

JONES, MARGARET

TRANSPLANT (N) Pop 75-1315;

LEONARD, GEORGE H.

ALIEN (N) Playboy 16378, 1977;

NADER, GEORGE

CHROME (N) Putnam 1978;

OWEN, RICHARD

THE EYE OF THE GODS (N) Dutton 1978;(fc)

RASPAIL, JEAN

THE CMAP OF THE SAINTS (N) S&S 1975; Ace 09120;

SABEN, LIONEL

REPLICA (N) Zebra 370, 1978;(fc 8/78)

SCHMIDT, DENNIS

WAY-FARER (N) Ace 87625, 1978;

SHELLEY, MARY WOLLENSTONECRAFT

FRANKENSTEIN: OR THE MODERN PROMETHEUS (N) (Brit 1818) Heritage 1953; Lion 146; Prmd R290; F1212; Coll H.S. 3V; Air Cl19; Bant FP165; +

VERCORS = Jean Bruller

THE INSURGENTS (N) Harcourt-B 1956;
SYLVA (N) Putnam 1962; Crest d586;
YOU SHALL KNOW THEM (N) Little-B 1953; Poc 1038; Pop 2202;
= THE MURDER OF THE MISSING LINK (N) Poc 1206, 1958; Pop 60-2202;

WALDROP, HOWARD

THE TEXAS-ISRAELI WAR (N) (with J. Saunders) BB 24182, 1974;

WRIGHTSON, PATRICIA

DOWN TO EARTH (N) HBW 1965;
THE ICE IS COMING (N) Atheneum 1977;
THE NARGUN AND THE STARS (JN) Atheneum 1974;

ANTHOLOGIES

BEFORE THE GOLDEN AGE BOOK 3
THE DARK BETWEEN THE STARS